Linguistics and the teacher

Language, Education and Society

General Editor
Michael Stubbs
Department of Linguistics
University of Nottingham

Linguistics and the teacher

Edited by

Ronald Carter

Department of English Studies
University of Nottingham

Routledge & Kegan Paul
London, Boston, Melbourne and Henley

First published in 1982
by Routledge & Kegan Paul Ltd
39 Store Street, London WC1E 7DD,
9 Park Street, Boston, Mass. 02108, USA,
296 Beaconsfield Parade, Middle Park,
Melbourne, 3206, Australia, and
Broadway House, Newtown Road,
Henley-on-Thames, Oxon RG9 1EN
Set in IBM Press Roman by
Academic Typing Service, Gerrards Cross, Bucks
and printed in Great Britain by
Unwin Brothers Ltd
The Gresham Press, Old Woking, Surrey.
A member of the Staples Printing Group

Library of Congress Cataloging in Publication Data

Linguistics and the teacher.

(Language, education, and society)
Bibliography: p.
Includes index.
Contents: Introduction – Linguistics in teacher
education / Michael Halliday / Linguistics and the
teacher / John Sinclair / Linguistics for education / Mike Riddle – [etc.]
1. Language and education – Addresses, essays,
lectures. 2. Teachers, Training of – Addresses,
essays, lectures. 3. Sociolinguistics – Addresses,
essays, lectures. I. Carter, Ronald. II. Series.
P41.L54   1982   400   82-12209

ISBN 0-7100-9360-8
ISBN 0-7100-9193-1 (pbk)

Contents

General Editor's preface

Simply a list of some of the questions implied by the phrase *Language, Education and Society* gives an immediate idea of the complexity, and also the fascination, of the area.

How is language related to learning? Or to intelligence? How should a teacher react to non-standard dialect in the classroom? Do regional and social accents and dialects matter? What is meant by standard English? Does it make sense to talk of 'declining standards' in language or in education? Or to talk of some children's language as 'restricted'? Do immigrant children require special language provision? How can their native languages be used as a valuable resource in schools? Can 'literacy' be equated with 'education'? Why are there so many adult illiterates in Britain and the USA? What effect has growing up with no easy access to language: for example, because a child is profoundly deaf? Why is there so much prejudice against people whose language background is odd in some way: because they are handicapped, or speak a non-standard dialect or foreign language? Why do linguistic differences lead to political violence, in Belgium, India, Wales and other parts of the world?

These are all real questions, of the kind which worry parents, teachers and policy-makers, and the answer to them is complex and not at all obvious. It is such questions that authors in this series will discuss.

Language plays a central part in education. This is probably generally agreed, but there is considerable debate and confusion about the exact relationship between language and learning. Even though the importance of language is generally recognized, we still have a lot to learn about how language is related to either educational success or to intelligence and thinking. Language is also a central fact in everyone's social life. People's attitudes and most deeply held beliefs are at stake, for it is through language that personal and social identities are maintained and recognized. People are judged, whether justly or not, by the language they speak.

Language, Education and Society is therefore an area where scholars have a responsibility to write clearly and persuasively, in order to communicate the best in recent research to as wide an audience as possible. This means not only other researchers, but also all those who are involved in educational, social and political policy-making, from individual teachers to government. It is an area where value judgments cannot be avoided. Any action that we take – or, of course, avoidance of action – has moral, social and political consequences. It is vital, therefore, that practice is informed by the best knowledge available, and that decisions affecting the futures of individual children or whole social groups are not taken merely on the basis of the all-too-widespread folk myths about language in society.

Linguistics, psychology and sociology are often rejected by non-specialists as jargon-ridden, or regarded as fascinating, but of no relevance to educational or social practice. But this is superficial and short-sighted: we are dealing with complex issues, which require an understanding of the general principles involved. It is bad theory to make statements about language in use which cannot be related to educational and social reality. But it is equally unsound to base beliefs and action on anecdote, received myths and unsystematic or idiosyncratic observations.

All knowledge is value-laden: it suggests action and changes our beliefs. Change is difficult and slow, but possible nevertheless. When language in education and society is seriously and systematically studied, it becomes clear how awesomely complex is the linguistic and social knowledge of all children and adults. And with such an understanding, it becomes impossible to maintain a position of linguistic prejudice and intolerance. This may be the most important implication of a serious study of language, in our linguistically diverse modern world.

In this book, *Linguistics and the Teacher*, Ron Carter has brought together a collection of articles by linguists and educationalists with national and international reputations. There are many books on language in education, the importance of linguistic knowledge to teachers, and so forth. However, this collection tackles explicitly and squarely several issues which other books ignore or touch on only slightly. All the authors are academic specialists in linguistics or language in education, but they have all thought seriously about the careful selection and presentation of academic knowledge which is required for practical educational purposes. This means: making specific proposals about syllabuses – not as definitive solutions, but to provide a realistic basis for discussion;

identifying the questions that teachers really do ask about linguistics – this is explicit in one article, but a theme of the whole book; and being constructively prescriptive about children's language abilities, by making judgments on the basis of the best knowledge available.

The area of linguistics in education, language in education, and teaching English as a mother tongue, is in considerable confusion. Ron Carter's useful introduction clarifies several misunderstandings which often muddle the debate. He shows clearly that in areas in which entrenched professional positions are at stake, it is the responsibility of academics to make clear what their positions are, and to present them as carefully as possible to those who need the knowledge in practice. This attempt to write clearly and to disseminate knowledge in appropriate ways is a major aim of the whole series.

Michael Stubbs
Nottingham

Acknowledgments

I have benefited greatly from discussion about linguistics and education with colleagues in a number of institutions and in particular with John Sinclair and Deirdre Burton (University of Birmingham), Margaret Berry (University of Nottingham), and John Edmonds and Terry Prince (Hertfordshire College of Higher Education).

I also owe a considerable debt to Michael Stubbs, General Editor of the series, for perceptive advice, encouragement and balanced judgment. He is also a never-failing source of original ideas and I have learned a lot from many discussions with him.

I must also thank the contributors to this book for their co-operation, resourcefulness and hard work. It is encouraging to work with a group of people who believe in the need for some fundamental re-evaluation of the role of language in education and teaching and who believe in the necessity for a sustained challenge to some dominant models of that relationship. Norma Hazzledine worked with me on the manuscript and organized me with exemplary patience, displaying her usual insight into the fine details of a book's scaffolding and preventing in the process many errors.

Lastly, my thanks go to Jane Carter and to Matthew, Jennifer and Claire for their affectionate reminders that this is only a book. And it is no exaggeration or contradiction to say that without them the book would not have been written.

The author and publishers are also grateful to the following for permission to reprint copyright material: Granada Publishing Ltd and Harcourt Brace Jovanovich Inc. for 'pity this busy monster manunkind' from *Complete Poems 1913–1962* by e.e. cummings; Eyre Methuen Ltd and Alfred A. Knopf Inc./Random House Inc. for 'Janet Waking' from *Selected Poems* by John Crowe Ransom; Faber and Faber Ltd for the extract from 'Mr Bleaney' from *The Whitsun Weddings* by Philip Larkin.

Notes on Contributors

Ronald Carter (editor) lectures in English at Nottingham University. He has published a book on W.H. Auden and several articles on literary criticism and twentieth-century literature. His main interests are in the relationship between linguistics and literature and linguistics and education. He is co-editor (with Deirdre Burton) of *Literary Text and Language Study* (Arnold, 1982) and editor of a collection of articles on stylistics entitled *Language and Literature* (Allen & Unwin, 1982). He has taught in a comprehensive school, colleges of further education and in a teacher-training college.

Michael Halliday is Professor of Linguistics at the University of Sydney, Australia, having previously held chairs at the Universities of London (University College) and Essex. He is the author of several books and articles on syntax, lexis and intonation and is known internationally as the founder of systemic linguistics. His most recent publications include *Cohesion in English* (with R. Hasan) (Longman, 1976) and *Language as Social Semiotic* (Arnold, 1978). His *Learning How to Mean* (Arnold, 1973) is just one example of his long-standing interest and research commitment to child language study and language in education.

John Sinclair is Professor of Modern English Language at the University of Birmingham. His main teaching and research interests are in stylistics, linguistics and education, discourse analysis, and, more recently, in computing and lexicography. He is the author of numerous articles in these areas. He is also the author of *A Course in Spoken English: Grammar* (Oxford University Press, 1972) and (with Malcolm Coulthard) of the influential *Towards an Analysis of Discourse: The English Used by Teachers and Pupils* (Oxford University Press, 1975).

Mike Riddle is Senior Lecturer in Linguistics at Middlesex Polytechnic where he has taught on modern English studies and teacher-training in-service courses. He is Chairman of the Committee for Linguistics in Education and has organised conferences on the teaching of linguistics. He has researched aspects of language testing and the teaching of punctuation. He is regularly invited to address conferences concerned with the application of linguistics to language teaching.

Arthur Brookes's career started in 1947 with teaching English in an Indian secondary school in South Africa. Since then he has taught in primary and secondary schools in a number of countries including Scotland, New Zealand and England. He was a lecturer at the start of the Waikato Branch of Auckland University (now the University of Waikato) where he lectured on modern English usage, and was for many years in teacher training at Bede College. He now holds a joint appointment in the School of Education and the Department of English Studies at Durham University. He was for some years on the Council of the National Association for the Teaching of English and represents them on the Committee for Linguistics in Education, and on the National Congress on Languages in Education.

Richard Hudson is Reader in Linguistics at University College, London, and is the author of several key text books including *Arguments for a Non-Transformational Grammar* (Chicago University Press, 1976) and *Sociolinguistics* (Cambridge University Press, 1980). In 1967-70 he worked as a research assistant on the Linguistics and English Teaching Project (under the direction of Michael Halliday) and has retained a strong interest in the dissemination of the findings of linguistics, especially to teachers.

Gillian Brown lectures in the Department of Linguistics, University of Edinburgh, having previously lectured in English Language at the University of Cape Coast, Ghana. She has also taught widely abroad (including India, Canada, Poland, Sweden, Norway and Greece). Her books include the widely acclaimed *Listening to Spoken English* (Longman, 1977). She has also published books and articles on phonology, dialect variation and intonation and is currently preparing a book on discourse analysis (with George Yule). She has a long-standing interest in the applications of linguistics to teaching and learning problems in both first and second language study.

Peter Gannon After graduating from Oxford in English Language and Literature, Peter Gannon taught in a Scottish secondary school for six years, during which time he became involved in working parties on linguistics and English teaching. Following a return to Oxford for four years' research in linguistics (syntax of the verb phrase in English) and some years in teacher training, he joined Her Majesty's Inspectorate with a special responsibility for English. He has, formerly, also taught French and Russian, as well as EFL. He is co-author (with Pam Czerniewska) of *Using Linguistics* (Arnold, 1980) and has written many articles on language and English teaching, book reviews, etc., as well as being involved, through lecturing and the DES short course programme, in in-service education and training.

Katherine Perera lectures in the Department of General Linguistics, University of Manchester. She has worked as a VSO teacher in Malaysia and taught English in schools on Merseyside for six years. She has also taught in a teacher-training college. Her main academic interests are the applications of linguistics to the fields of mother tongue learning (particularly reading and writing) and speech therapy and she has reviewed and written several articles in these fields. She is also the author of *Analysing Classroom Language: the Structure of Writing* (André Deutsch, forthcoming).

Michael Stubbs is Lecturer in Linguistics at the University of Nottingham, where he teaches the general principles and history of linguistics and sociolinguistics. His main research and writing interests are in language in education, and the analysis of spoken and written discourse. His publications include *Explorations in Classroom Observation* (Co-editor, Wiley, 1976), *Language, Schools and Classrooms* (Methuen, 1976), *Language and Literacy* (Routledge & Kegan Paul, 1980) and articles and reviews on language in education and discourse analysis. He is General Editor of the series on *Language, Education and Society*, in which the present book appears. He has taught in Australia, China and France.

Introduction

This book explores some relationships which exist between linguistics and education. The starting point for the authors of the articles is that linguistics should be a central element in the pre- and in-service education of teachers. It is therefore a programmatic book. It is also a fairly polemical book. But being programmatic and polemical should not be taken as a sign that all linguists are impossibly uncompromising about the relation of their subject to education, and that they do not consider debate or dialogue useful. For example, we do not claim a one-for-one correspondence between the analysis of linguistic facts and the solution of educational and learning problems; we do consistently claim, however, that not to undertake such an analysis can have dangerous consequences and that teachers should therefore be properly equipped in techniques for analysing language. In such debate and discussion a clear, unequivocal and programmatic statement by interested linguists can clarify positions so that further dialogue can ensue without fuzziness or misconstrual of principle.

Also, the authors of articles in this book do not proceed in ignorance of the ways in which linguistics is regarded in educational circles. Several articles attempt to answer objections which have been made against linguistics in education. This introduction could introduce these articles and outline their main points to help to orientate the reader. But a more useful orientation might be given by an attempt to focus and give context to the debate by posing and anticipating objections or questions and by directing readers to places in the book where the linguist's case is stated. There are many such questions, of course, but I shall list what I take to be the principal ones.

1 *There are already many courses in language and education. Why do linguists keep stressing the need for courses in linguistics in education?*

This is a matter of differences in emphasis. An essential difference between the two approaches is that courses in Language in Education select aspects of language which can be presented for study in a relatively uncomplicated or undemanding fashion. Often criteria of selection remain unclear but language is presented as something to be studied alongside sociology or psychology or philosophy or education. Generally facts about language are taught and valuable conclusions are reached. Teachers' and students' interest in language is undeniably heightened and consumers of such courses often find them highly interesting and absorbing. More important, they complete such courses with an increased awareness of the place language has in facilitating and inhibiting progress in learning. A good example of such a course would be the Open University Language Development Course PE232.

Linguists feel on the whole that teachers of courses in language and education are really saying that we must study language without excessive attention to the discipline of studying the language. In other words, those bits of linguistics are borrowed which do not presuppose any detailed or systematically organized analysis of the language.

This is a dangerous direction for a number of reasons. First, the argument is shaky. It is rather like constructing a teacher-training course about numbers which avoids doing too much mathematics. Second, it can be said to be patronizing. There is a presumption that teachers are incapable of doing real analysis of language because it is too difficult. Setting low expectations produces no more than low achievement. If language is a central element in learning then there seems little justification for encouraging low achievement in its study. Third, as a related point, it is often argued by the 'mediators' (as Sinclair terms them, (p. 17) of linguistics in language and education courses, that the 'demands of in-service or pre-service pedagogy' mean that there is little time, given a demanding curriculum, to go into the kind of analytical sophistication demanded by linguists. This is again a shaky argument. It can be countered by pointing out that time must be found if teachers are not to be sent back into schools interested in language but without the tools to develop or effectively solve the language problems facing them in the school.

So, the difference between language and linguistic study in relation to education is principally one of the degree of organization of language analysis to be undertaken. But the assumption that language problems can be effectively solved without linguistic analysis of the source of the problem does seem dangerously misguided. There seems little point in increasing teachers' awareness of language if they are not given the equipment to solve real language problems in the classroom. Further discussion of this question is found throughout the book but specifically in the articles by Riddle and Sinclair.

2 Look at all the diagrams and models linguists keep presenting. In particular, why is there so much jargon? Surely most teachers are right in finding the subject generally too abstract for their purposes.

This is another version of the argument that linguistics is too difficult for teachers. It is not just linguists who find such an argument condescending and anti-intellectual and one which places little confidence in the capabilities of the teacher. Linguists produce models and diagrams because it is often the best way of representing the workings of a phenomenon like language. Language is indeed subtle and complex particularly because it involves an interrelation of different linguistic levels such as syntax, phonology, morphology, discourse, lexis, etc., and each level has its own structure and organization. It is not just an amorphous entity which we should vaguely encourage to grow. The application of an approach which is sufficiently principled to be attentive to the multi-levelled nature of language organization is particularly well illustrated in the paper by Peter Gannon. It is a paper which is far from abstract. One feels that the pupil concerned would only benefit from working with a teacher able to analyse and prepare for such a systematic remediation of her difficulties with language. If it is still thought that linguistics operates in some remote realm and can never really be appropriately applied to real classroom problems, then readers should turn their attention to the teaching of English as a second or foreign language (ESL and EFL) or to courses in English for special purposes and special study skills and, in particular, to the kinds of materials produced both by linguists working in this field and by teachers whose training is much more directly informed by linguistics than is the case with training for English as a mother tongue (EMT).

To cite just one example from many, the University of Malaya project[1] contains a wealth of practical teaching materials for developing written and oral language skills. The materials are informed by current linguistic theory, are progressive in a linguistically principled way (which in turn allows for principled rather than wholly subjective means of assessment) and are designed to assist language development through real language use and practice. Some recent papers (e.g. McDonough and McDonough, 1978) and an NCLE report (1981) point to the advantages derived from mutual support and integration of EFL and EMT but it is one of the tragedies of current English teaching that so many mother-tongue teachers are either ignorant of work in EFL or consider it a poor relation which is anyway distinctly irrelevant to their needs and concerns. It is an even more distressing feature of teacher education courses in English and language teaching when one considers the multi-ethnic, multi-linguistic nature of our classrooms.

The argument that linguistics is jargon-ridden cannot really be a serious one either. Most academic disciplines have a specialist terminology; 'alliteration', 'terza rima', 'half-rhyme', 'sonnet' are familiar to English teachers (significantly most of the 'jargon' of English as a subject is to do with literary text study) but would be jargon to those outside the discipline. Most teachers are inoculated against the terminologies of their own discipline and in the context of teacher education linguistics is very much a new and therefore 'alien' discipline.

3 *The teaching of linguistics is often no more than the imposition of an arid formalism. It may have its uses in the categorization of features of language but its concerns are basically blinkered and anti-humanistic.*

This is an important objection. The argument for studying language as a living entity of which teachers should seek to give children experience rather than mere techniques of analysis is put very powerfully in a recent debate in the journal *English in Education*. In this debate a linguist is accused of draining away 'from language study the real strength that it can have when it is rooted in the world the pupils live in: that is, the strength to put into our pupils' hands the ability to control their environments by giving them insights into language interactions'.[2] *But* such a view of language study would be shared by many linguists. Despite what appears to be a common mythology about the subject, linguistics is *not* just a study of grammar. Nor is it Chomsky. It is surprising how widespread but anachronistic such a view of linguistics is. It dates from the 1960s when, it is true, linguists were for very good reasons developing theoretical models and when a lot of attention was drawn to the transformational-generative grammar developed by Chomsky and his followers. Rather disturbingly, a recent text book *Assessing Language Development* (Wilkinson *et al.* 1980) dismisses linguistics because of its excessive formalism and its concern with 'counting grammatical features'. Rather predictably, there are very few references in the text or bibliography of that book to the linguistic literature of the 1970s.

The past ten to twelve years have seen an expansion of interest in both the forms and *functions* of language. In particular, there has been an increase in study and research in *sociolinguistics* to the extent that some linguists would consider this to be linguistics proper. But whatever the arguments, language has been increasingly studied in context, that is, with reference to its uses, its interpersonal message, its styles and varieties. It has been systematically investigated for its social, moral and political importance, both in single countries and internationally. Michael Stubbs's proposals for a syllabus for modern English language studies reflects much of this work undertaken in the last decade. This kind of proposal requires language to be studied systematically and from clearly defined perspectives but it is in no way arid formalism. Such a syllabus does not preclude the insights into language offered by sociologists, psychologists, politicians or literary critics. Similarly, Ron Carter's essay devoted to the integration of language and literature study is concerned to relate language analysis to more informed awareness of and competence in the stylistic and 'creative' functions of language and to generate greater and more precisely accountable sensitivity to language use in literature.

For teacher education sociolinguistic analysis has very considerable advantages. It is not necessary to elaborate such advantages here since they form the basis of the paper by Michael Halliday in this volume.

Halliday is not arguing for removing linguistic formalism from a curriculum for teacher education. As many essays in this book demonstrate, linguistic analysis at different linguistic levels has a crucial role to play, however much such analysis is misunderstood. But he and many other linguists, including all the contributors to this book, would subscribe to the view that analytical concern with the social functions of language is of considerable relevance to teachers and to the development of children's language. Here the views of many concerned with language come together, if this common ground could only be recognized.

The *fusion* of an awareness of both linguistic forms and their socio-linguistic functions is a necessary element in lending support for an increasing concern teachers have for pupils' basic language skills (the 'back to basics' movement in Reading and Writing) but it should also ensure that concern with the role of the language user as an individual in a complex society does not evaporate either. It is a fusion which most linguists would want to support.

4 *Why even try to teach linguistics today when we read about constant disagreements among linguists from different branches of the subject concerning what really constitutes their subject?*

This is a good question but the proposition is a misguided and uninformed one all the same. It would be strange if everyone working in an academic discipline could agree or if there were not sub-disciplines or demarcated areas to a subject. I have already argued that sociolinguistics is of central relevance to education but most areas of linguistics have an appropriate application: psycholinguistics; grammar; phonetics; dialectology; lexicology, etc., etc. What unites linguists applying their subject or different areas of the subject is a recognition of the necessity for clarity and explicitness, for the provision of analyses which are replicable and retrievable and which resist counter-examples, and for teachers to feel the model of analysis to be authentic and generalisable to the data encountered in their own classroom examples. It must be admitted, however, that there is a vast amount of work being currently undertaken in linguistics which, without a lot more work, cannot be synthesised or presented in a relevant form in an educational context. There is also a lot of linguistic research which will prove irrelevant to education.

But this fact should not obscure how much agreement there is among linguists. The essay in this volume by Brookes and Hudson is useful in this respect. As a basis for answers to Brookes' questions Hudson supplies a paper which, in the light of a survey, summarizes many key linguistic facts and concepts over which there would be little or no disagreement among linguists. It is a particularly useful paper and, as Brookes demonstrates, one which can help teachers in all sorts of ways. At a time when pressure is increasing to standardize and set up assessment procedures for national minimum requirements in English, when the language needs of ethnic minorities are being given serious consideration and when such pressures are resulting in teachers and examination boards re-thinking the curriculum and the part played by language studies at 'O' and 'A' level, such a paper as this can be both a corrective to certain assumptions (for example, that there is a 'correct' English) and can give considerable impetus to the kinds of developments outlined here.

5 *Linguists would convince more if they took greater account of teacher-training pedagogy and made their material more directly relevant and practical. They seem too preoccupied with language as a knowledge content.*

This is basically a re-formulation of earlier questions. It is a durable objection, however. For a recent account of the whole question in the context of an Open University teacher education course in language see Carter (1980) and reply by Czerniewska (1981). Further evidence to support the linguists' case is provided in the two articles by Perera (p. 101 and p. 114) which show how a systematic grammatical and lexical analysis of reading material across the curriculum can provide teachers with important techniques and criteria for evaluating 'difficulty' and thus selecting books and designing work-sheets appropriate to particular groups of children.[3]

Along with 'language across the curriculum', 'talk' and 'assessing talk' regularly finds itself the subject of courses for teachers. Gill Brown's article demonstrates how a linguist's analysis can provide the kinds of sharp demarcation of spoken language forms and functions which can only be directly relevant and practical. Such papers as these seem a long way from a preoccupation with knowledge content.

But the point also needs to be made that it should not *always* be the task of the linguist to meet the demands of in-service pedagogy. Most linguists are teachers and, as shown in the teaching suggestions contained in a number of the articles in this book, have ideas about how language can be taught. Not all have experience of schools or teacher education. Linguists consider their experience qualifies them or disables them in different ways from such demands. To reiterate a point made above, there is no unequivocal or unproblematic fit between linguistics and education nor between theories of language and language teaching. This is another key reason why dialogue and debate are important.

It is in this light that the more programmatic sections of the book should be regarded. In some articles authors have appended syllabuses. This is not a prescription of a knowledge content. Their inclusion does not deny the role played by the teacher in generating a context in which pupils can discover a path for themselves through a subject. As a contribution to a debate and dialogue the author is simply giving his or her professional view concerning some basic requirements for studying that part of their subject. This is not a reflection of an uncompromising stand; it is simply a belief that discussion is best conducted on the basis of a clear articulation of principle and example.

Finally, there is a point about 'knowledge content' which must be cleared up. This specific objection against linguistics often takes as its starting point a quotation from the Bullock Report (DES, 1975, p. 162): 'There is no satisfactory evidence to show how far an explicit knowledge of the rules governing language can reinforce an implicit knowledge or substitute for it.' A number of different issues seem to become entwined in the light of statements such as this. Let me attempt to clarify them. First, there *must* surely be a distinction between teachers' knowledge and pupils' knowledge. 'The rules governing language' must be a vital part of the teacher's knowledge; otherwise pupils' engagement with language, whether it be in spelling or in poetry or in the lived experience of the individual, can never really be progressive, systemically developed, or properly evaluated and assessed. Language teaching *should* be about process rather than content; pupils *should* be encouraged to use language as a way to knowing. But if there is no determinable and accountable content, teacher and pupils work in a vacuum. It might be 'creative' but it is comparable to living in a house which is all bright attractive bricks but which has no foundations. Second, the fact that 'there is no satisfactory evidence' of the connection between teaching rules of language and the developing of language skills does not preclude such evidence. It all depends how it is done and how much explicit 'linguistics' is taught in schools and in what form. This is a point addressed directly in the article by Mike Riddle (p. 31).

Much more work needs to be undertaken before such conclusions can be presented as gospel. The whole question of 'knowing about' and 'knowing how to do' is a very complex one and much depends on the age, abilities, etc. of the pupils concerned. Teachers need to be alert to it and must decide how much explicit knowledge of the rules of language can help their pupils at different stages of their development. Third, there seems no reason why linguistics cannot be taught in schools as an academic discipline like physics, chemistry, sociology or English literature, cf. Hawkins (1979), Tinkel (1979). No one would surely wish to pretend to a direct connection between studying 'O' level English literature in its present form and the improvement of performance in reading and writing. But teaching linguistics and having linguistics as a foundation for classroom language teaching should not be confused.

The aims and scope of this book

Needless to say, it is impossible to fulfil the kind of catholicity of scope suggested by the title to this book. Had there been the space, I should have liked to include more material on some of the following areas of language education to which linguists have made important contributions: the teaching of reading; language acquisition; spelling; teaching the deaf and those with speech disabilities; adult literacy; discourse analysis and classroom interaction; bilingualism and bidialectalism; the language situation of ethnic minorities; the teaching of English as a second and foreign language, to name but a few major aspects of contemporary education studies. Some of these topics are taken up in further books in this series, but interested readers are directed to the bibliography for appropriate material.

This book offers some articles which lay a theoretical basis for the application of linguistics to education. The questions debated and discussed here are important and must be clarified so that application can take place without misunderstanding. The book may therefore be more theoretical and concerned with principle than some would like. But in the context of a complex area like language teaching it would be wrong for us to proceed without a clear and full statement of the position of the linguist.

Other articles concentrate on core areas of linguistics: grammar; lexis; phonology; the social basis of language. The orientation is toward 'secondary' or 'upper school' language study and teaching. There is thus a certain homogeneity about the different contributions to the book; the focus is necessarily narrow and it is hoped that it is also clear and fundamental.

Above all, it is hoped that this book will contribute to further discussion of the role of language in education which, just as it was in the 1970s, will be an undoubtedly central issue for the 1980s. It is our hope but also our conviction that by the end of this decade those concerned with this area will find that they have to use the combinations *linguistics* and education and *linguistics* and the teacher.

Notes

1   See *The University of Malaya English for Special Purposes Project*, ELT Documents 107 (British Council, 1980). For teaching materials associated with the project see E. Morais (ed.), *Skills for Learning* (Nelson, London, 1980).

2   The debate contains a number of contributions from interested parties including Colin Stork, Mike Torbe, W.H. Mittins, Peter Doughty and Tony Burgess. See Stork *et al.* (1980).

3   The articles by Perera have particular point in the light of this statement:

> For many pupils . . . the language of schools subjects becomes more and more alien during the years of their secondary education, and they participate less and less in its processes. When they do not understand the characteristics of language in the context of learning, they may fail to develop the confidence and incentive to participate that are vital if learning is to take place. (DES (1977), *Curriculum 11-16*, Working Papers by H.M. Inspectorate, pp. 20-3, 'Language'.)

1

Linguistics in teacher education

Michael Halliday

Introduction

This article reviews some issues in the language education of teachers during the past fifteen years and discusses the relationship between linguistics and education with particular reference to the training of teachers. The following main points are argued: that linguistics is not just a description of the formal features of language but is also a study of language 'as an institution' which can condition the way individuals see each other, both in and out of schools; that the social basis of language study (or sociolinguistics) should be a core element in the courses which linguists should work out with teacher educators; and that teachers' fears about linguistics are groundless – because of its *systematic* attention to language it can help solve many practical language problems in the classroom.

I would like to talk in the area of linguistics and teacher education. I do so without apology, because we were asked at this meeting to relate what we'd been doing to the field of teacher education; and I am, after all, a linguist. I've been sharing the boat with teachers now for seventeen years, very amicably; seventeen years in which, in our work on the principles and practices of language education, a very great deal has happened. Educational theory has moved away from formalism and excessive structure (educational practice had already moved away from it, at least in England – though not so much in Scotland, where I started). It's been through a period of child-centred liberalism which often took the form which I used to call benevolent inertia: the theory that, provided the teacher puts his feet up and does nothing to stop it, learning will take place by magic of its own accord. It is now searching for a new kind of structure which will, in some way, re-instate the teacher in his or her traditional dual role as a source of authority and of wisdom, but one which, this time, will be justified in terms of some prevailing theory of human learning or child development.

A lot has happened also in linguistics during this time. Linguistics has moved into, and then again out of, a period of extreme formalism; a period when it was discovered that you could talk about language as a formal system. The cost of doing this was that you had to pretend language was very different from what it really is: you had to idealize it to a fantastic degree, so that it bore very little relation to the way people actually talk and listen, or even the way they write and read. This was, historically, a resurgence of the Aristotelian tradition which has tended to dominate western linguistics, and in which linguistics is part of philosophy, and grammar is part of logic. (Philosophers of language don't call it grammar; they call it syntax.) This kind of linguistics has little relevance to education, as Chomsky, with whose name it is associated, has always made perfectly clear.

Over the past ten years the other western tradition, that of discourse and rhetoric, and linguistics oriented towards the speaker in the community, which starts from the fact that people not only talk but they actually talk to each other, has been popping up again and struggling back into the light of day. This kind of linguistics has a relevance for education because it is all about meaning. It is concerned with meanings, implicit and explicit. When it is said that 'linguistics' is currently concerned primarily with language forms', people are talking about the formal linguistics of ten years ago. If they had had the advantage as I did two months ago of spending a few weeks in California working there with linguists at different institutions, they would have found that those very linguists who, a few years ago, were trying to make rules for generating ideal sentences, are now studying what people actually say and write. They have abandoned formalism and all the barren distinctions that go with it: distinctions between competence and performance; between language and the use of language; and they're studying discourse and meaning, and accepting language as the typically human mixture of order and chaos that it really is. Those who glibly deny that linguistics has any relevance to the teacher at the chalk-face are invited, therefore, to look a little more closely at what linguistics really is and what it does, and maybe even to try and find out what questions linguists are exploring, and what problems they are trying to solve.

Right in the centre of the picture they'll find questions like the following (and these are only examples): how and why do children learn a mother tongue? What are the universals, the culturally specific features and the individual variables of the language development process? How do people interpret the situations in which they find themselves in such a way that they can effectively exchange meanings in those situations? How do people construct a model of reality, a picture of the world, through language, and what is it about the nature of language that enables them to do so? How is language related to social structure? What part does it play in transmitting, maintaining and modifying that structure? How do people agree on what is sense and what is nonsense, on what is literature, on what is good literature? and so on.

It would be hard to find questions more central to education than these, and in order to pursue them, we have to investigate language in all its aspects. At the heart of language are its semantic, lexicogrammatical and phonological systems; or what we call in everyday parlance the meanings, the wordings and the sounds. This is where grammar comes in. Language teachers - and I mean by that all teachers concerned with language education - ought to know something about grammar; though in my view, functional grammar is more useful than formal grammar for our purposes. (One of the objections to traditional grammar is that it is formal, not functional; another is that it is not very good formal grammar.) This is not, of course, so that they can teach grammar in the classroom. I was sceptical about the value of classroom grammar seventeen years ago, and nothing that has happened since has led me to change my mind. (I leave aside, however, the question of grammar in the upper two years or so of secondary school; there may be a place for it there, but that's a different question.) The purpose is so that they, as teachers, will understand about language and how it works. But even in linguistics, in the context of teacher education, it seems to me that grammar will play only a fairly minor part. For one thing I would consider semantics more important (although it should be said that functional grammar is, in any case, a semantic kind of grammar). I would put in, I think, just as much functional grammar as is necessary for the understanding of semantics and for explaining the meaning of a text - you need this, apart from anything else, for the appreciation of poetry. You can't really explain why a poem or any other piece of literature makes the impact it does without some grammar behind you. Grammar helps to overcome the purely private nature of literature as a school subject, where the pupil is simply left guessing as to what reaction to a particular work the teacher expects of him - an approach that may be derived from I.A. Richards's dogma that the meaning of a poem is between the lines. (A very slight but significant slip there - if he'd only said the meaning of a poem is *behind* the lines I would have said 'hear, hear'.)

I would want some basic phonetics and phonology in teacher education; about intonation, rhythm, prosodies and airstream mechanisms. A bit of segmental phonology concerned with phonemes, is, perhaps, also likely to be useful, especially in teaching English as a second language. In addition I would want something on language development in children, and on the relation between language development and cognitive development. (I needn't expand on this because it's a major theme for this whole conference.) Then I would want a deep study of language variation and varieties: dialects and registers, language types, language universals, and language variables; again with a special eye to the needs of those concerned with migrant and Aboriginal education. And then I would want a study of institutional linguistics – bilingualism and multilingualism, language development (in the other sense of nations and communities), and language planning. Finally I would want to explore the whole question of the place of language in the life of institutions, and in the value systems of the community: how language expresses ideologies and creates a culture as a complex of semiotic or meaning systems.

All this is linguistics. I don't know whether it's just linguistics, or sociolinguistics, or some other kind of hyphenated linguistics; it's simply the study of language, and I don't think we need be too concerned with where we draw these particular boundaries. In other words, I would like to reject categorically the assertion that a course of general linguistics is of no particular use to teachers. I think it's fundamental. But I don't think it should be a sort of watered down academic linguistics course. It should be something new, designed and worked out by linguists and teachers and teacher trainers working together.

But the place of linguistics in teacher education is not simply, in my view, its contribution to the teacher's professional expertise – that is one aspect of it. In this respect it resembles psychology and sociology; it is not something to teach, but something to enhance a teacher's understanding of the processes of learning and the content of what is being learned. A very simple example can be given from what has just been said: that, without some linguistics, you can't understand the regularities of the English spelling system. If this was all there was to linguistics perhaps people wouldn't be so scared of it. The strength of the reactions that the mention of linguistics used to provoke, and still does provoke in some quarters, suggests that a lot of people feel threatened by it; and if that is so, we need to understand why. Partly, no doubt, in the same way that I always felt threatened by philosophy and philosophers. A philosopher colleague once said to me that I'd been 'doing philosophy' all the time in my own work – I just hadn't been doing it very well; it was a do-it-yourself philosophy of a not very effective kind. I think the reason teachers feel threatened by linguistics is partly that they know they're 'doing' it all the time in their work, and yet doing it not very well. But there is also, perhaps, another reason: there is a real sense in which linguistics is threatening; it's uncomfortable, and it's subversive. It's uncomfortable because it strips us of the fortifications that protect and surround some of our deepest prejudices. As long as we keep linguistics at bay we can go on believing what we want to believe about language, both our own and everybody else's. We can go on believing that there must be something wrong with the mental abilities and thought processes of all those children who speak non-standard English, or are foreigners, or are Aboriginal speakers, or whatever else. We can go on believing that language criticism is a meaningful exercise; that notions such as that certain vowel sounds are inherently ugly, or certain modes of expression and grammatical patterns are inelegant and impoverished, are genuine opinions and feelings that we have arrived at for ourselves instead of being what they are, simply the received attitudes and slogans that we get from our culture and our sub-culture. Linguistics destroys these comforting illusions, forcing us to distinguish what are simply regular features of this or that language or dialect, on the one hand, from what are true failures of language where the meaning has been distorted or obscured.

But there's more to it than that. Linguistics is not only uncomfortable, it's also subversive, in that once we come to look at language as an *institution* – that is, at the relation between a language and the people who speak it – then we come face to face with what are often unpleasant and unpalatable truths about society. More than any other human phenomenon, language reflects and reveals the inequalities that are enshrined in the social process. When we study language systematically (and that is all that linguistics is), we see into the power structure that lies behind our everyday social relationships, the hierarchical statuses that are accorded to different groups within society – social classes, ethnic groups, the generations, the sexes, urban and rural populations, or whatever they may be; and it's not surprising that these structures are revealed by language, because they are maintained by language, both actively and symbolically. This is why people defend their language when it is under attack and try to maintain it in an alien environment. This is why migrants coming to Australia want to go on speaking their own language: not simply as an echo of the cultural past, but because it defines and protects their identity in the present and the future.

More than any other subject, linguistics forces us to face and acknowledge the multi-cultural nature of society and to do something about it. This can be a deeply disturbing experience, bringing to consciousness what is usually below the level of awareness both in our individual mental processes and in our forms of social behaviour and interaction. But for the same reasons that linguistics is threatening and disturbing, it can also be immensely rewarding. These then are some of the reasons why I believe that linguistics is not irrelevant to education.

Not everything that a linguist inquires into is equally part of the picture. Linguists are interested in interpreting language from all kinds of different standpoints, and some of the questions that they ask are asked out of pure curiosity, just from the desire to understand. Therefore we should beware of thinking that every subject exists simply to serve the needs of education. There is a tendency for educators to demand an immediate pay-off: if we can't apply these ideas directly here and now in our teaching, then we don't want anything to do with them. This attitude passes for a healthy pragmatism: we're practical people with a job to do, no time for the frills. In fact it is simply mental laziness – a refusal to inquire into things that may not have any immediate and obvious applications, but which for this very reason may have a deeper significance in the long run. Most of linguistics is not classroom stuff; but it is there behind the lines, underlying our classroom practices, and our ideas about children, and about learning and reality.

Note

This paper first originated in a talk given at a conference organized by Canberra Curriculum Development Centre as part of its National Language Development Project in Australia. The paper appeared in J. Maling-Keepes and B.D. Keepes (eds), *Language and Education: The LDP Phase 1*, Canberra, Curriculum Development Centre, 1979, and is reprinted here by kind permission of the Director of the Language Development Project.

2

Linguistics and the teacher

John Sinclair

Introduction

This article stresses the need for the implementation of recommendations made in the Bullock Report for teachers to receive a rigorous and linguistically systematic course(s) in language and learning, and does so in the light of some reasons why such courses have generally failed to materialize. The dangers of such a failure are very effectively highlighted by a mordant analogy with the professional training of doctors. The article is usefully supplemented by an appendix in which Professor Sinclair outlines, with reference to criteria established in the main body of the paper, the kind of content he thinks appropriate to linguistics in education courses.

The matter of expertise in English language as part of the professional training of teachers has led to a recurrent debate. Some movement can be observed in practice, not all in what I consider to be the right direction. This paper is a revision of a contribution to the debate some years ago, and I am glad to say that fairly extensive revision is necessary. Since 1975 we have had the Bullock Report (DES, 1975), well received but not well implemented, indeed stymied by the decline in provision of teacher education and the disbanding of the Area Training Organizations. Serious work in English language, not firmly enough established in the preceding four years, fell an easy prey to arguments about austerity, and the new autonomy of those former Colleges of Education that remain open weakened the external pressure to maintain and build up courses in English linguistics. Since 1976 too, we have seen the establishment of NCLE, the National Council for Languages in Education, which, in the five years of its existence, has begun to provide a useful centre for identifying important issues in the profession as a whole, and co-ordinating development. Although numerically heavily weighted in favour of teachers of western European languages, it is conscious of a need to broaden its base and get all the branches of language teaching to work together. From the learner's point of view – for example a child at secondary school – the language teachers speak with many voices, impose widely different methods, have different priorities and objectives, assess in a variety of ways. Because of the language situation in the UK, some variety is desirable and inevitable, but at present we have unplanned and often needless variety in approaches, and too little recognition of differences that really matter, like the different language backgrounds of the pupils.

This paper pursues the claim that knowledge of the structures and functions of language is essential in the professional education of a teacher. All teachers should be given access to a basic understanding of language in the classroom. Language teachers have to control a more complex discourse, and therefore need more detailed study of the processes of education through language. English teachers, whose subject is central in the educational system, require a comprehensive appreciation of the role of language in both institutionalized learning and personal development.

It must be recognized straight away that this view is not attractive to many who claim to speak on behalf of the silent majority of teachers. I shall call them the mediators. In the 1950s, they or their predecessors were downright hostile to the growing discipline of linguistics; as the climate of opinion gradually moved, and some approving gestures were necessary, the mediators became ready to admit some watered-down 'language study' into educational courses, while trying to isolate 'linguistics' as almost a dirty word. To be sure, the attitudes and pre-occupations of many academic linguists played into their hands as the 1960s became a period of intense development of theory and formal systems in linguistics. But during the last decade the development of, broadly speaking, communicative models of language has left the mediators with little more to work on than an instinctive dislike of systematic description.

The methodology of English mother-tongue teaching now looks distinctly backward, compared with other branches of language teaching. Many of its central tenets, particularly the accent on the individual's development of creative and critical skills, are well worth cherishing and are valuable correctives to methods which define narrower aims. But the unwillingness to admit new concepts from linguistics has impeded progress substantially.

One argument which attends every effort to introduce something new is the argument about timetable and resources. In schools, in PGCE courses, in examinations, the intellectual issues are often diverted into forbidding practicalities. Linguistics work in secondary schools, English language at 'A' level, Bullock's language across the curriculum, linguistics in teacher education, can all be blessed in principle but kept out or down in practice.

The fact is that any subject that establishes an aura of necessity in the education of a teacher will be fitted in somehow. Some subjects are there by tradition, some because of the status of the department, some by consensus and some by demand. For those subjects the timetable difficulties will be solved, the library will be adequately stocked, there will be proper accommodation and equipment. Students will get help if they find those subjects difficult; those subjects will be strongly defended if students protest about them.

The teacher and the linguist

A teacher in action is primarily a highly skilled verbalizer. He must so control and direct his own utterances, and those of his pupils, that the mysterious communication we call education takes place. Now there is a strong argument that linguistics, being the study of language for its own sake, must have a dominant position in the study of any human verbal behaviour. Linguistics is a subject developed by scholars who devote themselves to the explanation and detailed description of language phenomena, and adjacent or overlapping subjects ignore linguistics at their peril.

The other side of the coin is that a linguist must be prepared to show the relevance of his work, in his terms, to the enquiries of others. The main stumbling-block here has been the 'so what?' syndrome – the inability to correlate objective evidence with evaluative insight. Linguistics has to play down the natural understanding that people have about language, in order to gain precision in description. However only some extreme behaviouristic models attempt to edit out the human beings entirely. Most present-day linguists use a descriptive method which relies heavily on access to the intuitions of a native speaker, despite the variables that are difficult to control in the process. Texts are increasingly seen as merely a stage in a person-to-person-and-back interaction, requiring interpretation to be an essential component of description. With the development of discourse analysis, evaluation is a recurrent element of structure.

It is thus less easy to claim that the factual and systematic character of linguistic description renders it irrelevant to the acquisition of skills in verbal communication, which themselves are a prerequisite in education.

In recent years we have heard many propositions about the relations between language and learning – that certain kinds of language are important in learning, that talk itself is educational, that the social background of some children is more conducive to learning through language than that of others. We see pedagogical fashions attempting to get children to write long sentences, or increase their active vocabulary, in the belief that by such means they will be better educated, or there may be a fashion that regards impromptu verbalization as critical, or puts great store by stimulating the fantasy world of children. Teacher styles can be praised or blamed without the benefit of accurate analysis – this or that kind of questioning is good or bad; negative decisions on children's contributions have to be carefully disguised: 'Well, now, that's very interesting – we'll come back to that. What do the rest of you think?'

Surely a linguist must have a part to play in the evaluation of these trends, and in the elucidation of the precise relationship between language in use and the development of the mind.

Linguistics should, then, be accessible to a teacher and obviously relevant to his work. Unfortunately, the state of an academic subject at one point in time is rarely such that it anticipates practical needs. Accessibility should not be a major problem – if a subject is inherently complex but necessary, it can be made accessible. Either linguistics is in a state where it should be turned into a central discipline in education, or it is so irrelevant that it can be left out of account. We back it strongly, or reject it. What is not to my mind appropriate behaviour is to strain the subject through intellectual filters of mixed origin, or accept no more than some parts of its elementary stages.

Linguistics, like any other discipline, demands commitment. There are kind words like 'appreciation' and 'orientation' for courses which do not get inside the subject. There is a range of 'hyphenated linguistics' like sociolinguistics and psycholinguistics which are tricky to handle without a base in the central areas of theory and description, though providing valuable routes to applications.

But every teacher does not need to become a competent field linguist with experience in comparative theoretical approaches. The magic minimum seems to depend on an important concept in linguistics – that language is a finite apparatus with the potential for describing a limitless range of verbal behaviour. Knowledge of some or all of the finite apparatus is not universally motivating, but the ability, in some distinct area of language patterning, to be able to describe the limitless behaviour, and to have confidence in the skill, is the essential target. And in selecting areas of language patterning, what could be more relevant than the discourse that teachers and pupils actually use all day long?

If the curriculum does not make a generous allocation to language work, the skill target should take priority over a broader consideration of language factors in education. In general the time allowed is so small that we should beware multidisciplinary approaches. Education itself is multidisciplinary but it does not follow from this that its component subjects can be jumbled up. Linguistics can provide the language side with a coherent base, from which the categories of other disciplines can be viewed, and so can each of the other disciplines concerned. Only a handful of remarkable scholars manage to think creatively across a broad spectrum of subject areas; it is unfair on the student to expect him to generate a coherent intellectual framework from potted observations in several subject areas. His learning will perforce be a one-way process.

Objections

I now review some of the main arguments against linguistics as a central subject in the education of teachers. These are culled from years of talking to a very wide range of people concerned with every aspect of education, and they represent genuinely-held views, even if I state them somewhat sharply.

(a) Linguistics is too technical, too abstract, too complicated, too difficult for our students. They have to learn about so many other things, and they are not intellectually disposed towards all this quasi-mathematical stuff.

(b) (The Catch-22 clause.) Simplified linguistics is no good either, because the students will learn it without understanding it, and it could be a dangerous weapon in their ignorant hands. Slick shortcuts and descriptive breakthroughs are alike suspect.

(c) There isn't time to go into detail. We'll manage a few lectures on Chomsky and, well, maybe Bernstein. A teacher in preparation has so many calls on his time that he cannot move into the academic side of his work, but has to keep his low brow fixed on his own horizon.

(d) Linguistics makes claims of objectivity, but it is fairly obviously not objective in the scientific sense. So it has conned people into thinking that it is a science, whereas in reality it is a pseudo-science. Objective description is a laudable aim, but if that aim is not achieved the stages towards it have no greater interest or validity than those of a subjective argument.

(e) Linguistics is a vast arsenal of terms and axioms and techniques, with an enormous fire-power. We are mere mortals, with a fairly restricted job to do, but blessed with intuitions, which, though not of course in the same class as linguistic arguments, offer a home-spun alternative that gives fair results over the years, and even seems at times to pick out what is important, while linguistics blunders on along its pedantic path.

Many of these objections condemn themselves, and I do not want to refute each of them in turn. Instead, here is an analogy with another important profession and its training.

Medicine

Notice that a doctor's period of training is as long as it takes to master the curriculum. We need doctors just as we need teachers, and doctors have to learn about how to cure people. Let us examine arguments that they do not need to learn anything much about the structure of the human body.

(a) Subjects like anatomy, physiology and all that are much too technical. Everyone knows medical students are not from the top of the academic pile, and they'll soon get confused by all those long Latin names and cutting people up.

(b) We are very suspicious of all the new packaged aids to doctors, like computerised diagnosis, where it could be a dangerous tool in the hands of a non-expert. If a doctor doesn't fully understand any of his contributory subjects, he should not embark upon them.

(c) There isn't time for detail because of all the other things in the course, like a three-year main course on Bedside Manner, and special options like Diagnosis without Evidence, Natural Amputation and Badminton.

(d) Science is never fully objective. Microscope or telescope, there's always the same blur when you look inside. We are guessing all the

time, and even some of the firmest arguments may well be challenged – so really the rigour of medical science is bogus. And once
it is challenged, then the whole notion of scientific argument goes
out of the window.

(e) There's a lot in all this anatomy and stuff, and we must admire and
respect it, even though we do not use it ourselves. The plain fact of
the matter is that we might waste time paddling around in the
niceties of all these subjects when in reality anyone knows when a
chap's ill – you don't have to be a doctor to take his temperature –
and if a few of us get together for a chat we'll surely work out
what's wrong with him.

There is a very serious point to be made at this juncture. The arguments above are patronising in respect to the students and dismissive of
academic priorities. It is most regrettable if such attitudes are allowed
to circumscribe the intellectual opportunity of students on educational
courses. There seems a fair consensus that students in general live up
to or down to the expectations of those in charge of them. If the
mediators pronounce linguistics too difficult for teachers, they are
putting an artificial ceiling on the intellectual development of their
students.

The difficulty of linguistics

The question of the difficulty of linguistics is worth closer consideration.
Linguistics requires abstract conceptualisation, systematic thinking
and attention to detail. Human beings have a head start (almost liter-
ally) in linguistics compared with many academic subjects because of
access to their intuitions about language. It uses far too much and too
varied terminology, partly because it is a young subject and partly
because linguists have a tendency to be fussy or innovative about terms
– rather an occupational hazard. It uses a variety of symbolic notations,
which can be off-putting at first, but so is the alphabet, and literacy
teachers persevere. It uses language to talk about language, which is
potentially confusing, but so do language teachers, without undue
strain.

This is hardly a formidable picture. Properly presented, there should
be nothing untoward about a course in linguistics that achieves high
academic standards. Yet many presentations seem more of an inocula-
tion against the subject than a genuine attempt to teach it.

Some approaches avoid the rigours of linguistics by 'studying' the language informally. Teacher and student have full freedom to observe. The teacher does not necessarily have any expertise in linguistics or adjacent subject areas, such as philosophy, psychology, sociology.

This informal approach is very popular at present, and it is worth examination, because it often conceals misunderstandings about the nature of linguistics. For example, several times I have heard or read someone saying that simple counting of word-classes in transcribed speech was laborious and unproductive. Instead some more sophisticated categories had to be set up to describe the data. Good. What is not so good is that this is seen as a move away from, instead of towards, linguistics. Not many linguists spend their days producing raw counts of word-classes – my experience is that of resisting pressure from non-linguists to use such simplistic tools.

In fact the categories of analysis of present-day linguistics are far more relevant to educational research than they are often given credit for. They avoid the major pitfalls of intuition, while using linguistic intuition to the full.

There is an embarrassment of riches in almost any snatch of language; almost any observation can be made into a self-fulfilling generalization if the generalization is informal enough; categories can be made to shrink or expand or proliferate at will. One set of observations need not be related to any other; overlaps, cross-cutting criteria and unexplained gaps can be ignored.

We have been victims in recent years of a fashion of publishing scraps of tape transcripts alongside unstructured commentaries; or polemics supported by occasional transcribed examples. Video and audio equipment is frequently used in conjunction with casual notes. These presentations are often stimulating because people in action are interesting, but they are not likely to give usable insights into educational communication.

I should like to suggest certain minimum standards for the analysis and discussion of recorded human language. They are not difficult criteria to meet, and although they themselves do not guarantee success or even relevance, their acceptance would help students to judge descriptive systems.

A   The descriptive apparatus should be finite, or else one is not saying anything at all, and may be merely creating the illusion of classification.

If I pick up various common objects and name them with non-sense words, consider the different effect of these beginnings:

(i) This is a wonk, this is a dibble. . .

We do not know what is happening. Perhaps the English nouns are being simply recoded. We have no idea what will be said next.

(ii) I am going to classify everything into two classes. This is a wonk, this is a dibble. . .

We know a tremendous amount more. We can reconstruct the next utterance all but a simple choice of *wonk* or *dibble* and we shall have had even some guidance in guessing that.

B   The symbols or terms in the descriptive apparatus should be precisely relatable to their exponents in the data, or else it is not clear what one is saying. If we call some phenomenon a 'noun', or a 'repair strategy' or a 'retreat', we must establish exactly what constitutes the class with that label. The label itself is negligible – it is the criteria which matter. Consider (iii) below.

(iii) Anything with a right angle in it is a wonk. Everything else is a dibble. . . .

We don't need any more. The number of classes and the criteria are provided, and off we go. The classification is replicable and clear. There will be problems of interpretation, marginal choices, etc., but that is a feature of all practical classification.

C   The whole of the data should be describable: the descriptive system should be comprehensive. This is not a difficult criterion to meet, because it is always possible to have a ragbag category into which go all items not positively classified by other criteria. But the exercise of building it in is a valuable check on the rest of the description. For example, if we find that 95 per cent of the text goes into the ragbag, we would reject the description as invalid for the text as a whole. If we feel uneasy about putting certain items together in the ragbag, this may well lead to insights later on.

The effect of this standard is to stop commentators picking and choosing from a text with no regard for the total structure of the text.

D   There must be at least one impossible combination of symbols. This is the basic notion of linguistic structure, although here couched as a prohibition. A, B, and C above could be general standards for linear string analysis, but this one is linguistic. Language, it seems, never exhausts the possibilities in its structure, thus leaving elbow-room for two major features: style and change. So if a descriptive system of wonks (w) and dibbles (d) allows all two-symbol structures (ww, dd, wd, dw) then it is worth looking at three-symbol structures, perhaps to find only wwd, wdd, dwd, ddd. It is now clear that no three-symbol string can end in w, and we have made a structural statement.

There will probably be all sorts of limitations on four-symbol strings and above, but at the very least we can say that a descriptive apparatus which does not meet this criterion is certainly not showing anything of the structure of what it is describing.

I find that I cannot take seriously any textual description that does not attempt to meet at least these standards. So, to return to the original point of this part of the argument, the 'informal study of language' seems close to a contradiction in terms. Language is just not something that can be informally studied. This point is valid even at the most elementary stages.

Course design

If the main argument in this paper is accepted, the next question is what should be the syllabus of a suitable course in linguistics. There have been several designs proposed in recent years, and valuable suggestions are made elsewhere in this volume. The Bullock Report contains helpful designs (DES, 1975, pp. 343-6), and the Appendix which follows sets out a recent attempt of my own to outline the language content.

Appendix

1 *The sound system of English*

This component can be relatively self-contained. It involves students in:

1 Accurately listening to human speech.
2 Distinguishing between loosely-defined notions like 'consonant' and 'vowel' in speech and writing.
3 Classifying variation into (a) allophonic, (b) phonemic, (c) accent differences.
4 Acquiring basic notions of structure (e.g. syllable structure).
5 Learning and using a symbolic notation, i.e. a transcription.
6 Acquiring kinaesthetic awareness of articulation.
7 Recognizing visual clues to articulation.

8 Separating and combining components of articulation.
9 Noting the relation between segmental analysis and the continuous variation of the sound wave.
10 Studying stress and rhythm and some of the range of linguistic variation found, particularly, in Indian languages and West Indian Creole.
11 Recognizing the role of pitch variation in articulation.
12 Noting systematic variation in the speech of individuals in different circumstances e.g. assimilation.
13 Identifying slips of the tongue.
14 Noting common 'speech defects' and unusual articulations.
15 Discussing intelligibility criteria.
16 Evaluating notions of correctness and propriety in speech.
17 Gaining access to major authors and reference works.

2 *The syntax of English*

The aim of this component is to provide access to descriptive skills and to gain experience in using the skills in classroom activities. It is the central component, because it studies the most distinctive and characteristic patterns of organization in language, in their simplest form. It will involve students in:

1 Recognizing syntax-like constructs in nonlinguistic patterns.
2 Coping with the problem of terminology in syntax, via discussions of criteria for terminology, and systematic relations among sets of terms.
3 Identifying significant variation (hence some preliminary discussion of prescriptive grammar).
4 Acquiring basic notions of syntagmatic and paradigmatic organization, and open and closed choices in both dimensions (building on 1 above).
5 Learning and using a simple symbolic notation.
6 Exploring the notion of 'grammaticalness' and the principal types of syntactic deviation, through practical experiments.
7 Acquiring a grasp of procedures for problem-solving in syntax.
8 Separating and combining syntactic features.
9 Noting the relations between class and structure.
10 Studying some of the range of syntactic variation within English, with particular reference to classroom observation.

11 Discussing the inter-relationships between phonology and syntax, particularly concerning intonation.
12 Noting systematic variation in the syntax of individuals in different situations: basic notions of registers, genres, styles.
13 Studying idiomaticity and its relation to syntax.
14 Examining the syntax of the spoken language, using a number of examples.
15 Comparing the syntactic structure of speech and writing and discussing how to account for the differences.
16 Returning to prescriptive grammar (from 3 above) and re-examining notions of correctness and propriety.
17 Gaining access to major authors and reference works.

In this list of topics, there is nothing specifically mentioned about the imaginative and creative aspects of linguistic composition. It is not thereby excluded, but is seen as a cross-cutting dimension which is utilized and referred to as often as possible.

3 *The semantics of English*

The practical study of semantics will involve students in:

1 Isolating semantic patterns from other linguistic forms of organization.
2 Discussing 'meaning' and related concepts in a preliminary fashion.
3 Considering synonyms and paraphrasibility through examples – particularly those exemplifying communication difficulties.
4 Acquiring basic notions of semantic structures and relationships.
5 Investigating semantic congruence and oddity.
6 Comparing semantic classifications with lexical collocation and word-association evidence.
7 Separating and combining semantic features.
8 Noting some aspects of the historical development of meaning.
9 Noting some of the range of semantic variation within English, with particular reference to classroom observation.
10 Considering the possibility of generalization of semantic concepts, as against the cultural confines of meaning.
11 Discussing the relationship between semantics and syntax.
12 Noting systematic variation in the semantic usage of individuals in different situations.

13 Studying typical performance errors in meaning and the implications for how meaning is acquired and stored.
14 Investigating specialized areas of semantics, e.g. the creation and use of technical terms.
15 Considering the speech acts of naming and defining.
16 Returning to notions of meaning (from 3 above) and re-examining them.
17 Gaining access to major authors and reference works, and making tentative evaluations of the reference works.

4 *Written text*

This is a fast-growing field of study which has great practical potential in education. It will involve the student in:

1 Observing the surface structures and other organizing resources (layout, typography, inter-relations with nonverbal matter) that are available above the sentence.
2 Disambiguating the notion 'sentence'.
3 Classifying exponents of reference and cohesion.
4 Examining paragraphs and possible higher units.
5 Learning and using a simple analytical system.
6 Investigating the notion of coherence in texts.
7 Glancing at the genre of concrete poetry.
8 Studying the role of self-reference (language about language) in text structure.
9 Noting ways in which suprasentential structures and relations are signalled.
10 Studying the main types of variation within written English and making some effort to account for them.
11 Considering the skill of reading aloud from written text, what is added, what is omitted and what consistency there is between individuals.
12 Collecting and studying putative instances of poorly-formed paragraphs and reference networks.
13 Cross-referring to the spoken language and its larger structures.
14 Studying the flow of information in paragraphs, and how it can be adjusted.
15 Reviewing prescriptive literature on continuous writing.
16 Gaining access to a range of recent work in this field.

5 *Spoken discourse*

This component balances syntax (which is normally studied mainly in relation to writing) and provides in particular a basis for careful examination of classroom interaction. A descriptive system is offered at (5) which the student can use to examine his own behaviour, his pupils' and other instances of oral teaching. The component will involve the student in:

1 Accurately observing classroom language behaviour and para-linguistic signals.
2 Acquiring a precise basic vocabulary distinguishing terms like 'utterance', 'turn', 'move'.
3 Identifying significant variation, particularly in the intonation sequences.
4 Acquiring the notion of discourse structure being continuously created by more than one participant.
5 Learning and using a symbolic notation – simple enough to be usable, with practice, in real time observation.
6 Exploring the cohesive patterns of spoken interaction.
7 Studying the role of gesture, posture and other kinesic/proxemic factors in structuring discourse.
8 Separating and combining components of verbal interactions.
9 Considering overlappings, engagement and interruption.
10 Studying a variety of discourse styles shown by teacher and pupil.
11 Studying the contrasts when teacher and pupil adopt other roles (*not* in simulation).
12 Acquiring recognition competence in the intonation patterns which are structural in spoken interaction.
13 Identifying and studying breakdowns in the interactive aspect of discourse.
14 Noting putative tactics adopted by speakers over more than one utterance.
15 Considering what might be the reasons for observed conventions of talk.
16 Considering what might be indications of the competence of participants.
17 Making suggestions for improving classroom communication.
18 Gaining access to a range of recent work in this field.

6 *English in the school curriculum*

This is the only relational component, and so is structured in a slightly different way from the others. It includes general review material. It will involve the student in:

1　Observing spoken and written language in a variety of curriculum settings.
2　Discussing terms like 'transactional' and 'service' English and reaching a personal position on the matter.
3　Classifying variant types of curriculum-based language.
4　Discussing the so-called dichotomy of form and content.
5　Compiling a list of typical communication problems in a range of classrooms.
6　Looking for instances of effective uses of language in relation to academic subjects.
7　Using concepts and categories from other components to analyse the problems at (5).
8　Separating and combining linguistic forms and conceptual categories.
9　Noting the concerns of semiotic analysis.
10　Studying the effect on pupils of a range of different discourse styles.
11　Developing methods for evaluating the contributions made by pupils in speech or writing.
12　Considering the interplay between linguistic and nonlinguistic presentations of subject-matter, and mixed types.
13　Gaining access to a range of recent work in this field.

Note

This contribution is based on an article first published in the *Dudley College of Education Journal* in 1973, but has been extensively revised and updated.

3

Linguistics for education

Mike Riddle

Introduction

This article gives a useful account of the work of the Committee for Linguistics in Education of which the author is Chairman, and then goes on to offer practical suggestions for implementing linguistics-based in-service courses. Among the wide range of issues addressed by Mike Riddle are the teaching of linguistics as a school subject, the applications of linguistics to learning problems and to the teaching of English in particular, and the nature of the discipline of linguistics itself. The final part of the article contains a number of interesting suggestions for teaching activities which draw in a principled way on the subject of linguistics.

Whoever coined the expression Who is afraid of Linguistics? must have known from first hand the contention created by the entry of linguistics into the field of language in education. The fact that it came in, in the mid-1960s, just after the English teachers, whose responsibilities included English language, had begun their own revolution in language teaching, and that it appeared in a form reminiscent of traditional grammar (which English teachers were phasing out) did not ease its entry. Co-operation between linguists and English teachers was not helped by a parallel event: linguistics was at almost the same time doing it with an analytical objectivity that was, and still is, anathema to most English teachers. There were some legendary confrontations in print, and at conferences, over issues in both language and literature, but in spite of these the influence of linguistics continued to grow, and, if anything, has accelerated in the last ten years.

The main reason for this is that many of the problems in language teaching have appeared to be intractable. Administrators, lecturers and advisers and inspectors of English, as well as teachers, have turned to

linguistics for assistance: the DES has taken a lead in organizing conferences and courses on language and linguistics; within the National
Association for the Teaching of English (NATE), many of its members
have become convinced of the need for some linguistics in English
teaching; the National Association of Advisers and Inspectors of English
(NAAIE) numbers among its members several committed linguists, and
many others who are sympathetic to the subject. And recently, the
National Congress on Languages in Education (NCLE) was launched to
explore problems across the boundaries that divide the language skills
subjects: English Mother Tongue (EMT), English as a Foreign Language
(EFL), English as a Second Language (ESL) and Modern Languages
(MLs).

The two linguistics associations, the British Association of Applied
Linguistics and the Linguistics Association of Great Britain, were slow
to respond to the language teaching problems of secondary and primary
schools: BAAL's main interest was with EFL and ESL; LAGB was
principally concerned with the development of the subject at university
level. But in 1978, the two associations jointly sponsored a seminar on
linguistics in schools, at the North Worcester College in Bromsgrove,
and as a result of this the Committee for Linguistics in Education was
set up. Its purpose was twofold: to maintain momentum and direction
in the contribution that linguists can make to the teaching of languages,
and to maintain contact with initiatives taken by other bodies, such as
those already mentioned. Accordingly, CLIE organized and ran two
seminars in April 1980 at the same venue, on the following subjects:
(a) Linguistics as a School Subject (Bromsgrove 80a); (b) the contribution of Linguistics to the teaching of EMT (Bromsgrove 80b). Further
seminars are planned for 1982, 1983 and 1984. The long-term aims of
the committee are to get linguistics better known within education, and
to remove barriers between it and the other agencies working for the
same ends – the improvement of language teaching. Therefore, the
committee co-opted members from the DES, NATE and NAAIE; it
has also established links with NCLE.

My intention, in contributing to this collection of essays, is to reflect
on the thinking of those linguists brought together, in seminar and committee, by the joint initiative of BAAL and LAGB. Also I would like to
take up some questions that interest me and I think need further discussion, such as: Is there a subject called 'language', separable from linguistics? Which is more cost effective – in-service or initial training? Which
strategies for teaching linguistics are likely to be most successful? Is
linguistics one subject or several?

'Language' or linguistics?

I want to deal with this question first because it provides me with an opportunity to give a brief account of the context within which the other questions need to be considered. It was in the late 1950s that the current fascination with language emerged as a national phenomenon – in literature and in the media. This was not an arbitrary happening, but was the result of decades of academic research in such subjects as anthropology, linguistics, philosophy, ethnography and information theory. The education system was, naturally, affected by the new thinking and its long-standing concern for the values of reading, writing and correct speaking took on a much more sophisticated appearance. Language came to be seen as a mediator in the personal and social lives of individuals. Its potential as an area for development was readily appreciated, particularly by English teachers, many of whom replaced literature with 'language', as their main focus of attention.

Meanwhile, the academic research that fuelled this interest did not slacken; on the contrary it intensified and, particularly in the case of linguistics, became very specialized and inaccessible to any but trained linguists. As research developed in the linguistic theory imported from America, the transformational grammar associated with Chomsky, a gap opened up between the 'transformationalists' and those linguists working in the descriptive linguistics traditional in Britain, particularly in registers, varieties and the functions of language. It was the latter type of linguistics that made an impact on teachers in training and eventually on language teaching in schools.

Departments of English and professional studies in colleges and institutes of education came under pressure to provide courses in 'language'. For their syllabus content, staff drew on current work in descriptive linguistics and on the increasing amount of research in language carried out by sociologists and psychologists. The 'language' courses that resulted were not founded on the phonological, syntactic and semantic models that supported the descriptive studies of varieties and functions, but on selected facts derived from them, and especially on the social and cultural factors that determined code variation and choice of registers. The effect of this on teachers in training was predictable: students entered teaching with an appreciation of the role of language in education; but without a foundation in language analysis they found it difficult to apply this general knowledge to detailed linguistic problems in the classroom.

On the other hand, it would be wrong to suggest at this point that there were no 'language' courses with a linguistics base; qualified linguists in colleges and institutes constructed syllabuses that included some linguistics. But even with these courses results in the form of classroom application were not encouraging. The gap between courses on grammatical analysis and the actual day-to-day problems of the classroom was too large for the probationer to bridge, because the linguistics input was generally insufficient to constitute a basis on which to create any marked change in the methods of teaching. But the parts of the syllabus devoted to textual description of varieties and functions did make an impact and served to reinforce in the schools the demand for more relevant and contemporary syllabuses in 'language', particularly at 'O' and 'A' level. In the schools, where changes in atti-tude to language teaching were having an effect on syllabuses and examination content, the descriptivist/functionalist model was in tune with advanced thinking among English teachers, who were able to prepare examination proposals along these lines, but without know-ledge of grammatical systems or experience of analytical procedures, were not able to underpin them with adequate structural description of the linguistic systems involved. As a result of this, analysis and comment on the texts studied were very much open to the influence of literary evaluation and of unsupported functional analyses. But language syllabuses were prepared and examinations negotiated for at 'A' level.

To summarize the position at the end of the 1970s, a subject called 'language' had become part of the curriculum of colleges and institutes of education. Teaching staff were able to consolidate its status by borrowing from linguistics those bits they could take without having to study the subject itself, and by retaining control over the course content. By the inclusion of items such as the distinction between spoken and written styles, language acquisition, the functions of language and the nature (sic) of language, syllabuses were able to give the impression that an adequate grounding in the study of language was being provided, and that all that tiresome stuff about syntax, phonology and semantics was not to do with 'language' at all, but to do with linguistics. And in the schools, the syllabuses for 'A' level 'language' were doing much the same thing.

Reactions among the linguists at Bromsgrove 78 and 80 to the 'A' level 'language' proposals were mixed: some linguists saw them as a halfway house to 'A' level linguistics; others felt that to support them would reduce still further the slim chances of launching an 'A' level linguistics. The attitudes of members to 'language' courses in general are implied by the statements made in the seminar reports, some of which are summarized in a later section. The question of what kind of syllabuses were suitable for teacher training courses was not fully considered. It was evident, however, from the recommendations of Bromsgrove 80b that linguistics and not 'language' was held to be a prerequisite for teachers who wanted to make use of linguistics-based teaching materials, and profit from the research into aspects of language usage in schools.

On the other side of the coin, it was clear from the seminar discussions that there had been little concerted movement among linguists to discover which aspects of their subject were applicable to language teaching, or how appropriate courses in linguistics could be developed. One method of developing appropriate syllabuses was discussed at Bromsgrove 78, where it was suggested that linguists who were not directly involved in teacher training could develop small research projects at local and regional level, with the co-operation of advisers and inspectors of English and interested teachers. As this kind of re-training has considerable potential for the education of teachers in linguistics, I want to devote the next section to it.

In-service education in linguistics

Collaboration between linguists and others concerned with language in education is clearly desirable and practical but it does not constitute a formula for action on a national scale aimed at educating language teachers in linguistics. If, as one of the invited speakers at Bromsgrove 80b pointed out, the time is long overdue for the provision of effectively trained teachers of languages then a national policy should be worked out to ensure that this is done. But in a period of shrinking budgets, the question is bound to arise: where is the major effort to be made, at initial training or at in-service re-training? It could be argued that the obvious answer is to introduce linguistics to students in initial training, so that the whole output of new teachers will enter schools each year with a sound understanding of language. But even if there were no obstacles to this policy, such as the independent status of the process of course validation, and the immobility of staff caused by cutbacks in the educational budget, there would be several other drawbacks. Not least amongst these is the nature of the intake at the initial training. Conditioned by current 'language' attitudes in school, students on initial training are generally unreceptive to the objective and analytical methods characteristic of linguistics; furthermore they lack the first-hand experience of the extent of language's role in learning and in the social and personal development of children.

Those who believe that the major effort should be directed to increasing in-service provision, point to the greater receptivity of teachers on post-experience courses: they have come to a more realistic evaluation of their own resources in relation to the task in language teaching they have to undertake. In-service courses have the advantage that the classroom is constantly in view; even where students study full-time, a familiar classroom with its familiar problems is generally near at hand. However, there are drawbacks to in-service re-education: because they differ in themselves in various ways – by length, by intensity, by standard of work and by qualification awarded, in-service courses are much more difficult to organize into a coherent structure. The question to ask is whether any sequencing can be introduced into the types of course so that the teacher could be taken, for instance, from a 'sampling' day seminar, via short course, to a full- or part-time qualifying course in linguistics.

The key role in an undertaking of this kind belongs to the advisers and inspectors of English at regional and local level and to the HIMs at national level. Already a great deal has been accomplished by their efforts, and formulas for increasing in-service effectiveness are being worked out. Through their representatives on the Committee for Linguistics in Education the initiatives of the DES and NAAIE could be linked to the resources of BAAL and LAGB, and ways could be explored to provide a grading of course awards, so that all concerned could place a value on the time and effort required of the teacher who opts for in-service re-education in linguistics.

Before leaving this topic I would like to return to the question of collaboration between linguist and English adviser. Perhaps the most critical point for the linguist collaborating with the adviser is the first encounter between linguist and teachers. Things can go badly wrong if both linguist and language adviser are poorly briefed as to the other's expectations. Therefore, a pre-seminar negotiation is needed for each to understand what the other is offering. The adviser will want to know how the linguist intends to present his material so that he makes con-tact on a practical level with the teacher's needs. The linguist will want to know whether he will get any feedback, at a later date, when the teachers will have had the chance to try out the material, preferably in the form of small-scale research projects in school. If the adviser is planning to follow the introductory seminars by a course in linguistics then he will want to know if the linguist has the time to carry this through. A successful partnership between linguist and English adviser can provide a pattern for structuring in-service re-education.

What contribution can linguistics make?

Whether linguistics is introduced at initial or in-service training, the process of education in the subject is unlikely to yield lasting results unless a substantial amount of time is given to it. The teacher needs to know linguistics before he can apply it. One of the more unfortunate myths about linguistics has been that it can be applied successfully by some agency outside the classroom with the teacher as instrument within it (cf. for example, Doughty, Pearce and Thornton, 1971). Any teacher who has been asked to stand in for a colleague in another subject knows how difficult it is to elaborate on its central concepts. Each subject has its own conceptual framework within which a teacher operates, and in language teaching knowing how to use one's own language is not equivalent to having a conceptual framework to draw on to explain how it works. Without a background in linguistics it would be very difficult for a teacher using linguistics-based materials either to elaborate on them, or to repeat the linguist's formula in new material, or to capitalize on points raised in discussion or to hold to a coherent line of description and explanation.

Several of the speakers at Bromsgrove 80b illustrated this theme. A member of the team that prepared the Open University course on Language Development (Czerniewska and Twite, 1979) stressed how important it was to give students a map of linguistics and to alert them to the ways in which the subject could be made use of in the classroom. The course contains self-learning material which the student uses and afterwards can take into the classroom for use with his pupils. Two other speakers at the seminar presented material that could be of value to teachers; they both made use of the same range of knowledge of language structure, viz. the grammar of the complex sentence and the grammar of connected discourse. In the first lecture examples of complex sentences in connected discourse were analysed to show how a language of non-fiction, as in text-books, contains structures which put maximum strain on children's short-term memory, whereas fiction, by reversing the structural design, relieves the strain. The second speaker explained that the aim of the materials which he had developed for use in the classroom was to assist children to think about structural alternatives in complex sentences and discourse, so that, from a range of structures, they could select a design which would achieve the effect aimed at by the writer. In order to make full use of both these sets of materials, a teacher would need to have a knowledge of models of complex sentence structure, discourse structure and the relation of syntax to intonation.

The members of the working groups at Bromsgrove 80b assumed in their discussions that the teachers who would implement their proposals would be equipped with an adequate knowledge of linguistics. The three groups covered the ages 5 to 11 years, 9 to 14 years, and 14 to 18 years. Their brief was to consider the ways in which linguistics could contribute to the teaching of English Mother Tongue. All groups were agreed that an education in linguistics, with its emphasis on empirical description and theory construction, would alter a teacher's whole approach to the nature of language and its role in the lives of children. Instead of seeing language under evaluative labels such as 'correct English', 'bad grammar', or 'good style', he would see it as a complex structure of linguistic systems, related in systematic ways to the environment within which children learn and play. His image of language would be integrated because it would be founded on a description of these systems which could be applied in a consistent manner to the way in which language mediates meaning in social structure, in face-to-face communication, and in written texts. For a teacher equipped with this knowledge any instance of language use will bring into focus a map of the whole area of the subject that will help him to give a rational account of the diverse things children say and write. He will, in effect, base his teaching on a broad foundation of descriptive and predictive theory, drawn from the 'linguistic sciences', instead of on a narrow response of either prescriptive injunction or unspecific encouragement. These points were well illustrated in the report prepared by the 5 to 11 years working group, who looked at two instances of 'bad English' found in the personal 'book' of young children. They considered how a teacher would develop a consistent way of dealing with such usage as the following:

(1)   It hit his bum.
(2)   Gladys kick the ball through the window.

What is the teacher to do with this usage, allow it or not? The nature of his habitual response could very well influence his pupils' attitude to the language of learning. In both instances the language used belongs to the domains of family and friendship (cf. Fishman, 1972), where informal usage is accepted; but in the domain of education usage of this sort will eventually be unacceptable. It is instructive to contrast the two instances. In (1) the informality of 'bum', as a vocabulary item, is readily exchangeable for a more formal word, without doing damage to a child's ties with home and friends. But in the case of (2), since 'kick' is part of the syntax of the child's dialect, the form is more deeply rooted, and an alteration affects all other instances of the same form. In (2) there is a stronger tie between usage and culture; the form 'kick' would occur in a range of situations from informal to semi-formal. A denial of its cultural value to the child using it could have the kind of adverse consequences suggested above, so that an alternative strategy is required. The strength of the usage argues for some kind of co-existence of mutual respect whereby (2) is recognized for all purposes except for those which the teacher and the child agree lie within the domain of education.

Making consistent distinctions of this kind, and making them available to the children themselves, is likely to increase their chances of success as they progress into secondary schools. By the comprehensiveness of his explanation the teacher makes the children 'privy to the process' of language in its relation to the different domains within which it functions: family, friendship, education, religion or employment. In the last resort it is the individual pupil who chooses, and it is educationally sound to give him a rational basis for his choice.

I have found that some teachers misunderstand the intention behind explanations like that above, and accuse linguists of allowing standards to fall, of not being fair to children by letting them think that any kind of language will do. This is not the linguist's intention, however: in the model he is using the language 'that will do' is the language that is congruent with all factors in the domain in which the speaker finds himself.

In the 14-18 years working group, members gave numerous examples of models of language structure that could assist a teacher to contextualize his pupils' writing within such categories as correctness, appropriateness and stylistic appeal. They claimed that a teacher who knew the structure of language would be able to guide his pupils in their selection of vocabulary and grammatical constructions. Members also suggested that a teacher could employ wider frameworks of descriptive analysis such as discourse analysis, content structure analysis, together with theoretical frames derived from sociolinguistics and stylistics.

At the beginning of the section I referred to the conceptual framework that is possessed by someone who knows a subject. The framework consists of terms whose meanings are defined both by reference to the data and by their relation to each other, so that learning a subject is partly a process of familiarization with its terminology. A teacher with an education in linguistics will have acquired a formidable meta-language (i.e. terminology). The question which members of the 9-14 years group took up was: how much of the meta-language should be passed on to pupils in their lessons in EMT and MLs? This resembles the familiar question: Why teach grammar? which implies that a knowledge of the terms for parts of speech or clauses in sentences has no transfer value for pupils' performance in writing. Members of the group pointed out, however, that some use of meta-language by the teacher was unavoidable, because children pick it up from other sources – even infants might use the word 'word'. But they warned against the use of esoteric terms, when adequate terms were already in use.

The purpose of meta-language was seen not as a means of improving performance, but as a kind of shorthand for discussing meanings in different structures. Members were reminded that meta-language did not stop at the familiar grammatical terminology but included such labels as role, register, domain, metaphor, alliteration, and symbol; and that the teacher's aim should be to bring out the meaning of the concepts signified by the labels so that the pupils could construct some conceptual framework for analysing and commenting on linguistic phenomena. In this connection it is interesting to note current thinking concerning the place of meta-language in the proposed sixteen-plus 'Unitary' English examination. One suggestion would have candidates tested in (a) their performance in writing and interpreting English, and in (b) their ability to analyse and comment on others' performance (using meta-language), but not in (c) the description and evaluation of the theories and models associated with the meta-language concerned.

Linguistics as a school subject

Any teacher who is interested in his subject will find it difficult to restrict its use in schools to the subsidiary role of facilitator in the teaching of some other subject. A teacher whose knowledge of linguistics develops to meet his needs in language teaching will be tempted to elaborate on features of the models he is using beyond the point necessary to enable his pupils to analyse and comment on their own and others' performance. He will want to explain models and theories and discuss them with his pupils. To take an example referred to earlier, a teacher might find himself considering, with older pupils, the predictive value of domain theory, when what originally set him going was a practical question on 'appropriate choice'. There is more to this than the time-honoured 'red herring' principle: at secondary and primary level there is an easy modulation, in many subjects, from description to prescription and back again. This overlap between the two functions of the same subject is endemic in subjects concerned with human behaviour.

It was evident from the way many of the linguists at Bromsgrove 78 were talking about the role of linguistics in schools that they were confounding the two functions. In its planning for Bromsgrove 80, CLIE separated them, so that, if the contribution of linguistics to language teaching was rejected, that of linguistics as a school subject in its own right would be retained.

At Bromsgrove 80a the kinds of linguistics appropriate at different age levels within schools were discussed by members of the working groups: Early Years (5-9), Middle Years (9-14), 'O' level and 'A' level. Each group was asked to consider the principles underlying linguistics as a school subject, and to produce specimen syllabuses that illustrated them. The 'O' level syllabus was very ambitious: it contained items such as, Communication and Language, Language and the Individual, Language and Society, Purposes of Using Language, and of course, the Nature of Language (its syntax, semantics and phonology). Members recommended that the items should be more rigorously defined. However, their intention was clearly to broaden the base of linguistics so that its appeal was not limited simply to an elite. They believed that 'the content would ensure that what was regarded as desirable common knowledge would be made available to all children within the age range'. In practice, the influence of a syllabus of such scope and depth would extend downwards to the lower secondary and primary levels. The Middle Years group produced an integrated scheme covering some of the same ground: it linked the study of sentence and discourse structure to the purposes of language, and both of these to facts about language as a social and cultural phenomenon. In the Early Years group the same sorts of links were made, but in a much less formal manner: they proposed to integrate their language syllabus within the social, historical and environmental projects characteristically found in upper primary curriculum.

There were other points of agreement between the groups. All were confident that their method of presenting the subject, that is, through an emphasis on the role of language in the lives of the children, would draw out from their pupils the range of knowledge of language possessed by children in different age levels. They were also agreed on the principles that should underlie a linguistics syllabus: it should train pupils to 'observe, discover, make appropriate hypotheses, and draw conclusions about contemporary language usage'. They believed that a course in linguistics could be made both cumulative and coherent, provided that it adhered to the principles of the subject.

The proposals for the 'A' level syllabus were markedly different; they followed fairly closely the conventional format of a university undergraduate course, containing two sections: Language Structure, including phonetics, phonology, syntax and semantics; and Language Variety, including dialect differentiation and the factors affecting it. The aim of such a syllabus would be to make students aware of certain facts about language and to familiarize them with the meta-language needed to discuss them.

One of the main themes at both Bromsgrove 78 and 80 was the beneficial effect that the introduction of linguistics would have on the processes of learning. At both seminars members stressed the fact that a linguistics-based course would constitute a training in thinking. At Bromsgrove 78 a discussion took place on the relative merits of the deductive and inductive methods of teaching. In my report on that seminar I wrote:

> The two methods were characterised as follows: the deductive method consisted of presenting models of what language is, and of using these models to select the significant features of its structure; the inductive method consisted of presenting instances of language and of drawing out from them significant features of its structure. . . .
>
> During the course of this debate, claims that the inductive method, with its stress on observation and discovery, provided better motivation for learners were countered by the warning that most learners, at some stage in their courses required some signposting and mapping of the direction of their studies, which the inductive method would find difficult to furnish. . . . Some common ground was discovered [between the inductivists and the deductivists] : the inductivists conceded that the teacher, as linguist, cannot in practice confront language data with a mind bereft of any theory, and that the learners would in practice carry forward from one lesson those inductive generalisations that could furnish hypotheses for the next; the deductivists conceded that models could be presented as hypotheses, and that the alternative constructs of learners could be matched, for plausibility, with the model introduced by the teacher.

Some very usable material for inductive learning can be found in *The Growth of Word Meaning* (Anglin, 1971). This book is a report of a series of sorting experiments which Anglin conducted to investigate certain hypotheses about the structure of vocabulary. If the vocabulary items he used are typed on to cards, they can be presented, first, as a class or group exercise on sorting and classification; second, the data can be used as the basis for discussion of the sorting strategies employed. Each time I have used this material, students have made discoveries about their own intuitive structuring of word meanings; in discussion, they have argued over the merits of competing strategies of classification: by association, by syntagmatic combination or by paradigmatic selection. Here is a sample from the 20 items Anglin used:

laugh, horse, dead, white, girl, idea, during, grow, flower, above, etc.

An interesting stage in the formulation of inductive generalizations is the process of reaching a consensus. By this process students can determine whether it is the intuition collectively derived from the 'community of users' or the intuition of the individual that furnishes linguists with the rules of a language. Another exercise can be added: it consists of arranging the words (now grouped into sets) into hierarchies. I give three examples in Figure 3.1.

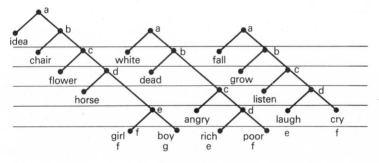

Figure 3.1

At this point, either of two strategies can be attempted: either inserting category labels for each set at the points marked a – f; or taking words from the sets and combining them into sentences:

(3) The white flower grew.

In the first exercise the labelled categories can be interpreted as distinctive features in a representation of some of the relations of similarity and difference that constitute the basis of vocabulary structure, e.g.:

boy = +HUMAN −ADULT +MALE
mare = +ANIMATE −HUMAN +ADULT −MALE

This leads naturally into a consideration of the value of componential analysis as a method of representing meaning (Leech, 1974). In the second exercise, hypotheses can be formulated and tested, e.g. when items from different hierarchical sets are combined, a downwards sequence is less grammatical the greater the number of steps between the items selected:

(4) The white flower cried.
(5) The white idea cried.

This group of exercises, based on Anglin's research, combines very neatly with similar exercises based on a classification of metaphor (Levin, 1977). In his chapter on Modes of Construal, Levin lists six categories of metaphor, with three examples of each category. Cards containing the eighteen examples can be given to students for classifying. I give some examples below:

(6) The bridge groaned under the weight.
(7) The boy froze with terror.

The first exercise consists of grouping the metaphors into classes; this is followed by a discussion of the reasons for the classifications made. Levin's hypothesis, which is too complicated to describe in detail here, proposes that metaphors are classified according to the kinds of changes that take place in the meanings of the words that are metaphorically related, for example, by the direction of the feature shift. The complicated nature of the hypothesis makes this a very difficult exercise, particularly if it is combined with a test of the hypothesis itself. I have only used this and other exercises of the same sort with students in H.E. However, the format used can be replicated with much simpler linguistic data, of the sort illustrated in the specimen syllabus of the Early Years group at Bromsgrove 80a.

What is valuable about this kind of investigation into language structure is that an experience of genuine discovery is possible because our knowledge of language is an unconscious knowledge, that is, we produce and interpret meanings without being able to make explicit to ourselves the structures we have internalized that enable us to do this. Making explicit to ourselves the knowledge of language that we possess is a dual experience of discovery: we experience the process of discovery as we follow the steps in the inductive method, and we are affected by the subtlety and complexity of the linguistic competence that the discovery reveals. It is on grounds like these that linguists claim that their subject should appeal to advocates of both an increase in science-based study in schools, and of a human orientation towards it.

Which linguistics for schools?

To what extent have linguists learnt from experience that it is pointless making claims about the potential of their subject, if, when it is introduced into schools, the choice of content undermines the very claims they are making? In this section I want to consider how the richness and variety of linguistic theory provide several alternative teaching strategies for introducing the subject. One of the most persistent myths about linguistics is that it is merely a more complex and unnecessarily jargonized version of traditional grammar. To a linguist this is a travesty of what he values in his subject, namely its orderly, precise and rigorous descriptive accounts of linguistic phenomena. But when a linguist, in his role as teacher, presents what he values in his subject, directly and unmodified, to pupils, it may very well 'come across' as something very similar to the parsing and analysis associated with grammatical exercises of a past era. Such precise and penetrating enquiry into the nature of syntax draws its justification from its relation to the goal of linguistic theory. Undergraduates and pupils at 'A' level would be expected to confront the complex and abstract methodology involved, because a proper grounding in descriptive theory is essential for all branches of the subject. But for all other age ranges, there is sufficient richness in the tradition of linguistic theory for alternative strategies to be used.

Modern linguistics has been in existence for about seventy years. During that time there have been several different approaches to the study of language. Though current transformational-generative theory has radically altered the nature of the subject, it has not obliterated previous approaches. In most cases it has strengthened them. The sociological, anthropological, semiological and philosophical traditions remain strong, and continue to contribute to our knowledge about language.

Taking a very broad survey of the development of the subject from the time of de Saussure, the founder of modern linguistics, we can see two separate traditions of study deriving from his work. His theories concerning language as a sign system have shaped the development of

European linguistics, whilst his theories concerning language as a system of structures have been taken up and developed in American linguistics. It is interesting to compare the different emphases that have come from this distinction. In the American tradition, linguists stress the structural properties of language systems and link them to the innate linguistic principles of the human organism that have helped to form human culture. Linguists in the European tradition stress the meaning-bearing capacity of linguistic signs and link it to specific cultural systems that determine the range of meanings that a language deploys. Modern developments in sociolinguistics, stylistics and communication studies borrow from both these traditions. A general education in linguistics could acknowledge both these traditions. In the rest of this section, I will try to develop this notion a little. My intention is to outline a pedagogic model for linguistics below 'A' level (but with 'A' level in mind) which avoids hybridism, responds flexibly to the needs of pupils and their teachers, and does not abandon or diminish the centrality of the study of the structure of linguistic systems.

In that branch of linguistics where language is studied in its context in a community, there are linguists (Labov, 1972a; Trudgill, 1978) who investigate varieties of usage determined by such variables as, class, sex, ethnic group and location. Their aim is to learn from actual usage 'more about what language [is], how it varies and how it changes'. Their emphasis is on the variety found within structures co-existing within a linguistic community. On the other hand there are linguists (Ferguson, 1959; Blom and Gumperz, 1972; Platt, 1977) working with the same data, whose interests lie in the semiotic function of language or dialect choice, that is, the meaning conveyed to members of a community by alternative choices within a system. In a similar vein, there are studies of address systems (Brown and Ford, 1961; Ervin-Tripp, 1976) based on kinship, social status, or cultural conventions, which illustrate how names and titles are invested with meanings derived from relations between members – relations of familiarity or distance, or solidarity or power. Studies of this sort are very much in accord with the common-sense knowledge of what language does, as perceived by children at school, and they can be used as entry points for systematic enquiry into language structures, such as the system of pronouns in languages which have a choice of 'thou' and 'you' (Brown and Gilman, 1960). Other examples would be the uses of 'must', 'should', 'may', etc. (Lakoff, 1972) as a means of expressing obligation and permission, and of different sentence types expressing various intentions between members of differing status (Ervin-Tripp, 1976; Searle, 1976). The main emphasis in these studies is on the meaning-bearing capacity of the choices made.

In stylistics, linguists working on textual analysis (Sinclair, 1966a; Halliday, 1971) show how the organizational power of language systems shapes the meanings we interpret from literary texts. In 'In Taking a Poem to Pieces', Sinclair says that he is taking his readers to the very brink of linguistics. His intention is to use a knowledge of the syntactic resources of the language to reveal the density and complexity of meaning in poetry. There is no reason why a teacher should not use this procedure also as a means of entry into a discussion of the resources of language available to creative writers. If the inductive method is preferred, a text can be presented in such a way that the literary devices used by the writer to achieve his meanings are made evident. Examples of this would be the following extracts from a sermon by Donne and a poem by e.e.cummings. These can either be presented in a conventional layout, or set out as below, so that attention is directed to the linguistic organization characteristic of poetic texts, rather than to their status as prose or verse:

Where be all the splinters of that Bone,
Which a shot hath shivered
And scattered in the Ayre?

Where be all the Atoms of that flesh,
Which a Corrosive hath eat away
Or a Consumption hath breath'd
And exhal'd away from our arms and other limbs?

In what wrinkle,
In what furrow,
In what bowel of the earth
Ly all the graines of the ashes of a body burnt a thousand years
    since?

In what corner,
In what ventrical of the sea,
Lies all the jelly of a Body drowned in the generall flood?

What cohaerence,
What sympathy,
What dependence maintaines any relation any correspondence
Between that arm that was lost in Europe,
And that legge that was lost in Afrique, or Asia,
Scores of years between?

> Extract from 'A Sermon Preached at the Earl of Bridgewaters
> House in London on November 19 1627'

The unconventional layout draws attention to the parallelism on the syntactic level, which creates positions for further parallelism on the phonological and semantic levels (cf. Levin, 1962). The unity of the text is fashioned out of linguistic resources, which can be readily identified and can furnish material for subsequent investigation of the systems involved.

> Pity this busy monster, manunkind, not. Progress is a comfortable disease: your victim (death and life safely beyond) plays with the bigness of his littleness - electrons deify one razorblade into a mountainrange; lenses extend unwish through curving wherewhen till unwish returns on its unself. A world of made is not a world of born - pity poor flesh and trees, poor stars and stones, but never this fine specimen of hyper magical ultraomnipotence. We doctors know a hopeless case if - listen: there's a hell of a good universe next door; let's go.
>
> A complete poem by e.e. cummings

Here, the unconventional layout poses a problem: how to reconcile the deviations in language usage with the normal paragraphing. The solution involves recognizing some conventional devices of versification at the level of phonology (together with some special effects characteristic of e.e. cummings) and perceiving unifying effects at the linguistic levels of morphology (word structure) and lexicology (word meaning). There is also a series of sociolinguistic questions: what speech act is being performed, with what knowledge, in what form, to which audience, etc?

Taking a different approach to poetry, that is, through a theory of literary 'competence' (Culler, 1973) we can read the following axiom: 'where there is knowledge or mastery of any kind, there is a system to be explained'. Literary 'competence' in Culler's theory (Culler, 1975) consists of an internalization of the system of literary strategies and devices, such as metaphor, parallelism, irony, fictionalization, etc. Related to these on one side are the abilities with which we interpret them, and on the other side the linguistic resources drawn on in the process of creation and interpretation. That is, we demonstrate our 'competence' through our performance in the complementary processes of writing and reading poetic works.

Similar but not equal processes of creation and interpretation can be found in the everyday use of language by children - in their jokes, their colloquial imagery, their sarcasm, expletives and graffiti. What children respond to in literature is of course more complex, more structured and more carefully fashioned than anything in their own conversation, but the aesthetic devices are not different, the mastery differs only in degree, and the linguistic knowledge not at all. Explaining the system of aesthetic devices amounts to a diagnosis of the make-up of our human nature, in so far as it demonstrates how different cultures react in a consistent way to the universal principles of artistic creativity – parallelism, deviation and structural unity. Alternatively, a teacher using the deductive method can propose the existence of these principles in order to promote a discussion of the wide range of cultural resources available for communicating human intentions and needs; these include costume, personal appearance, characteristic non-verbal communication, and the artifacts people surround themselves with. The meanings that are intended by the choices that people make can be investigated and classified into functions – social, ritual, aesthetic, erotic, practical; in this way new points of entry are opened up for the analysis of the different forms that correlate with these functions and of the semiotic resources out of which they are fashioned. The extract below (Bogatyrev, 1972) illustrates the importance attached to form in studies of costume. This serves to reinforce the centrality of adequate descriptions of linguistic structure when 'functional' approaches are adopted in the study of language:

> The interdependence of a costume's form and its function, or rather, the structure of its functions, is clear. The relationship which manifests itself most strongly in a costume is that which unites the costume's form and its dominant function . . . . In a costume whose dominant function is that of holiday wear, details which emphasise that function will stand out quite clearly.

My last example is taken from the work of Chomsky. His special interest is language and its relation to cognitive psychology. For him (Chomsky, 1979) serious psychology is about 'domains in which human beings excel', 'language [being] one such case'; language's unique properties make it 'the most interesting case we have' of evidence of at least one 'exceptional human capacity'. In Chomsky's theory, whose influence Culler acknowledges, the emphasis in Culler's axiom is reversed: instead of 'where there is knowledge or mastery of any kind there is a system to be explained' we have: where unique properties are discoverable in human performance we have to create a hypothesis that explains them. In the case of language, the hypothesis created to explain its unique properties is the nativist hypothesis, involving an innate mechanism of language acquisition. As an example of the kind of human performance that Chomsky has in mind we could take the language of infants. The collection and classification of the linguistic data would not be a random exercise, but would be directed by a hypothesis about language acquisition such as the following (Chomsky, 1972):

> In formal terms, then, we can describe the child's acquisition of language as a kind of theory construction. The child discovers the theory of his language with only small amounts of data from that language. Not only does his 'theory of the language' have an enormous predictive scope, but it also enables the child to reject a great deal of the very data on which the theory has been constructed.

In the same way, in literature and in the other arts data collection and the formulation of generalizations would be directed by appropriate hypotheses. The extract below (Jakobson, 1960) illustrates how a hypothesis about the essential nature of poetry can be constructed on a knowledge of the structure of language:

> What is the empirical linguistic criterion of the poetic function? In particular, what is the indispensable feature inherent in any piece of poetry? To answer this question we must recall the two basic modes of arrangement used in verbal behavior, selection and combination. If 'child' is the topic of the message, the speaker selects one among the extant, more or less similar, nouns like child, kid, youngster, tot, all of them equivalent in a certain respect, and then to comment on this topic, he may select one of the semantically cognate verbs – sleeps, dozes, nods, naps. Both chosen words combine in the speech chain. The selection is produced on the base of equivalence, similarity and dissimilarity, synonymity and antonymity, while the combination, the build up of the sequence, is based on contiguity. The poetic function projects the principle of equivalence from the axis of selection into the axis of combination. Equivalence is promoted to the constitutive device of the sequence.

I would like to suggest that the philosophical position adopted by Chomsky in relation to his subject could provide a paradigm for teaching linguistics in schools, both at 'A' level and the age ranges below it. This consists in discovering the essential nature of systems of human behaviour, and relating the unique features of these systems to theoretical principles concerning the nature of the human organism. At 'A' level, where language structure is given priority, enquiry into linguistic phenomena is linked directly to significant principles in linguistic theory, thereby giving insights into the nature of linguistic competence. Where cultural systems are given equal prominence, as they should be for the age ranges below 'A' level, linguistic phenomena are linked obliquely through conventional formulations in linguistic performance to significant principles in cultural theory, thereby giving insights into social communicative and aesthetic 'competences'. To put it another way, language presents itself as the obvious case study in the manifestation of social, communicative and aesthetic 'competences', because it is 'a domain in which human beings excel'.

To be able to carry out a programme of teaching of this sort a teacher of linguistics needs to have for his subject what literature teachers are accustomed to having for theirs, namely, a map of the essential concerns of their discipline and of the related areas that enhance its value. But there is something else which linguists could borrow from literature teachers and that is a vision of the relevance of their subject to those who study it, so that an encounter with language is an encounter with life. All that has been said about the nature and role of language in the lives of children requires that linguistics teachers possess the same breadth of knowledge and imaginative approach as their literature colleagues.

The ultimate justification for this broad approach to the study of language lies in its recognition of the interrelatedness of language and the socio-cultural life of a community. But its justification in the eyes of the linguist as a teacher is found in the fact that the central importance of the study of language systems is not denied, but is paced according to the capacities, preoccupations and awakening interest of pupils at different age levels in their school career.

4

Do linguists have anything to say to teachers?

Arthur Brookes and *Richard Hudson*

Introduction

This paper consists essentially of two separate documents which were produced independently for a seminar in April 1980. The first is a list of claims about language to which most linguists might reasonably be expected to subscribe, and which all have some possible relevance for school teachers. The list contains 83 separate points, covering all aspects of language from its structure to its external relations, and it appears to represent the views of a cross-section of British linguists to whom it (or an earlier version of it) was shown. We hope this list will be useful for those teachers (and teacher-teachers) who would like to know more about the findings of linguistics, but are struck by the ability of linguists to disagree with one another and to change their minds on major issues. The second document is a list of questions which tries to cover the main areas on which teachers might hope to be enlightened by the findings of linguistics. The questions deal with matters such as the superiority (if any) of standard English, the pros and cons of teaching several varieties of English, the nature of West Indian creole, how much the teacher should talk in class, the developmental stages through which the child's language should be expected to pass, the relations between linguistic forms and their functions, the relations between passive and active language skills, the nature of comprehension, the relations between speech and writing, readability, the need for a metalanguage, and correctness. After each group of questions, a brief paragraph relates them to the list of claims in the first document, and highlights any points of contact between the documents. If these two documents can be taken as representing what teachers want to know, and what linguists can tell them, then it seems clear that linguists do indeed have a lot to say which should interest teachers, even though there are, not unexpectedly, a number of areas where linguistics does not make the major contribution.

In April 1980 a pair of seminars were held in Bromsgrove, Worcestershire, for which we were each asked to prepare a paper, and the following is a composite of the two papers. The seminars were organized by the Committee for Linguistics in Education, a joint committee set up by the British Association for Applied Linguists and the Linguistics Association of Great Britain, but now supported also by the National Association for the Teaching of English and the National Association for Advisers in English.[1] Brookes represents NATE on this committee and Hudson represents LAGB, so the committee asked us to put the point of view of the teacher, in Brookes's case, and of the linguist, in Hudson's. The seminars were concerned with the possible applications of linguistics in schools, so it was hoped that the papers we prepared would help give content to the discussion. Specifically, Brookes was asked to produce a list of questions that teachers tend to ask about language, and Hudson to produce a list of statements about language (and a few about the nature of linguistics) on which most linguists would be agreed, and which might be relevant to the interests of teachers. The participants at the seminars found the two papers helpful, so we were encouraged to revise them for publication as a joint document.

In preparing our initial lists we worked more or less independently, rather than aiming at parallel lists of matching questions and answers. It was then an interesting task to try to match the two lists, and this has been done in Brookes's paper, where he comments at the end of each group of questions on the extent to which they find answers in Hudson's list. We have made no attempt to cover over the mismatches, as will be seen from Brookes's comments, so the points of contact that we did find can presumably be taken that much more seriously. At the same time, it should be clear to those familiar with linguistics that there are in fact far more points of contact than we have identified in Brookes's comments. We could have made the list of statements about language much longer by including points that not all linguists would accept (though many would), and many of these extra points would have supplied answers to Brookes's outstanding questions – and the answers might well have been correct, too. However, we felt it was important to confine the list to statements that would be accepted by virtually all linguists, as we are very conscious of the problems that teachers face when they try to apply the findings of linguists who cannot agree among themselves. We hope that by aiming at widely accepted points of view, we shall also have picked out some relatively permanent ones, which have a good chance of still being widely accepted among linguists in ten years' time.

SOME ISSUES OVER WHICH LINGUISTS CAN AGREE
(by Richard Hudson)

The following is a list of 83 points which seem to be acceptable to most if not all linguists in Britain, and possibly in other countries too. The basis for claiming that they are so widely acceptable is that the list has been seen and commented on by a reasonably large number of British linguists, and I think the revisions I have made to successive versions of the list mean that it should be compatible with the views expressed by those who gave me their comments. Specifically, I had comments on at least one of the half-dozen versions which were circulated from each of the following linguists (some of whom would probably be happier to be referred to as applied linguists): J. Aitchison, R. Allwright, M. Breen, A. Brookes, G. Brown, K. Brown, C. Brumfit, C. Candlin, N. Collinge, G. Corbett, A Cruse, A. Cruttenden, L. Davidson, M. Deuchar, N. Fairclough, D. Ferris, A. Fox, M. French, P. Gannon, G. Gazdar, M. Harris, R. Hartmann, R. Hogg, J. Hurford, G. Knowles, R. Le Page, J. Lyons, J. Mountford, W. O'Donnell, K. Perera, G. Pullum, S. Pulman, R. Quirk, M. Riddle, R. Robins, S. Romaine, G. Sampson, D. Sharp, M. Short, N. Smith, M. Stubbs, G. Thornton, L. Task, G. Wells, M. Wheeler, D. Wilson, J. Windsor Lewis. Between them, these linguists cover just over half the linguistics departments in British universities (15 out of 26), and there is no reason to think that the other departments would have presented a significantly different set of views. (All departments were in fact circulated with copies of the list, and a request for comments.) Moreover, any reader who knows the work of linguists in the list will agree that they cover a very wide range of views on such questions as the proper balance between theory and description and the pros and cons of competing linguistic theories. This diversity of views on controversial questions makes me all the more confident about the list of views on which they can all, apparently, agree. I should like to take this opportunity of thanking them all for their help.

1 The linguistic approach to the study of language

(a) Linguists describe language empirically - that is, they try to make statements which are testable, and they take language as it is, rather than saying how it should be. (In other words, linguistics is descriptive, but not prescriptive or normative.) (See 2.1a, 2.3a, 2.4b, 3.2e.)

(b) The primary object of description for linguists is the structure of language, but many linguists study this in relation to its functions (notably, that of conveying meaning) and in relation to other psychological and cultural systems. (See 2.1b, 2.7a.)

(c) Linguists construct theories of language, in order to explain why particular languages have some of the properties that they do have. Linguists differ in the relative emphasis they put on general theory and on description of particular languages. (See 2.1d.)

(d) An essential tool of linguistics (both descriptive and theoretical) is a meta-language containing technical terms denoting analytical categories and constructs. None of the traditional or everyday meta-language is sacrosanct, though much of it is the result of earlier linguistic scholarship, but many traditional terms have in fact been adopted by linguists with approximately their established meanings. (See 3.2a, 3.3e, 3.4a.)

(e) The first aim of linguists is to understand the nature of language and of particular languages. Some linguists, however, are motivated by the belief that such understanding is likely to have practical social benefits, e.g. for those concerned professionally with the teaching of the mother tongue or of second languages, or with the treatment of language disorders.

2 Language, society and the individual

2.1 *Language*

(a) Language is amenable to objective study, with regard both to its structure and to its functions and external relations. (See 1a, 3.2c.)

(b) We learn our language from other individuals, so language is a property both of the individual and of the community from which he learns it. Consequently, both social and psychological approaches to its study are necessary.

(c) A language consists partly of a set of interacting general constraints, or rules, and partly of a vocabulary of lexical items. (Some linguists prefer to take a language as a set of sentences, and would apply the preceding description to the grammar of a language, rather than to the language itself.) (See 2.3d,f, 2.5a, 2.6e, 3.)

(d) There are features common to all languages (linguistic universals) which involve the organization of their grammars and also the types of patterning found in sentences. (See 1c, 2.2d, 2.4a, 2.6e,f, 3.)

(e) Although all speakers know at least one language, and use this knowledge ('competence') in speaking and understanding, very little of their knowledge is conscious. Knowledge of structural properties (e.g. rules of syntax) is particularly hard to report in an organised way. (See 2.5.)

2.2 *Languages*

(a) There is no clear or qualitative difference between so-called 'language-boundaries' and 'dialect-boundaries'. (See 2.3c,d,i.)

(b) There are between 4,000 and 5,000 languages (though no precise figure is possible because of the uncertainty referred to in (a) above.) They differ widely in their number of speakers, ranging from a few individuals to hundreds of millions; and nations differ widely in the number of languages spoken natively in them, ranging from one to many hundreds.

(c) In many communities it is normal for every speaker to command two or more languages more or less fluently. Such communities exist in Britain, both in the traditional Celtic areas and in areas of high immigration. (See 2.3b.)

(d) There is no evidence that normal human languages differ greatly in the complexity of their rules, or that there are any languages that are 'primitive' in the size of their vocabulary (or any other part of their language), however 'primitive' their speakers may be from a cultural point of view. (The term 'normal human language' is meant to exclude on the one hand artificial languages such as Esperanto or computer languages, and on the other hand languages which are not used as the primary means of communication within any community, notably pidgin languages. Such languages may be simpler than normal human languages, though this is not necessarily so.) (See 2.1d, 3.3i.)

(e) Only a minority of languages are written, and an even smaller minority are standardized (i.e. include a variety which is codified and widely accepted as the variety most suitable for formal writing and speech). English belongs to this small minority. (See 2.3a,h, 2.4c, 3.2.)

(f) The present position of English as a world language is due to historical accidents rather than to inherent superiority of the language's structure. (Similar remarks apply to other world languages, notably French, Spanish and Russian, and to the 'Classical' languages such as Greek, Latin, Arabic and Sanskrit.) (See 2.3e, 3.5e.)

2.3 *Varieties of language*

(a) Spoken language developed before written language in the history of mankind, and it also develops first in the individual speaker; moreover, many languages are never written. These factors lead most linguists to believe that in linguistic theory priority should be given to spoken language, and many linguists give further priority to the most casual varieties of spoken language, those which are least influenced by normative grammar. (See 1a, 2.2a, 2.2e, 2.4e.)

(b) Every society requires its members to use different varieties of language in different situations. (See 2.2c, 2.3h, 3.1d.)

(c) The different 'varieties' referred to in *b* may be so-called 'languages', 'dialects' or 'registers' (i.e. roughly, 'styles'). (See 2.2a, 3.4c.)

(d) All varieties (including the most casual speech) are 'languages', in that they have their own rules and vocabulary, and they are all subject to rules controlling their use. (See 2.1c, 2.2a.)

(e) The prestige of a variety derives from its social functions (i.e. from the people and situations with which it is associated) rather than from its structural properties. (See 2.2f, 2.7b, 3.4b.)

(f) All normal speakers are able to use more than one variety of language. (See 2.2c, 2.5f.)

(g) Different varieties are often associated with different social statuses, whether these are the result of birth (e.g. sex, region of origin, race) or of later experience (e.g. occupation, religion, education). (See 2.5g, 2.7b.)

(h) There is no reason for considering the variety called 'Standard English' the best for use in all situations. (See 2.2e.)

(i) Standard English subsumes a wide range of varieties, and has no clear boundaries *vis-à-vis* non-standard varieties. (See 2.2a.)

(j) In particular, there are many different ways of pronouncing Standard English (i.e. different 'accents'), one of which is particularly prestigious in England and Wales, namely 'Received Pronunciation' ('RP'). (See 3.1a, 3.2f.)

2.4 *Change*

(a) The only parts of a language which are immune to change are those which it shares with all other human languages. (See 2.1d, 2.6b, 3.5d.)

(b) Change in a language is normally a matter of becoming different, rather than better or worse. (See 1a, 2.4d.)

(c) It is normal for language to change from generation to generation even when subject to the conservative influence of a standardized variety. (See 2.2e, 2.6c, 3.2e.)

(d) Change in the language may reflect the influence of non-standard varieties on the standard one as well as vice versa. (See 2.4b, 2.6a.)

(e) Language changes for different types of reason: sociolinguistic, as when one variety influences another, or communicative needs change, or institutions such as schools intervene; psycholinguistic, as when one group misperceives or misanalyses the speech of another; structural, as when disrupted patterns are restored. (See 2.3a, 2.5a, 2.6a, 2.7a, 3.5c.)

2.5 *Acquisition*

(a) When children learn to speak, they learn a language (in the sense of rules plus vocabulary) which is an increasingly good approximation to the language of their models; however, direct repetition of model utterances plays only a minor part in their speech. (See 2.1c, 2.4e, 3.1b,c, 3.2.)

(b) In learning their language, children's main source of information about the model is the speech of older people. No explicit instruction by the latter is needed, though parents often simplify their speech when talking to children, and correct some of the children's mistakes in a haphazard way. (See 2.4f.)

(c) By primary school age, children are commonly taking their peers rather than their parents as their dominant linguistic models. (See 2.5g,h.)

(d) There are considerable differences between children in the speed at which they acquire active use of specific parts of language. Such differences may be in part due to differences in their experience of language used by older people. (See 2.7a,c.)

(e) A child's poor performance in formal, threatening or unfamiliar situations cannot be taken as evidence of impoverished linguistic competence, but may be due to other factors such as low motivation for speaking in that situation, or unfamiliarity with the conventions for use of language in such situations. (See 2.7c, 3.4c.)

(f) By primary school age children already command a range of different varieties for use in different situations. (See 2.3f.)

(g) Some parts of the language of children are indicators of the status of being a child, and will be abandoned by the time the child reaches adulthood. Some such features are learned almost exclusively from peers, and may have been handed on in this way for many centuries. (See 2.3g, 2.5c.)

(h) Mere exposure to a model different from that of his peers or his parents will not in itself lead a child to change his own speech; the child must also want to accept the model as the standard for his own behaviour. Many people go on using varieties which they know are low in prestige, and which they believe are deficient, because these varieties are the only ones which they can accept. (See 2.5c, 2.6a, 2.7b.)

(i) The amount of knowledge involved in mastering a language is very great, although its extent is masked from ordinary adult speakers for various reasons, such as the unconscious nature of much of the knowledge. Children normally acquire a high proportion of this knowledge before they reach school age. (See 2.2d, 3.3d.)

2.6 *Relations between languages and dialects*

(a) Whenever speakers of two languages or dialects are in contact with one another, the languages or dialects concerned may be expected to influence each other in proportion to the extent of the contact, the social relations between the speakers, and the practical benefits of such influence for the recipients. (See 2.4c,d, 2.5h.)

(b) Such influence may be profound, going well beyond the borrowing of individual lexical items. (See 2.4a, 2.6g.)

(c) Since languages and dialects are indicators of group membership it is common for a community to resist and criticize such influence, and to pick out particular aspects of it for explicit complaint. (See 2.4c, 2.7b.)

(d) Some aspects of language are more susceptible to external influence than others. Possibly certain areas of vocabulary are the most susceptible, and the least susceptible may be inflectional morphology (i.e. variation in the form of a word to reflect its number, tense, case, etc.). (See 3.3c, 3.4a,b.)

(e) Alongside the similarities among languages, there are many gross differences. Such differences are most obvious in the arbitrary relations between the pronunciation of a word and its meaning and/or its syntactic properties, which are covered partly by the vocabulary and partly by the rules of morphology. (See 2.1c,d, 3.3a, 3.4d.)

(f) Apparent similarities between languages may turn out on thorough investigation to conceal significant differences, and vice versa. (See 2.1d.)

(g) If two languages are similar in their structures this need not be because they developed historically from the same earlier language, nor need historically related languages be similar in their structures. (See 2.4a, 2.6b.)

2.7 *Speech as behaviour*

(a) There are many possible reasons for speaking, only one of which is the desire to communicate ideas to an addressee. Other purposes include the establishing or maintaining of relations with the addressees, and the sorting out of the speaker's own thoughts. (See 1b, 2.4e, 2.5d, 3.5a.)

(b) The variety of language which a speaker uses on a particular occasion serves as an indicator of the speaker's group-membership and also of the speaker's perception of the type of situation in which the speech is taking place. A speaker's choice of variety is not wholly determined by social factors beyond his control, but may be manipulated by him to suit his purposes. (See 2.3e,g, 2.5c,h, 3.1a,c.)

(c) No speaker uses speech equally fluently or effectively for all functions (i.e. for all purposes and in all situations). Skill in speaking depends in part on having the opportunity to practise speech in quite specific functions, rather than on general linguistic ability. (See 2.5d, 3.2b.)

(d) When people comprehend speech, they may actually need to perceive only a proportion of the total utterance, since they can fill in the gaps with what they expect to hear.

3 The structure of language (see 2.1c,d)

3.1 *Pronunciation*

(a) Pronunciation differences are especially closely associated with social group membership differences, and consequently they are especially value-loaded. (See 2.3j, 2.7b.)

(b) Pronunciations which deviate from the prestige variety are generally learned from other speakers, and are not the result of 'slovenly speech habits'. (See 2.5a, 3.1d.)

(c) The precision with which speakers unconsciously conform to the linguistic models which they have adopted in pronunciation (as in other areas of language) goes beyond what is required for efficient communication (e.g. for the avoidance of ambiguity.) (See 2.5a, 2.7b.)

(d) All speakers, in all varieties, use pronunciations in fast speech which differ considerably from those used in slow, careful speech, and other aspects of the situation, such as its formality, may have similar effects. Rapid casual speech is skilled rather than 'slovenly'. (See 2.3b, 2.7d, 3.1b.)

(e) The analysis of pronunciation takes account of at least the following: phonetic features of vowels and consonants, the order in which these occur, and the larger patterns which they form (syllables, words, intonation patterns, etc.).

(f) Intonation does not only reflect the speaker's attitude, but is a particularly important indicator in spoken language of an utterance's structure, and also of its contribution to the discourse. (See 3.2b.)

(g) Intonation is regulated by norms which vary from variety to variety. Children start to learn the intonation patterns of their community's variety in the first year of life.

3.2 *Writing*

(a) Written language reflects a linguistic analysis in terms of categories (e.g. sentence, letter) some of which are not related simply or directly to categories needed for spoken language. (See 1d.)

(b) The skills needed for successful reading and writing are partly distinct from those needed for speaking and listening, and the relevant linguistic patterns are also partly different. Such skills and patterns have to be learned as part of the acquisition of literacy, so the latter involves much more than learning to spell and to recognize single words. (See 2.7c,d.)

(c) The English writing system is only one of many such systems, each of which is amenable to objective and systematic study. Not all writing systems are alphabetic, and not all alphabetic systems are like English in the way they relate writing to other parts of language structure. (See 2.1a.)

(d) Spelling is only one part of the English writing system, which also includes e.g. punctuation, handwriting and the numerals. (See 3.3c.)

(e) Spelling is probably the most immutable part of English, and the part where prescriptivism is most easily accepted by linguists. (See 1a, 2.4c.)

(f) English spelling does not reflect RP any more directly than it does other accents, so it is no easier for RP speakers to learn. (See 2.3j.)

3.3 *Vocabulary*

(a) The relation between the meaning of a word and the pronunciation (or spelling) of its root is usually arbitrary. (See 2.6e, 3.4d.)

(b) Items of vocabulary ('lexical items') include not only single words but also idioms (combinations of words whose meaning cannot be derived from the meanings of the individual words) and other longer structures such as clichés. (See 3.5b.)

(c) The specification of a lexical item must refer to at least the following types of information: its pronunciation (and its spelling, if the language is a written one), its meaning, the syntactic and semantic contexts in which it may occur, and how inflectional morphology affects its form (at least if it is irregular in this respect). (See 2.6d, 3.2d.)

(d) There is no known limit to the amount of detailed information of all such types which may be associated with a lexical item. Existing dictionaries, even large ones, only specify lexical items incompletely.

(e) The syntactic information about a lexical item may be partially given in terms of word-classes, some of which correspond closely to traditional parts of speech. However, a complete syntactic specification of a lexical item needs much more information than can be given in terms of a small set of mutually exclusive word-classes like the parts of speech. (See 1d.)

(f) The boundaries between word-classes tend to be unclear even when defined by linguists.

(g) Many lexical items have meanings which cannot be defined without reference to the culture of the language's speakers.

(h) Vocabulary varies greatly between registers, so a child may use in the classroom only a small portion of his or her total vocabulary. (See 3.4c.)

(i) It is very difficult to measure a person's vocabulary meaningfully,

partly because of the difference between active and passive vocabulary, partly because it is possible to know different amounts of
detail about any given item, and partly because it is possible to
know more vocabulary relevant to one area of experience than to
another, so that measures based on just one kind of vocabulary do
not give a sound basis for estimating the total vocabulary. (See
2.2d, 3.3d, h.)

3.4 *Syntax*

(a) The analysis of syntactic structure takes account of at least the
following factors: the order in which words occur, how they com-
bine to form larger units (phrases, clauses, sentences, etc.), the
syntactic classes to which the words belong (included those marked
by inflectional morphology), and the specifically syntactic relations
among the words or other units, such as the relations referred to by
the labels 'subject' and 'modifier'. (See 1d, 2.6d, 3.5b.)

(b) Although English base has little inflectional morphology, it has a
complex syntax. (I.e. it is not true that 'English has no grammar'.)
This is true of all dialects of English. (See 2.3e, 2.6d.)

(c) Syntax, like vocabulary, is particularly sensitive to register differences, so a child's use of syntactic constructions in the classroom
may reflect only part of the total range of constructions that the
child knows, and uses under other circumstances. (See 2.3c, 2.5e,
3.3h.)

(d) The relations between meanings and syntactic structures are less
arbitrary than those between the meaning and pronunciation of a
single word. However, even this limited arbitrariness allows very
different syntactic structures to be associated (either by different
languages, or within the same language) with similar meanings, and
vice versa. (See 2.6e, 3.3a.)

(e) Syntactic complexity is only one source of difficulty in understanding spoken or written language. (See 2.7e, 3.2b.)

3.5 *Meaning*

(a) The information conveyed by an utterance of a sentence on a
particular occasion may cover many different types of 'meaning',
relating to the conditions for the sentence's being true, the assumptions made by the speakers, the utterance's social function as a

statement, a suggestion, a request, etc., and other factors. (See 2.7a.)

(b) Part of this information is the literal meaning of the sentence uttered, which reflects the meanings of the lexical items in it and the syntactic relations between them. Part of it, however, derives from the context in which the sentence is used. (See 3.3b, 3.4a.)

(c) To a greater extent than other parts of language, meaning may be negotiated by speakers and addresses, e.g. by defining terms or by modifying established meanings to suit special circumstances (See 2.4e.)

(d) The meanings of lexical items change with time, and there is no reason to take the etymological meaning of a word as its true one, or indeed as part of its meaning at all. (See 2.4a,f.)

(e) There is no evidence that any language is any more 'logical' than any other. (See 2.2f.)

THE KINDS OF QUESTIONS TEACHERS TEND TO
ASK OF LINGUISTS
(by Arthur Brookes)

The selection of questions relevant to any topic is a major task. Most of the questions we normally ask are quite rightly concerned with the day-to-day decisions we have to make in particular circumstances and the answers to these are often primarily methodological, and take into account a whole series of practical considerations, which, in the case of teachers, include such things as timetable constraints, class numbers, and attitudes in the staffroom.

However, many of these matters of daily concern can be grouped into those which are ultimately the province of one discipline or another. The knowledge that the answer is potentially available in a certain area (in this case linguistics) lies behind the selection of the particular set of questions that follows.

Having matched the questions to the relevant discipline, it is important to ask the right questions within that discipline. If we consider the teaching of reading, for instance, we might note that in the final chapter of Fries (1962) the whole of the major central section is devoted to answering the two questions 'How do children learn the letters?' and 'How do children learn the spelling patterns?' In the 1980s there might be minor disagreements with some of Fries's analysis, but far more probably we would be asking different questions.

The asking of apt questions is likely to be the result of dialogue. Teachers with the same interests from different institutions begin to frame questions that are not so concerned with the particularities of their individual circumstances when they are in dialogue with each other. Similarly those concerned with education in one form or another are likely to change and refine the questions they ask as they embark on dialogue with linguists. The original set of questions used at Bromsgrove, for instance, has been carefully revised as the result of the dialogue there.

Dialogue, however, is not possible except in an atmosphere of cautious trust. The trust that linguistics has an important part to play in directly or indirectly informing the thinking of teachers has been growing. Language is patterned and systematic and linguists constantly test their hypotheses about the nature of such systems, their relations to each other and to the world. Without this there would be no yardsticks for teachers to test the assumptions they have about language. Furthermore, as a discipline, linguistics is able to provide a framework into which to put the various language topics otherwise sometimes dealt with by teachers in a slightly haphazard way.

While trust has been growing, caution is, however, also necessary because it is not always obvious which elements of linguistics are helpful and at what level. Furthermore, the limits of the usefulness of such insights in relation to other considerations in teaching need to be very carefully considered. It is also important to recognize that dialogue is a two-way process. Linguists may also benefit from dialogue with teachers.

The questions asked in the 1940s and 1950s may well have seemed faintly obsolete in the 1960s and 1970s. It will be interesting to see what new questions are thrown up in the 1980s and 1990s and whether the list below will remain relevant in changing circumstances.

The questions are grouped under sub-headings and tend to move from the general to the more specific and from spoken to written English. The concerns of primary and secondary school teachers were taken into consideration. It should be pointed out that the sub-headings are not an exhaustive list any more than the questions themselves are.

The questions themselves with brief comments

1 *Curiosity about language*

Is linguistics a discipline that encourages curiosity?

Does it provide the framework for eager and objective exploration by children?

The objectivity of the linguist is commented on in 1a and 2.1a above. All objective study calls for the collection of genuine data. It also requires a framework for that data even at a simple level, and this is dealt with in 3.

2 *Language, society and the school*

What language norms do social groups expect of their members?
Should all these different norms be exploited/resisted in the classroom?
How far is a prestige form like Standard English superior?
Should it be consciously taught in the school?

The question of Standard English is crucial in many teachers' minds. There is a clear statement of linguistic fact in 2.2e, though some teachers feel the status quo has political overtones, strictly outside the province of the linguist. The growing awareness of varieties (as in 2.3) already influences many teachers' attitudes. The causes of differing pronunciations are dealt with simply and clearly at 3.1 a–c.

3 *Varieties of English*

Could linguists help with good definitions of 'variety', 'register' etc.?
Should the teacher teach several varieties of spoken and written English?
What is the optimum number at each developmental stage?
What features are particularly important in distinguishing one from another?

The statement itself does not define 'variety', 'register', etc. very fully and indeed the questions here are particularly searching. However, there are many useful pointers towards an answer. The section on varieties (2.3) is clearly helpful, and 2.6b shows the place played by factors other than vocabulary in distinguishing one variety from another. It is clear that a fuller examination of this field by linguists and educationists together is long overdue since the useful pioneering work done by the *Language in Use* team.[2]

4 *Language as identity*

How can a child be given a sense of value about the varieties of English he brings from home?
How can these be categorized?

How far should the teacher express his own identity through language? Alternatively, how far should he modify it to bring it nearer to that of the children?

The questions are not all directly linguistic ones, but there are helpful answers to some points in the section on 'Speech as behaviour' (2.7).

5 *Dialect*

What is dialect?

Is there such a thing as a 'broad' dialect?

How far should a teacher discourage/encourage dialectical speech in the classroom?

The section on 'Languages' (2.2) and 'Relations between language dialects' (2.6) are both helpful.

6 *West Indian patois*

Does Creole have regular rules?

Can it express the full range of intellectual or emotional meaning?

Is it possible to store Creole receptively while employing normal British dialects in speaking?

Should such receptive knowledge be ignored?

Should those who speak a form of Creole be discouraged from speaking it or writing it?

The type of question is a reflection of the number of teachers who have in their classrooms pupils of Caribbean origin. The linguist can certainly help answer the first two or three questions and 2.2d is particularly explicit on the ability of most languages to convey complex meaning just as 2.3d helps to establish that there are rules within a variety. This, in turn, has implications for attitudes to 'correctness'.

7 *Bilingualism*

Do bilingual children progress as fast as monolingual children?

What proportion of the work should be taught in each language?

Are the answers to these questions the same for Welsh children as, say, Pakistani children?

The move towards mother tongue teaching of ethnic minority groups in EEC countries makes the answer to this type of question important. The statement (2.2c) outlines the situation.

8 *Language interaction in the classroom*

How much should the teacher speak? What varieties of teacher-speech are there?
In what ways and adopting what roles can the children speak?
Which of these should be developed and for what purpose?
For instance, what kind of speaking is most related to learning?

This type of concern is reflected in the Bullock Report (DES, 1975) (*A Language for Life*) pages 47–50, and the Hudson section on 'Acquisition' (2.5) has some pertinent things to say about this area.

9 *Developing a child's spoken language*

Is there anything that is known about children's language acquisition that can be applied to the development of the child's spoken language at school?
Can the stages the child passes through be categorized?
What part can drama play in developing a child's spoken language?
What factors prevent a child progressing in all or part of his spoken language?
Can the different sub-skills be satisfactorily identified?
Can (and should) the different varieties of English be developed at uneven rates?

Some teachers tend to ask the above type of question while others are more concerned with clarity and correctness in speech. Clearly the work of Tough, Crystal, and others has made teachers think more along the lines of this section and the next. The statement certainly has useful things to say at 2.5–2.7.

10 *Form or function*

Can linguistics clear up the muddled area of notions and functions?
In determining how competent a child is in using the language, is it better to look at the forms of the language a child can use or the functions he can use them for?
Is there any sound way of relating form to function?

The questions are, of course, also of considerable importance in second language learning. The relation of form to function is explicitly commented on at 1b and 2.1a, though neither provides in itself all the answers sought for in this section, as most work has been done on either form or function and rarely on the connections between them.

11 *Profile of a child's language development*

It is useful to be able to provide a profile for diagnostic purposes or to keep a check on linguistic development.
Can linguistics help in sorting out what is possible, what is helpful, and what is practical in this field?
Can this be done for the active modes of speaking and writing?
Can it also be done for the passive modes of listening and reading?

This group of questions reflects a desire on the part of some teachers (particularly those who favour more informal methods in the classroom) to be able to record the child's linguistic development accurately; and undoubtedly the questions in number 10 continue to be of importance in these concerns too. Many of the answers can be found in section 3 of the statement, but once again the questions of practicality lie in the co-operation between the linguist and those close to the classroom.

12 *Listening and receptive skills*

Is there much passive knowledge of language which the speaker can't make active?
How can we know which items of language are only in the passive mode?
Is it necessary to try to turn all passive language into active language?
How does one turn passive language into active language?

There are useful references to receptive skills in section 3.

13 *Comprehension*

What is the full range of meaning we can get from a piece of spoken English?
Can we find out what goes on in our minds as we try to understand it?
How can we exploit this as teachers in the strategies we adopt in the classroom?
Can linguistics answer any of the above points in relation to written English?

Is comprehension personal or active in any way or is it simply learning to understand the speaker's/reader's full meaning?

How can we frame questions about a 'text' really to test the learner's understanding?

The questions are beginning to move from oracy to literacy and this group of questions directs itself to both and looks for its answers partly to psycholinguistics, partly to semantics. Section 3.5 on 'Meaning' obviously has some useful things to say in reply as has 2.7d. The last question points to the very common use of passages and questions for the teaching of comprehension, though it may point to different levels of meaning in the text and how to identify these.

14 *Speech and writing*

Are there any significant differences between written and spoken English?

What are they?

Does developing spoken English help with written English?

Are there any areas where the primacy of speech might be disputed?

The relation between written and spoken English is a crucial one at every stage of schooling though it is particularly important in the teaching of initial literacy. The beginning of the section on 'Writing' in the statement (3.2) is relevant.

15 *Beginning reading*

Can linguistics help with initial literacy?

How helpful is the development of oracy as an aid to promoting literacy?

Which criteria in constructing and selecting reading schemes come within the scope of linguistics and which do not?

Are alternative strategies in teaching initial literacy (other than through the extensive use of the reading scheme) supported by linguistics. Which are not?

In what sort of ways can linguistics help in determining the amount and nature of overt teaching of 'phonics' in helping children learn to read?

Some of these questions overlap with those in the previous section. Clearly there are a number of answers already known, and linguistically informed materials such as *Breakthrough to Literacy*[2] have helped to start changing the climate of opinion.

16 *Readability*

Which elements of readability can linguistics tell us about?
Which of the commonly-used readability tests is most respectable linguistically? .
What can linguists say in general about the readability of non-fiction texts as opposed to fiction texts?
What analysis of technical jargon can be made and how does this relate to readability?

It is useful to note that science teachers and others are asking this type of question more frequently. Linguists are, of course, working in this field and there are some useful pointers towards the end of the statement.

17 *Literary and non-literary language*

In what terms can linguistics help us to describe these two types of writing?
Can such a description of the language be related to the reader's response?

The answers to this type of question might lead to more informed literary criticism and to a differential treatment of fiction and non-fiction in the classroom. Stylistics, not reflected as such in the statement, might well provide some answers. Crystal and Davy (1969) and Widdowson (1975) provide some linguistic guidelines for looking at these two kinds of language.

18 *Metalanguage*

Most schools employ linguistic terms like 'sentence' but rarely words like 'tagmeme'.
Where between the two do we draw the line with children?
How useful are the names for the parts of speech?
Are some more useful than others?
Are they the right terms for the right concepts?
Is it helpful to teach *about* language?
If the answer is 'yes', how young should one start?

Meta-language is referred to in 1e. Many teachers are not aware that common expressions like 'word' and 'sentence' are linguistic terms that can be discussed rationally with quite young children. The study of language up to the 'A' level stage is the subject of continuing debate.

19 *Vocabulary and spelling*

If we are actively extending vocabulary, are words better taught by exposure to more language in a random way or by some conscious programming on the part of the teacher?

If the latter, is it important for the word to be seen in several different contexts?

What kinds of things can a linguist tell us about a particular lexical item? What part have dictionaries to play?

To repeat a question from 14, are some words learned through reading first and do they need to become part of the spoken vocabulary?

Is spelling helped by a morphological study of words and their connections to each other?

Are there enough regular rules to make the teacher take these into account when teaching spelling?

Does correct spelling matter?

If it does, what in our strategies as teachers of initial literacy will help or hinder learning to spell correctly?

Clearly this is an area of considerable concern. The two groups of questions on vocabulary and on spelling reflecting sections 3.2 and 3.3 in the statement have been conflated, partly because of the tendency of some teachers to take questions of spelling in isolation even in making work. 3.5d has a most valuable point to add to the questions about the meanings of words.

20 *Syntax and correctness*

Does the child go through stages in his readiness to process and use increasingly complex syntax?

Can the linguist give guidance on how to assist the child in moving on to the next stage of complexity in sentence structure?

Is this a helpful thing to do?

Is there such a thing as *correct* syntax in English?

Or is it simply a question of using the appropriate variety?

This document relates 'correctness' to 'syntax' but questions about correctness are dominant in many teachers' minds and it forms part of their questions about language and language teaching. Similarly there are answers scattered throughout the statement, for example at 1a, 2.3b, 2.3h, 2.5b and c, 3.1d, 3.2e.

Conclusion

The compilers of the two sets of items working at first independently were interested to find what an intricate relationship there was between teachers' questions and linguists' convictions. We were also interested to note that, where teachers had seen the Hudson document, it had itself triggered off new questions and new lines of thought in certain areas.

It is, however, also true that by separating out the linguistic from the other elements in the teaching programme and then subdividing both the linguists' beliefs and the teachers' questions into apparently distinct items a false impression may have been created. We would like to make it clear, first, that we attach considerable importance to the inter-relations between different aspects of linguistics itself. Second, we do not wish it to appear that we fail to recognize the importance of the learner himself in the educational process. Finally, we recognize the holistic nature of educational programmes and materials. Clearly each element within a programme has its part to play, but many materials we have looked at either lack a proper linguistic input or more often assume beliefs about language that do not bear linguistic scrutiny.

Holistic activities may themselves be of two kinds. The first kind is the *particular* activity. We may decide, for instance, that a class is at the stage of needing to look at the media with a careful and critical eye. One part of this activity may well be to look at the way in which two or more papers report a news item. There will be non-linguistic considerations such as which page the report appears on, the length of the report, the size and prominence of the headline, or, indeed, the political bias of the report. But there will equally be linguistic elements such as the variety differences produced by the demands of space, by the nature of the readership, by the degree of formality, by the level of generality, or even the way in which the political bias is reflected in the language. Whether these are best taught by observation and discussion or by some sort of writing in the style of different newspapers or perhaps by a combination of both methods is largely a pedagogic question. This is precisely the kind of exercise envisaged by the authors of the *Language in Use* materials we have already referred to.

The second kind of holistic activity is of a different nature. One example is the question of comprehension. This is clearly an on-going process during the child's school life of interest both to linguists and psychologists. Here the linguistically sound awareness in the teacher of the processes of comprehension may well inform the teaching of a wide range of school subjects. Furthermore, the interest of the linguist in spoken English may alert the teacher to the importance of listening as well as reading comprehension. Included in this generalized on-going process will no doubt be some more formal lessons where units of spoken or written material are subjected to careful scrutiny. Once again linguistics will take its place by the side of other considerations in helping the teacher with the selection of material, the framing of tasks to help the learner grasp as much of the full meaning as he is ready for, and the language in which those tasks are formulated.

The linking of the items on our two lists to these two types of holistic activity is unfortunately beyond the scope of this chapter, but we are certain there is still important work to be done in this field. At a simpler level, the more the two compilers have worked together and discussed the material, the more we have become convinced that there is fruitful dialogue possible between linguists and teachers.

Notes

1 Further information about the Committee for Linguistics in Education and its work may be obtained from the Hon. Secretary, John Rudd, 92 Bath Road, Worcester WRS 3EW.

2 *Language in Use* (Doughty *et al.*, 1971) and *Breakthrough to Literacy* (Mackay *et al.*, 1970) are two of the outcomes of the Programme in Linguistics and English Teaching which took place at University College, London, from 1964–70 under the general direction of Prof. M.A.K. Halliday. These are two of the best known linguistics-based projects from that programme. The former is an ideas book for secondary teachers and the latter is a method of linking speaking, reading, and writing for those involved with literacy at the initial or remedial stage.

5

The spoken language

Gillian Brown

Introduction

This article begins by questioning some commonly held assumptions
about the nature and value of 'talk' in school and goes on to propose
a crucial difference between primarily 'listener-oriented' speech and
primarily 'message-oriented' speech. Gill Brown discusses the forms and
functions of these two types of talk and argues that 'message-oriented'
speech is not explicitly taught in schools in spite of its importance to
an individual in the performance of a wide range of tasks in a literate
society. In the latter part of the article she discusses the kind of criteria
which should inform the explicit teaching and principled assessment of
message-oriented speech. Such syllabi will need to take into account a
number of variables including the addressee, how much the addressee
knows about what the speaker is talking about, how familiar the topic
is to the speaker, how complex the topic is, and how much the structure
of what the student/pupil has to talk about is provided by the nature
of the task itself.

1 Common assumptions

There is a widespread assumption in the linguistic literature that native
speakers of a language all learn naturally to speak their own language
(apart from a minority of tragic exceptions). It is assumed that all
normal children will become articulate adults. In much sociolinguistic
and educational writing, on the other hand, we find a rather different
picture. We find a picture of a large group of children in any literate
society, whose manipulation of the spoken language is held to be
inadequate, judged by the norms of their successful peers. Let me
emphasize that, as far as I can tell, it is in literate societies that these
deficits or disadvantages are perceived. I shall return to this point.

The reaction by educationalists and sociologists to the evidence of 'disadvantaged' speakers has been to create schemes which would extend the exposure of children to thoughtful talk by adults, and to give the children the maximum opportunity for expressing themselves orally within the educational system. Many educational reports have, since the early 1960s, laid stress on the importance of 'talk' in the educational curriculum, often with the implication that if children can't learn to express themselves in writing, at least they should be able to express themselves in speech, and conversely, if they can't extract information from the written word, at least they should be able to extract information from the spoken word. In many of these reports there seems to be an assumption that it really doesn't matter too much if the children can't cope with the written word comfortably and fluently, because this lack can be compensated for by fluency in the spoken mode. There seems to be then, an assumption that, for all practical purposes, spoken and written language are performing the same sort of tasks and that you can perfectly well develop spoken language skills in the absence of written language skills, and the spoken language skills will in some sense 'stand in for' the functions that written language fulfils in a literate society.

This seems a plausible point of view at first blush – it must be, since so many people have fallen for it. After all you can point to non-literate societies and observe that full lives appear to be lived by people with only a spoken mode available or, indeed, you can point to individuals in a literate society who live full, social lives and are vividly articulate in speech, even though they have only a marginal command of written skills.

2 Functions of spoken language:
listener-oriented and message-oriented speech

I believe that the argument I have represented here is a misplaced one, based on the belief that to be articulate in one sphere of spoken language activity implies that you will also be articulate in another sphere. Any teacher knows that this doesn't follow. Children who chat vividly and amusingly with their peers about what they've been doing over the weekend, are reduced to almost total inarticulacy if invited to develop an argument to the class, or justify a particular viewpoint in conversation with their teacher. It is easy to suppose that the crucial factor at issue here is the interlocutor, the person who the child is talking to. It would be wrong to deny that this has an effect on the speaker. What is usually ignored, however, is the effect of the different kind of activity that is involved in chatting in an informal mode on the one hand, and expounding a coherent position on the other.

I am going to propose a simple-minded two-way distinction between the main functions of spoken language. I shall suggest that there is one type of speech that is primarily *listener-oriented*, and another type of speech that is primarily *message-oriented*. I assume that in primarily message-oriented speech the main point of speaking from the speaker's point of view is expressing the message. He intends to bring about some specific change in the listener's state of knowledge (for example he wishes to make it clear that he refuses to co-operate with a friend, or he wishes the doctor to understand his symptoms, or he wishes to buy a railway ticket for his intended destination). His utterance is goal-directed. It matters to him that the listener understands what he is saying, and that he understands it correctly. In listening to primarily message-oriented speech, we may judge it to be successful if the message (the point of view) is satisfactorily communicated to the listener. The point of the utterance may, then, be held to be the speaker's communication of a propositional or cognitive (information-bearing) message to his listener. Of course it is nice if the listener also ends up feeling friendly to the speaker, but there is a sense in which this may be considered to be a happy side-effect, rather than the reason for the utterance.

Primarily listener-oriented speech, on the other hand, has as its main intention the establishment and maintenance of good social relations with the listener. It is often the case that speakers in primarily listener-oriented dialogue don't actually seem to be talking about anything very much. The topic keeps changing, they are untroubled by surrounding chat or deafening music, and they sit and smile and nod happily away to each other. What is crucial in this sort of dialogue is that a good deal of agreement goes on. In listening to primarily listener-oriented speech, we may judge it to be successful if the participants succeed in maintaining friendly relationships. Of course it may be the case that speaker A finishes up knowing that speaker B prefers holidaying in the Scottish Highlands to walking in the Pennines, and that Mrs March down the road has to go into hospital but, again, this information may be considered to be almost an accidental side-effect of the main business of the dialogue, which was to be friendly.

Note that I am not claiming that we normally participate in any conversations which are all and only message-oriented, or all and only listener-oriented (though you may think of some that lie very nearly at the ends of the scale – instructions to an inferior rank in the army (or medical profession), versus chatting to a stranger at a bus-stop). What I shall maintain, however, is that the more the conversation is listener-oriented the less of it is, of its nature, highly structured, whereas the more a conversation is message-oriented the more it is, of its nature, highly structured. In the next section I shall explain what I mean by 'structured'.

3 Forms of spoken language

In the last few years a considerable amount of linguistic descriptive work has been done on the different forms of spoken language which are produced in different conditions of use (cf. Givon, 1979; Ochs, 1979; Goody, 1977; Brown, 1977, 1978). The conclusion which I draw from these diverse studies is that if you take any articulate adult out of a literate society and analyse the forms which he produces in primarily listener-oriented speech and primarily message-oriented speech, you will find quite startlingly different norms of use. I list below some of the characteristics of listener-oriented speech.

1 The rate of delivery is slow, broken into short chunks, with a good deal of pausing.
2 The short chunks are frequently structured so that only one thing is said about a referent at a time (simple case-frame, or one-place predicate): *It's a biggish cat* + *tabby* + *with torn ears**, i.e. the information is not densely structured.
3 The relationship between the short chunks is rarely syntactically marked – there is rather little subordination, and little use of logical connectors other than *and, but, then, if.* The speaker assumes the listener will work out the conversational relevance of each succeeding chunk: *I'm so tired* + (because) *I had to play hockey* + *all this afternoon.*
4 The topic is frequently announced in an independent phrase which is followed by a comment: *my father* + *he was furious, the cats* + *did you let them out.*
5 In talk about the immediate environment, the speaker may rely on physical context – for instance, gaze direction – to supply a referent: (looking at the rain) *frightful* + *isn't it*?

*The symbol + indicates a pause in the stream of speech

6 The speaker uses many non-specific deictic (demonstrative) expressions: *I haven't done this before, that's all there is to it.*

7 The speaker replaces or refines lexical items as he goes along: *this man + this chap she was going out with.* He typically uses many general words like *got, nice, do, girl, chap, a lot of,* etc.

8 The speaker repeats the same syntactic form several times over: *he's about 6 feet + he's quite tall + he's quite well-built + he has very nice manners.*

9 The speaker produces a large number of interactive, prefabricated 'fillers': *I think, I mean, you know/remember, do you know/think, of course, what I mean is.*

10 The speaker frequently repeats what he has already said.

11 The speaker may change the topic or produce an extended parenthesis on some different topic, and long stretches of the dialogue may have no settled topic since the participants are trying out several possibilities to find out what will mutually interest them.

12 The speaker may fail to make it clear precisely which of several referents he is referring to – partly because he's using a lot of pronouns or very general lexical items.

13 The speaker will not produce any extended argument or justification or explanation but, typically, expressions of opinion and short narratives often relating to the speaker's own experience or the shared experience of speaker-listener: *do you remember Mrs Jones? Well, she . . . .*

This list is by no means exhaustive and of course it is only indicative of norms – it is not prescriptive. (Some readers will be reminded of some of the features of Bernstein's restricted code, Bernstein, 1959.) Observe, however, that the cumulative effect of the general tendencies I have listed here will be to create language which is rather generalized and non-specific, where it is sometimes quite difficult to identify the point of the speaker's remark. However, the listener rarely interrupts to identify precisely who or what is having what said about them – one's general impression is that the listener is often only doing a fairly sketchy interpretation of what the speaker is saying and, when his turn comes to speak, he will produce similar rather general comments, which may not hold together too well with what the previous speaker has said, or indeed may be inconsistent with the remarks he himself has already made. In friendly relaxed chat about whatever topic turns out to be of mutual interest, it doesn't matter too much if the speaker doesn't make his meaning crystal clear.

If we turn to primarily message-oriented speech, we find the articulate adult producing forms of language which are characteristically different from those I have listed. The delivery is typically more structured, in that more is said about a referent within one chunk, there is more syntactic marking between sequences (or propositions) – more subordination and more logical connectors (*because, therefore, it follows that, however, so,* etc.). The vocabulary is typically more specific (*my solicitor* rather than – *a man I know*) and the speaker takes pains to make it clear precisely who or what he's talking about at any given point. The topic changes much less frequently because, after all, it's the topic, the message, that is the point of the utterance. In this sort of dialogue we may find extended argument, justification, explanation, and so on.

Clearly, it would be possible to draw much finer distinctions than the gross distinctions I have drawn between primarily message-oriented speech and primarily listener-oriented speech (and I am not even claiming that these two gross categories are discrete categories). We would find, for example, that there are some characteristics typically associated with argument, but not with narrative, and vice versa, that there are some speech functions where negative sentences, questions, passive sentences or directives abound, and others in which they occur rarely, if at all. That is to say we would find that different formal features of language are to be associated with different modes, the sort of phenomenon that has been described under such headings as 'style' or 'register'. That sort of finer detail does not concern me here. In what I want to go on to say, I shall adhere to my gross two-way distinction.

It seems reasonable to suggest that we all have the ability to use spoken language to express ourselves in primarily listener-oriented speech. Anyone brought up in a social environment will acquire some level of social competence, varying somewhat according to the personality of the individual, or the customs of his family, or that of his particular speech community. Our expectation is that all speakers in a nonliterate society will have this ability, just as we expect that all speakers in our own society will have this ability. So we find speakers who, in a formal context, say a school context, have very little to say for themselves, but may be highly articulate talking to their friends in the corridor or outside school. There is, of course, every reason to set a very high value on this ability. It is clearly fundamental to social life. On the other hand, it is essential to realize that to be articulate in listener-oriented speech does not guarantee that an individual will also be articulate in message-oriented speech. You may well consider that the social value of listener-oriented speech is so great that we can afford to ignore what I am calling message-oriented speech. You will have, however, to admit that a member of a literate industrialized society like our own is necessarily limited in the possibilities open to him if he does not control those forms of language typical of message-oriented speech.

Some linguists, who in my view ought to know better, have expressed the hope that society (in particular, schools) will become more tolerant of 'self-expressive' modes of expression (where I take it 'self-expressive' means very much what I mean by 'listener-oriented'). This view arises from a fundamental misunderstanding of the functions of language in society. Of course self-expressive speech is adequate and appropriate, for all of us, *in situations where self-expressive speech is appropriate*, but we can all think of dozens of everyday situations where self-expressive speech is not appropriate. Consider the following situations: a doctor explaining to a mother the possible side-effects of her child's treatment, a journalist phoning in a report on a traffic accident, a trades union representative arguing for better working conditions, a master decorator explaining to an apprentice why it's necessary to soak wallpaper before hanging it, a teacher explaining a maths problem to a child, a nurse reporting on a patient's behaviour following an operation, a driving instructor explaining the effects of putting the clutch in, a travel agent outlining holiday options. In all such cases we would think it quite unsatisfactory if the speaker was not able to express what he wanted to say reasonably concisely, making it quite clear what it is he wants to say. There are times in a complexly structured, technologically developed, literate society, when it is necessary to be able to produce a clear description, a straightforward narrative, or a complicated argument laying out pros and cons. There are times when we need to be able to pack information efficiently, and to use the structural resources of the language to make the meaning clear. It is misleading to pretend that self-expressive speech (listener-oriented speech), which is of course a rich and infinitely varied instrument in its own domain, is adequate to handle all these functions.

It is clear that the articulate adult needs to be able to control a range of different modes of spoken language which will have typically different functions. The ability to produce and to understand highly structured speech, with information relatively densely packed, while remaining sensitive to the listener's state of knowledge and ability to draw relevant inferences, represents a very complex skill. It is a skill that the

majority of the population does not acquire without a good deal of
help, unlike listener oriented speech which most of us begin to acquire
without special tuition in our earliest years. It is a skill which relates
very closely to the written language (cf. Goody, 1977). Indeed it may
reasonably be argued that this highly structured language is parasitic
upon written language, and that it is extremely hard to develop it in the
absence of control of written language skills. Certainly mere exposure
to written language or to message-oriented spoken language will not
guarantee its acquisition. It is a skill that most children are going to
have to acquire in school, if they acquire it at all.

It is crucial, then, that it is thoroughly understood by teachers that
it is not sufficient simply to give the child more opportunity to 'talk'
in school, since the child may merely be practising that type of 'talk'
that he constantly produces outside the school. What we need is a
proper programme to extend the ability of the child to talk, to express
himself in a way that is, quite properly, highly valued by the society
he is part of.[1]

4 Constructing a programme

If we accept that it really is necessary to teach children to produce
message-oriented speech, we urgently need to find out more about the
characteristics of such speech. On the basis of studies undertaken so
far, it seems reasonable to suggest that there are far more urgent priorities than sentence-length, control of complex syntax, learning extensive
vocabulary, though there is no doubt that the control of these formal
features does greatly improve the chances of successfully developing
message-oriented speech. However, the first and fundamental priority
has to be enabling the child to make it clear what he wants to say. At
the simplest level it means insisting that he identify clearly what he is
talking about. Initial control in this area can be practised by having the
child identify verbally, without pointing or nodding, a particular
individual out of a set of rather similar individuals. You could try
this with photographs of different people, or by taking a set of assorted
pencils, the same colour, but set out in a distinctive configuration, so
that it is necessary to identify 'the one at the top left-hand side' and
so on. From the message point of view, there is no point in the child
saying anything, if it is not clear what he is talking about. Of course
language is highly redundant, and in many cases the sympathetic listener
can work out what the child must mean. However, the child is being

prepared to live in a difficult world, where people in a hurry may not have time to stop and work out what he means. The first priority is clear initial identification of what he wants to talk about.

I am not at all sure what the next priority is. I have a list of competitors which all seem to me urgent.

1 Obviously it is important that the child should make it clear what comment he wants to make on his chosen topic.
2 He has to make clear what is the *point* of his message, why he is bothering to speak at all.
3 He has to learn to select, to put first things first.
4 He has to learn to construct a rational sequence of observations, using expressions like *because* and *so* in a careful manner.
5 Once he has established his initial reference, he has to distinguish any later referent that he introduces, and maintain that clear distinction between competing references as he goes on talking. Thus if he is explaining how two cars came to be involved in an accident, he has to make it quite clear which of the two cars he is talking about at any point.

These seem to be such basic skills that many members of our community find it astonishing that all school leavers have not mastered them. Yet it is clearly the case that many school leavers have not done so. Part of the reason may be that, because they share so much knowledge with their friends and families and teachers they can 'get away with' very inexplicit language, since their usual listeners are either prepared to make a great deal of effort to understand them, or else assume that, since what they are talking about is so unclear, it can't matter very much anyway. It is important then that the child should practise talking, not only to people whom he has every reason to believe know everything that he knows on a subject, but also to listeners who don't know what he knows. There is little motivation for a child to be very explicit when he is asked to describe what is going on in a series of pictures which his interlocutor is looking at as well. Why should he bother, since his listener can see what is going on just as well as he can? Similarly there is no point, the child may well feel, in telling his teacher what the teacher obviously knows already.

Many sympathetic teachers have rumbled this one and decide therefore to set the child to talk on some topic where, they feel, he has privileged information and has to be telling them something that the teacher can't possibly know. Many an unfortunate pupil is asked then to talk for two or three minutes on 'my interests' or 'my favourite subject' or 'what I do at the weekend' or 'my holiday last year' or 'what I did at Guides'. The bright articulate child has often no problem and rattles away on such topics, leaving the teacher to despair at the other children who are unable to cope with what seems such a pleasant and sympathetic task. After all they are only being asked to talk about what they know. In fact, this is a difficult and complex task.

To begin with, the child has to assess how much his listener is likely to know in general terms, about his topic. Does the listener know Liverpool, what happens at Guides meetings, what it means to be a Sea Scout? This assessment of how much the listener is likely to know is a really sensitive skill, and we all frequently get it wrong. For a child who is used to talking to members of a rather closed community this can provide a formidable problem. In a normal conversation between articulate adults, there is a mechanism by which the speaker can find out how much the listener knows – he can ask questions. The problem for the child, who believes he should answer the teacher's question as quickly as possible, is that the possibility of taking the conversational initiative, and finding out about the teacher's knowledge of his topic, doesn't even occur to him. Yet, without this essential preliminary, it is very unlikely that the child will not either assume more shared knowledge than he has warrant for, or tell the listener what he already knows.

The next problem that faces the child is what, out of the large and rich topic-area that he has been allocated, he should select to talk about. It requires considerable sophistication to be able to select from your wealth of experiences, some one particular experience which will provide you with something interesting to say. If a child fails to identify one (or two) particularly striking and interesting topics, the result of the exercise will tend to be a random list of topics with perhaps a comment or two on each. Having selected a topic to talk about, the next problem is what to say about it to begin with, if it has no natural structure. Suppose you are asked to talk about 'your interests'. Having chosen an interest, do you begin by saying why you like it (and it's hard to imagine a more difficult task than that) or by saying what pursuing this interest involves – and where does the pursuit begin?

It seems clear that rich, unstructured topics of the sort I have listed present formidable difficulties to the child who is not confident in message-oriented speech. It produces for him a situation of communicative stress, in which he is unlikely to learn very much, or perform very well. What we require, I suggest, is a 'communicative stress index' which would allow us to identify a situation in which the child would feel most at ease, and is likely to perform most efficiently. Then, using this as the point of departure, we could construct a syllabus which would enable the child to cope with carefully controlled increases in communicative stress.

We can list at least some of the relevant variables. I suggest that the speaker engaged in message-oriented speech finds it least taxing to produce coherent speech under the following circumstances:

(a) *Listener* – where he is talking to one listener and the listener is a friendly and co-operative person of the same status.

(b) *Context* – where they are talking in a pleasant, familiar, private context, face to face.

(c) *Shared knowledge* – where the speaker has some idea of, or is able to find out about, how much the listener knows about the topic.

(d) *New knowledge* – where the speaker knows the new knowledge and his listener does not.

(e) *Structure of information* – where the information to be imparted provides its own structure.

(f) *Type of information* – where the type of information is familiar, concrete rather than abstract.

(g) *Type of task* – where the task is concerned with answering questions like *when, what, where, who, which* (which may involve identification, narration, description, etc.) rather than questions like *how* and *why* (which involve the development of strategies of argument in justifying, explaining, etc.).

An easy task, defined by these variables, would be, for instance, where a child who is used to playing cards is explaining to a friend, also used to playing cards, a card-trick which the speaker is very familiar with and the hearer does not know. The shared knowledge (names of cards, structure of tricks) is known, the speaker is in sole charge of the new information and cannot be challenged, the information structure is provided by the sequence of actions which constitute the laying-out of the trick, so there is external support for the language, and the type of task simply involves an ordered set of instructions.

Tasks can be made more difficult by boosting the stress under any variable. The listener may be unfamiliar, which imposes a different set of roles and may alter (c) above. The task may be being taped, or performed in front of other people. The listener may share the same knowledge, thus reducing the motivation for explicitness on the part of the speaker, and making him vulnerable to being challenged about the correctness of what he is saying. The card trick task can be made more difficult by taking away the cards and relying on memory. The problem can be made more difficult by providing tasks with less and less structure. The type of information can be made more difficult by being chosen from an area which is less familiar to the speaker. The task can be varied as well by changing its demands – rather than simply reporting that action X happened before action Y, the speaker may be asked to explain why this order is significant, or how Y is affected by X.

Summary

In the first part of this paper, I tried to make the point that it is not sufficient to say that children should produce more 'talk' in schools, and assume that any old 'talk' will do. We need to distinguish between primarily listener-oriented language and primarily message-oriented language. We can draw the distinction on formal grounds, in terms of descriptive linguistic categories, and we can draw it on functional grounds in terms of different social functions. Primarily listener-oriented speech is naturally acquired in a social setting, and is just as naturally acquired by members of a nonliterate society as by members of a literate society. Primarily message-oriented speech plays a very important part in technologically advanced, literate society, is not naturally acquired by the majority of the population, and needs to be explicitly taught.[2]

In the second part of the paper, I suggested that we need to develop a syllabus for teaching message-oriented speech, which begins from the type of task which involves least communicative stress for the speaker, and which gradually increases the difficulty of the task that is required of the speaker. Some of the variables which seem likely to affect the performance of the speaker are discussed.

In the present state of our knowledge, we are still only making educated guesses about the major variables which affect a speaker's performance.

Notes

1 It may be argued, correctly, that the child's local community does not value message-oriented language particularly highly. There is no doubt that this constitutes an enormous extra barrier for the teacher. However, from a purely economic viewpoint, the restricted access to most forms of well paid employment that a child who cannot

control such language suffers from is surely sufficient evidence of its importance to society at large.

2 It is a curious irony that most foreign language teaching is concerned with message-oriented language, which is taught to children who may not be competent in message-oriented language in their mother tongue.

Acknowledgments

This is an extended version of a paper first presented to a seminar organized by the National Foundation for Education Research in Cambridge, 1980. I am grateful to members of that seminar for helpful comments. I am indebted to many friends and colleagues for conversations on aspects of the topic of this paper, in particular to Keith Brown, Jacqueline Schlissinger, Hilary Smith and George Yule.

6

Responding to children's writing

Peter Gannon

Introduction

This article illustrates a way of looking at children's writing that is informed by an awareness of linguistic structure at different levels. Many teachers, when marking pupils' work, concentrate on spelling and punctuation, to the exclusion of other and often more important features of the language used. Some children have a confused notion of the relationship between speech and writing; some have difficulty with word-structure; others find it difficult in writing to vary their sentence-structures, while some write quite 'correctly' but in sentences that do not quite hang together. The article puts forward the view that by regarding error as an opportunity for the teacher to help with linguistic features that are erratically or insecurely displayed by children, it is possible to be more powerfully constructive about writing development. To do this, it is important for teachers to know as much as possible about the structure of the English language at the traditional linguistic levels of phonology, morphology, syntax, semantics and discourse. For too long, there has been a gap between the theoretical work of descriptive linguists and the attempts of teachers to improve the language performance skills of pupils. By applying basic linguistic principles to a piece of writing by a 13 year old, this paper seeks to show, in an informal and simple fashion, how a linguistic approach may illuminate the teacher's responses.

It is not uncommon to find children of all levels of ability in our secondary schools who, in their last two years of statutory schooling, have written up to 200,000 words of prose (see DES, 1979, chapter 6). Yet teachers' responses to those vast quantities of written work are frequently vague and unhelpful. The very term used in schools to refer to the process of assessment – 'marking' – is indicative of typical response. To mark a piece of work may mean little or much. In fact, there is a predominance of effort devoted to correcting surface features of spelling and punctuation and relatively little helpful assessment. One may describe the situation diagrammatically (Figure 6.1). Between these two extremes, one may find varying approaches; sporadic help with sentence-structure, suggestions for more appropriate word choices, sympathetic expression of interest – all are to be found as teacher response to the vast bulk of writing produced by children.

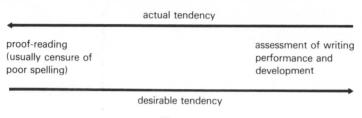

actual tendency

proof-reading
(usually censure of
poor spelling)

assessment of writing
performance and
development

desirable tendency

Figure 6.1

It is the purpose of this chapter to consider a not untypical piece of writing by a child in the middle of her secondary education and the teacher's response to it, and then to consider some of the implications with regard to what English teachers should know and do in the light of current linguistic knowledge. The chapter also starts with three main assumptions that should be made explicit: first, that if teachers are concerned with children's linguistic development, whatever else they may be interested in, then it is important for them to know as much as possible about not only the children they teach and how children typically develop, but also language itself; next, that since there is a discipline in which language is the object of study, namely linguistics, then it is the duty of both teachers and of linguists concerned with education to explore the discipline's applications to the main theme of this chapter, viz. the teacher's assessment of children's writing; finally, that a specifically linguistic assessment in no way precludes other necessary responses, whether they be concerned with motivation, emotional sensitivity, grading for examination purposes, or whatever.

Let us start by looking at a piece of written work. In a third year secondary English class, the teacher had read aloud a story about an old tramp, whose cheerfulness and ability to converse with other poor people, as well as his love for animals, bore testimony to a life of curiosity and speculation, despite its material poverty. The children were asked to write on what they thought the story was about and what they felt about it. Here is an extract from the work of a girl whom we may call Emma, designated by the teacher as of average ability. The lines are numbered for ease of reference.

1 The story showed many things about ordinary life, one was
2 that the old man had got not much educatin
3 but he felt things just the same as other people.
4 Another thing is how the animals were like pictures
5 of ordinary everyday people and poor workmen could
6 talk to the old man in not at all boring ways even
7 if they hadnt of been to school like him.

The teacher's comments and corrections were as follows

(a) 1.1 Full stop inserted after *life*, with the initial letter of *one* corrected to a capital.

(b) 1.2 *educatin* crossed out and 'Sp' (spelling) entered in the margin.

(c) 1.6 *not at all boring ways* underlined and a superscription entered which read 'interesting ways'. G (grammar) entered in the margin.

(d) 1.7 *hadnt of been* crossed out and 'had not been' inserted. G in the margin.

(e) At the end of the piece was the comment 'Too many careless mistakes! Watch your grammar.'

The teacher had conscientiously marked all the pieces and returned them to the class of 28 children before proceeding to another topic.

It is always difficult, when commenting on isolated classroom events, to assess the importance of the missing variables, particularly the context of development. That is to say, one may be unaware of the developmental rate of progression in the individual child or of the development of the teacher-pupil relationship, etc. However, even if, in Emma's case, the teacher was well aware of her rate of progress and even if her written work were talked about in a relaxed and trusting way, this example illustrates four things. First, the typical teacher comment is not as efficacious as it might be; second, more effective comment could be made with an awareness on the teacher's part of differences in *levels* of linguistic error; third, it is important for the teacher to know what could have been written as well as what is wrong with what has been written; fourth, more powerful and productive comment is likely to result from an appreciation of basic linguistic principles.

The five teacher comments are of three kinds. There is the proof-reading correction of (a) in which the *o* is changed to *O*, and (b) where the abbreviation 'Sp' calls attention to a spelling error. Then there is the corrective nature of (c) and (d) where more acceptable alternatives are added. The hortatory comment in (e) is, I suspect, no more than a teaching ritual. To ask a child to watch her grammar is akin to saying 'Be careful!' when she leaves the house to go to school, or 'Have a nice day.' Such utterances are almost phatic in their generality. They serve merely to signal a recognition that an interpersonal process is going on, whether it be the reinforcement of a parent-child relationship or a teacher-pupil relationship. They make everyone feel better, especially the speakers.

For a correction of a writing error to be effective, three conditions must ideally be met: the comment should be comprehensible to the reader; it should relate to a genuine error, i.e. one that is systematically recurring rather than one which is the result of speed or inattention; it should lead to improved performance. Of the comments made about Emma's writing, it is likely that the first two will be comprehensible to her as to most children, but not so with the rest. One might paraphrase the five comments thus

(a) You should have begun a new sentence here.
(b) This is a spelling mistake.
(c)
(d) } What I have written is better than what you have written.
(e) You must find out how to write better in future.

Emma's errors may or may not be systematic – we have no way of knowing – but it is difficult to see how the comments made might lead to improvement. Such comments are, in my experience, quite typical of much that is written in response to writing done in classrooms. It should be stressed that this does not reflect adversely upon the conscientiousness of teachers. It is mentioned to emphasize that most 'marking' is intuitive, imprecise and, above all, negative (see DES, 1979, p. 89).

Let us consider in a little more detail Emma's piece of writing. We should all agree that line 1 contains an error. She ought to have put a full stop after *life*. Perhaps a mere reading aloud of her own work would have reminded her to do so; perhaps the teacher's insertion was enough. But if this is a systematic error in her work, it is not a question of not knowing what a sentence is. There is nothing wrong with the syntactic structure either of *the story showed many things about ordinary life* or of *one was that the old man had got not much educatin* (we shall come later to *got not much*). The business of full stops is rarely to do with knowing about sentences; it is to do with marking the beginnings and ends of sentences. Geoffrey Thornton (Thornton, 1980, pp. 50–4) has suggested classroom activities to take account of this very point and quotes Crystal (Crystal, 1976) on the importance of relating punctuation systematically to the intonation system of the language. Punctuation is partly intonational, in that it serves in writing to indicate relationships that in speech are signalled by intonation patterns. It is, of course, also partly grammatical, as when commas are used to mark off what are called non-restrictive elements in a sentence. In, for example

My girl friend, who is in Rome, has just telephoned

who is in Rome is non-restrictive. That is, its function is not to restrict the semantic reference of *My girl friend* for purposes of definition or identification. In the absence of commas, *My girl friend* is being identified by the fact of her being in Rome (and is being distinguished from others who may be in different places). So, in line 1 of Emma's piece, we have an error which, if it is to be remarked upon and no matter how simple it may seem, calls for some knowledge on the teacher's part of the punctuation system, its relation to the phonological system and aspects of English syntactic structure.

What of *educatin* in line 2? It may well be that this is a mere slip of the pen, an omission of the letter *o*. There is no way of knowing whether Emma meant to write *education* or whether she had in mind *educating*. If the latter, then obviously a more serious grammatical error is involved. But ignoring that, and supposing that it is a spelling error, and supposing further that it occurs more than once in her writing (otherwise, it seems trivial to 'mark' it), it may be that there is a need to remind here that *tion* behaves in a morphologically consistent way. Stubbs has addressed this point in a very clear fashion (see Stubbs, 1980, pp. 52-3) showing how in this case spelling is related to grammar, and also how the written forms of word-final phoneme sequences differ according to the semantic relationships involved. Hence, na*t*ive/na*t*ion but suspe*c*t/suspi*c*ion, etc.

It could be argued that in line 6 there is nothing wrong with *not at all boring ways*, although the teacher has substituted *interesting ways*. We should possibly all agree that had the phrase been *not boring ways*, it would more certainly have seemed odd. Why should that be? One answer may lie in the behaviour of the negative marker *not*. If *not* is regarded as a special kind of adjunct (a syntactic class including adverbs) akin to *very, hardly, scarcely*, etc., then its scope, i.e. the stretch of utterance negated, can be determined syntactically. *Not at all* is an intensified variant of *not* and its scope is restricted to the item *boring* (see Quirk *et al.*, 1972). The single item *not*, however, lacks the feature of intensification supplied by *at all* and usually its scope is less well defined. We can test this by changing the position of *at all*, which can normally be moved to a position following the scope of the negation. When *not* lacks intensification, its scope is less well defined. When the teacher substitutes *interesting* for *not at all boring* he is expressing a stylistic preference, not pointing to a purely syntactic error as is implied by his marginal G.

The situation is quite different in line 7, however. The teacher's marginal G is justified, but one wonders about the reason. For there are two separate but related errors here; one is syntactic and the other is primarily phonological. The syntactic error lies in the verb phrase structure itself. It seems that *of* is Emma's representation of the perfective aspect modifier HAVE (capitals are used to indicate that some form of the item may be used, e.g. *has, had* are subsumed by HAVE). So that her phrase in its uncontracted form reads *had not have been*, which does not occur in written English. The structure of the verb phrase is dealt with elsewhere (Quirk *et al.*, 1972; Palmer, 1974; Gannon and Czerniewska, 1980) but it may be noted here that in contracted speech forms it is fairly common to find utterances such as 'He'd've come if you'd've asked him'. (He would have come if you *had have asked* him). This is because the contraction *'d* can stand for either *had* or *would*; people confuse the two and so we find the kind of mistake made by Emma. Her second error here is not so much one of syntax caused by phonological confusion but is rather phonological in nature. It is increasingly common to find children who write *could of* for *could have*. This seems to be due to the fact that all unstressed vowel sounds in English have a tendency to reduce to the neutral sound known as schwa, written phonemically as /ə/; both *have* and *of* are, unless stressed, pronounced / əv /. It is interesting to note that when children do stress *have* in the verb phrase, they have a tendency to say / ɒv / as in *of*. In these matters, learners (and teachers) are not helped by the relative poverty of English morphology. We may note that we have only one phonological form for all of the following:

1	regular plural marker of nouns	cat*s*	/s/
2	third person present tense marker	he kick*s*	/s/
3	possessive marker	cat*'s*/cats'	/s/
4	contracted form of the copula	it*'s* a cat	/s/
5	contracted form of auxiliary BE	what*'s* happening	/s/
6	contracted form of auxiliary HAS	Kate*'s* left	/s/

So we have six distinct grammatical forms with only one phonological realization, and in four of those (3 - 6) one graphological realization, i.e. *'s*. It is not then so surprising that some people have a little initial difficulty in representing their meanings unambiguously in writing. It may be that in a few decades the perfective verb modifier HAVE may be realized in writing as *of*. Meantime, however, children have to be taught to use current forms if they are not to be branded as half-educated. For the teacher, then, it is important to have clearly in mind the reasons for the errors, strategies for remedying them and clear objectives for the inculcating of good practice, however unfashionable that may sound.

Emma's mistakes occur at different but related levels of language. In commenting on this short extract, one has referred to phonological, morphological, syntactic and semantic levels of the language system. But it is interesting to look at what the teacher has not commented on. A feature of the text which it might be felt appropriate to mention is the choice of words, or lexical items, at different points. Emma uses the word *thing* (or *things*) three times, in lines 1, 3 and 4 respectively. It might be argued that the dullness of such a general noun tells us something of her experiential or even cognitive development. Present research lacks any coherent theoretical framework within which to discuss the relation between cognitive and linguistic development, but a number of psycholinguists have addressed themselves to it (e.g. Morehead and Morehead, 1976; Fletcher and Garman, 1979) and despite theoretical inadequacies, the aim of 'extending vocabulary' is one familiar to most teachers in both primary and secondary schools. It may seem more sensible for educationists to skirt the jungle of cognitive psychology and think rather of experiential variety, including, of course, variety of linguistic experience. Whatever the theoretical background may be, Emma's teacher might have been better pleased had she not used the word *thing* three times but had had recourse to more easily specifiable semantic fields. A semantic field is, crudely speaking, a paradigm of words assembled on the basis of related meanings. Thus, *thing* can enter a large number of semantic fields, e.g.

	monster	
The	thing	advanced towards her
	creature	
	apparition	

	object	
The	thing	can be analysed later
	substance	
	article	

	by-product	
The	thing	of/about his story is the
	concomitant	excitement generated
	feature	

Etc.

The semantic scope of *thing* is very large and in Emma's text we have only the linguistic context to tell us what she intended.

Another feature of her writing is to be found in line 5, when she uses the phrase *ordinary everyday people* (apart from the fact that she uses the word *people* twice in three lines). The fact that it sounds like a cliché may have to do with the radio programme *The Archers*, a 'story of ordinary, everyday country folk', but in any case the two noun phrase modifiers *ordinary* and *everyday* are, like *thing*, unspecific. Now, the linguist is not able to offer remedies for limited vocabularies. Children extend their vocabularies by using language frequently, for purposes important to them, in a wide range of situations. They build up their lexical repertoires by encountering, imitating and modifying rich lexical usages, in speech and in writing, and in many other ways. Teachers do not have to teach children to speak (I assume that the absurd notion that children from poor social backgrounds 'have no language' is now abandoned by all) but when things go wrong at school, the teacher has to be able to advise and help with appropriate remedies and suggestions for more effective word choice. To do that powerfully, it helps to know something of meaning relations in English lexis, in order to devise techniques that are more useful than adding to an essay the comment 'poor vocabulary!'.

A different kind of linguistic feature must be mentioned in order to explain the ambiguity, not noted by the teacher, in the last phrase, *like him*. *If they hadnt of been to school like him* may mean either (a) If they had not been to school as he had been to school, or (b) If they had not been to school, just as he had not been to school. What accounts for the ambiguity here is Emma's use of ellipsis. Informally, ellipsis is the omission from an utterance of items which can be replaced, while preserving the grammaticality of normal discourse. When the meaning of the utterance becomes obscured, ellipsis becomes pathological; if the meaning remains clear, then ellipsis is a useful device. The process is categorized by Halliday and Hasan (Halliday and Hasan, 1976) as one of the grammatical features of text which serve to render successive utterances a meaningful stretch of language, a cohesion device which can help to create a unit larger than the sentence. Their work on cohesion, in the 1976 volume, can be of great help in clarifying notions about such writing processes as paragraphs, achieving fluency, concision and balance and the avoidance of ambiguity. But to return to Emma – her first use of ellipsis is in line 3, where *just the same as other people* has to be understood, in its reconstituted form, as 'just the same as other people felt things'. Her second instance is in line 5, where she avoids the repetition of *how* before *poor workmen*. In this case, we have not a text-making device but a usual way of avoiding what could become intolerable repetition. One has only to consider what conversations would be like in the total absence of elliptical usage. Compare the following:

Elliptical	Non-elliptical
A Do you like swimming?	A Do you like swimming?
B Yes, I do.	B Yes, I like swimming.
A So do I.	A So do I like swimming.
B Mind you, not when it's cold.	B Mind you, I don't like swimming when it's cold.

Her third instance is the one already mentioned in line 8. It may be possible to capitalize upon this propensity for ellipsis (see Gannon and Czerniewska, 1980) in the shaping of narrative – allowing that the teacher has some knowledge of the cohesion ties used in the connecting of one sentence with another.

From a consideration of the factors so far mentioned, it is possible to produce a diagrammatic picture of the process of assessment rather different from the crude figure at the beginning of the chapter.

— situational constraints on writing tasks
— relationship between child's experience and rate of linguistic development
— child's perception of the nature of the writing task
— possibilities (and constraints) of the language system, at different levels, in relation to the child's linguistic development
— distinguishing between systematic and occasional errors, at different linguistic levels
— selection of errors for comment
— comment, made appropriate to child's understanding and nature of error

} Assessment of and response to pupils' writing

Such a list is neither exclusive nor exhaustive, but it is certainly more powerful, when marking work, than merely to have in mind spelling, punctuation and a rather hazy notion of 'structure', undifferentiated as to level.

In this relatively brief address to one piece of a 13 year old's writing, desiderata are implied concerning a teacher's model of how the English language works. In linguistic terms, knowledge of the following levels of the language system has been mentioned as having value: phonology, morphology, syntax, semantics, the organization of text (discourse), the relations between speech and writing, the graphological system, and various aspects of the interrelationships of these sub-systems. If that seems to be a rather daunting list for a busy teacher who may not have had any formal training in linguistics, then it may be well to bear in mind three things. First, it is important to accept that in other areas of intellectual or pedagogic activity, such complexity is taken for granted. Both teachers and pupils in, say, a chemistry class, will expect to have to become familiar not only with a fairly complex terminology (as well as a system of notation) but also scientific methodology - to formulate hypotheses, to make accurate observations, to measure intuitions or estimates against empirically observed phenomena within the framework of a theory and to arrive at conclusions. The study of language and children's use of it is just as complex and it is, I believe, time to accept that in the light of what has been learnt about language in the last few decades, intuition and goodwill alone will not suffice. Second, there is no need to wait until one has reached degree level in linguistic theory before applying sound linguistic principles to the assessment of children's language use. Every time a teacher makes a red mark in an exercise book, recourse is being had to some judgmental criterion, however inexplicit. By devoting some attention to even a quite limited area of concern, e.g. what linguistics has to say about the relationships between intonation and punctuation, one has entered into the field of linguistics applied to education. Through gradual familiarization with the available literature, and other means, one realizes after a time that one is becoming increasingly explicit about different aspects of language structure. It would, of course, be absurd to suggest that teachers have not managed well without a knowledge of linguistic theory in the past. They have done so and are doing so now. But it is equally absurd to refuse to test one's intuitions. Even if one's intuitive approach is effective - and many approaches are not - by the acquisition of further insights and knowledge, it is possible to refine and sharpen what may well be already quite effective strategies. The third point is that there is a curious confusion, quite widespread, between the way a theory is described and how one uses theoretical principles in teaching. Because a theory is necessarily expressed in highly abstract terms, that does not mean that the same terms have to be used in e.g. commenting upon a pupil's essay. Theoretical concepts have to be abstractly described, because they have to achieve a maximum generality. But one should never confuse theoretical presentation, usually written for theoreticians, with pedagogical presentation.

So, given that there exists sufficient motivation, and allowing for the fact that no person will be expert at everything, what, in sum, does this imply for the teacher of English? I think six things are desirable.

1 A knowledge of linguistic theory sufficient to allow an appreciation of the systematic nature of language *at different levels.*
2 An appreciation of the nature of speech and writing, of their differences and interrelationships.
3 An appreciation of how meaning relations operate in English.
4 A knowledge of the linguistic features which make utterances cohere as a text.
5 A familiarity with the main stages of language development in children and the ways in which those stages are manifested.
6 A knowledge of how situation, purpose and readership determine choice among the styles and varieties of written English.

Some open-minded teacher who has read this far may well be saying, 'Well, yes. I accept all that, but I was trained in English literature. No one at college told me about linguistics. Where do I start?' That is not an easy question but it is an important one. The answer cannot be simple either. There are now many readable books in print. In-service courses are few but they do exist: one of the most accessible and worthwhile sets of materials is to be found in the correspondence texts of the Open University course on Language Development (PE 232). Local authority advisers in some areas are playing a vital role through the organization of study groups and work projects. The Committee for Linguistics in Education (see chapter 3) now exists, under the auspices jointly of the Linguistics Association of Great Britain and the British Association for Applied Linguistics. The present volume is part of an increasing participation by both linguists and educationists in the task of enabling good theory to inform and inspire good practice. In short, the answer to the question has to be, 'Start wherever you can, but try using one of the above.'

This chapter has limited itself to one area of teaching activity, viz. responding to children's writing. It is an unfortunate reflection of the polemicism which permeates educational writing that the selection of one thing is taken to imply devaluation of others. I have made no mention of a large number of other factors which determine what a child writes and what response is elicited. Writing ability is measured pragmatically by the reader's perception of its effectiveness. Any written composition is characterized by a number of pre-linguistics principles – involving choices which are prior to any kind of linguistic formulation – and they are related to what the writer wants to say, the logic, the relevance, the importance and the associations clustering around the things to be said. So, in responding to and assessing writing in school, it is important to have in mind such questions as 'Why was the task set?', 'How was it introduced?', 'For what purpose?', 'For whom?', etc. We do no service to pupils by allowing them to write the first thing that comes into their heads, to continue handing in scribbled drafts that pass as finished copy; we shall serve them ill if we enthuse over ill-conceived and slovenly trivia, or fail to prepare them for the linguistic and communicational demands of adult life. Some years ago, a child in school confided to me that his class liked above all writing poetry. He enjoyed the smile that greeted the remark; he enjoyed even more telling me why poetry-writing was so popular. 'It's easy. All you have to do is to write a lot of words in pairs and make the second one have -ing at the end.' And he was right. There were dozens of 'poems' being enthused over in that school, all of them of the form

> Leaves falling
> Smoke swirling to the sky
> Babies crying
> . . . ad nauseam

The children had early realized that to some teachers Noun plus Participle minus Verb equals Poetry. We can do better than that. In order to do so, we have to give thought to all those variables not dealt with in this chapter – purpose, relevance to the writer's knowledge and experience, readership, preparation, classroom organization, and so on. The linguist has nothing to say, *qua* linguist, about educational aims and objectives, but when the teacher's pedagogic expectations have been fulfilled as well as possible and when the final copy comes in – that is the point at which the linguistic knowledge and awareness that I have been concerned with becomes of real importance. Of course we must be concerned with imaginative and emotional development and expression, of course we must encourage any initiative, however modest, but if we do not at the same time help children to make the most effective use of their complex mother tongue, we are being complacent. Teachers who do not wish to be complacent should know how linguistics can help them to help their children.

7

The assessment of linguistic difficulty in reading material

Katherine Perera

Introduction

Teachers have to assess the linguistic difficulty of a text in order to be able to provide pupils with reading material at an appropriate level. It is argued that informed judgments by a thoughtful teacher may have advantages over the application of a readability formula. The measures of word difficulty and sentence length that are used by the formulae are shown to have weaknesses: short or familiar words are not easy to read in all contexts, and long sentences are sometimes easier than short ones. An awareness of grammatical constructions which can cause difficulty gives the teacher a principled basis for simplifying a text.

The need for assessments of linguistic difficulty

Teachers have to make some kind of assessment of the linguistic difficulty of reading books, subject text books and work cards for at least three different purposes. The first is when they are choosing sets of books to buy; linguistic difficulty will be one of the factors to be considered, along with interest level, presentation, suitability of content and so on. Such a task does not arise particularly frequently; far more often it is necessary to select, from stock, the right book for the right pupil – to match text difficulty to the pupil's reading ability. To do this is particularly necessary where pupils are working individually (either in school or for homework) or in small groups, as there is inevitably less support available from the teacher. The Bullock Report (DES, 1975) comments (p. 113):

> a particularly important teaching skill is that of assessing the level of difficulty of books by applying measures of readability. The teacher who can do this is in a better position to match children to reading materials that answer their needs.

The third situation is when the teacher is faced with the task of simplifying an existing text, in order to make some source material accessible to a history class, perhaps, or to increase the readability of work-cards, written instructions and examination questions. Successful rewriting will only be possible if the teacher recognizes difficult constructions and knows how to simplify them.

Various methods are used to make these assessments of linguistic difficulty. One is to apply an objective measure, such as a readability formula. Generally, this involves working out a numerical value for word and sentence difficulty and inserting these figures into a mathematical equation. The result gives a readability score or a reading-age level for the book. (For a review of more than thirty formulae currently available, see Klare (1974). There is an interesting account of a cross-validation study of nine of the most commonly used formulae in Harrison (1979)). Another method is to make a subjective assessment of a text, using a combination of common sense, intuition and experience. Harrison (1979) has shown that, whereas the pooled judgments of readability level by a group of twelve teachers are fairly reliable, individual judgments of the reading age needed to understand a passage can vary by as much as nine years. The purpose of this paper is to outline some of the linguistic factors that may contribute to reading difficulty and that are *not* taken into account by readability formulae, in the belief that there is great value in teachers improving the accuracy of their subjective judgments.

Some weaknesses of readability formulae

The most well-established readability formulae (e.g. Dale and Chall, 1948; Flesch, 1948) have a correlation of approximately 0.7 both with pooled teacher judgments of readability (Harrison, 1979) and with pupils' scores on standardized multiple-choice comprehension tests (Klare, 1974). This means that such formulae are broadly reliable when used to find the average reading level of a number of books. They therefore have value for the research worker. However, they do not give a dependable reading age for any one book. This has been clearly demonstrated by Stokes (1978) who has shown that, although there are high correlations between the six published formulae he studied, the reading age predicted for a single book may nevertheless vary by nearly five grade levels, depending on the formula used. Furthermore, the scores given, by just one formula, to a large number of passages from one book may vary by seven grade levels. Thus, both the choice of formula and the choice of sample passages from the text can critically affect the result. There is also evidence that the reliability of formulae decreases sharply on some types of written material. For example, Bormuth (1966) has pointed out that they cannot be validly applied to small samples of language, such as questions on work-cards and examination papers, instructions, picture captions, chapter titles and so on. Poetry, too, produces misleading results. Harrison (1979), using the Flesch formula, reports a reading level of 12.5 years for *Macbeth* and for T.S. Eliot's poem 'The Journey of the Magi'. Commenting that this level is too low, he says that most readability formulae 'fail to register any extra difficulty associated with unusual sentence structure or compression of language, which are common in poetry' (p. 84). (There are examples below which show that these features are not peculiar to poetry.) Similarly, mathematics books receive scores which suggest that they are easier to read than they really are, because they are written in 'terse and condensed prose'. Pyrczak (1976) used the Dale-Chall formula to measure the readability of the instructions accompanying a US Income Tax Return Form and recorded a reading level of 14–15 years. However, when 35 post-graduate students were given comprehension questions on the instructions, they scored, on average, only 46.6 per cent, which again suggests that the formula had underestimated the reading level. Because of a growing awareness of the special reading difficulties presented by certain styles of writing, there is an increasing number of new and adapted formulae to assess specialist text books; for example, science subjects (Jacobson, 1965) and religious education books (Stocker, 1971-2). So, although a readability formula can be used to assess the relative difficulty of a group of books on the same subject, a teacher cannot be sure in the case of any one particular book that the formula will give a valid measure of absolute difficulty.

Another weakness of readability formulae arises from the fact that the score is derived for a whole passage (usually about 100 words long) and this averaged score can hide a wide range of variation. It would be possible for two passages to achieve the same readability score when one had, perhaps, three very difficult sentences and four very easy ones while the other had seven relatively straightforward sentences. Although the two passages would have the same degree of *measured* difficulty, it is most unlikely that they would cause the reader the same amount of actual difficulty; we have to read one sentence at a time and, although skilled readers can make use of forward context, young or inexpert readers are not helped over a difficult section by easy sentences further on in the text. In an attempt to assess the extent to which the difficulty level fluctuated within any one passage, Kaiser, Neils and Floriani (1975) selected twelve extracts which all had the same score on the Fry Readability Formula (Fry, 1968). They then analysed them using the Syntactic Complexity Formula devised by Botel, Dawkins and Granowsky (1973). This is a different type of readability measure which gives a score to a wide range of grammatical constructions on a scale from 0-3, and is worked out for each sentence in the chosen text. Kaiser *et al.* found that in some passages, measured sentence complexity was nearly constant, varying by only one point, whereas in others there were five full points difference between the easiest and the hardest sentence. Thus, all twelve passages had the same average score but they varied considerably in the level and range of difficulty of individual sentences.

As the smallest unit that can be assessed by most readability formulae is the 100-word passage, it is obvious that they can be used only to give a global score and not to pin-point the source of difficulty. This will be sufficient if the teacher is wondering whether or not to buy a set of books; it is clearly inadequate if the books have already been bought and have to be used. Then it is no help for the teacher to learn that the readability level of the text is three years ahead of the average reading age of the class (that is probably all too apparent anyway). What is needed is some indication of the aspects of the language that cause reading difficulty so that appropriate teaching can be provided to give the pupils some strategies for tackling the text.

A related weakness is that the formulae do not give any insights into the kinds of rewriting that will simplify the language. Klare (1974) emphasizes that word length and sentence length (the features used by the formulae in assessing reading difficulty) do not *cause* difficulty: 'Consequently, altering word or sentence length, of themselves, can provide no assurance of improving readability. How to achieve more readable writing is another and much more complex endeavor' (p. 98). Bormuth (1966) says, 'experiments have shown that [readability formulae] have little, if any, validity when they are used as style guides for "adjusting" the difficulty of materials' (p. 82). In the same vein, Harrison (1979, p. 102) describes how the Resources for Learning Development Unit in Avon discovered that using a readability formula to rewrite passages for particular reading levels could produce such unnatural, jerky language that the new version was actually harder to read than the original.

Another drawback of most formulae is that they are unable to take account of conceptual difficulty and interest level. There is a danger that teachers who have laboriously worked out readability levels will then accept the results at face value. After all, you can use readability formulae without actually reading the text at all - that is why they can be successfully applied by computers. On the other hand, a teacher who tries to make an informed subjective assessment of a passage has to read it very carefully and is bound to consider a wide range of non-linguistic features.

Readability formulae generally use the two factors of word difficulty and sentence length, with varying weightings, to arrive at a score. I shall now outline some types of difficulty that are not revealed by these two measures.

The assessment of word difficulty

Word difficulty is assessed in one of two ways: either by the length of the word, on the assumption that long words are harder than short ones; or by the familiarity of the word, on the assumption that familiar words are easier than unfamiliar ones.

(a) *Short versus long words*

Word length is measured in various ways by different formulae: some count the number of letters, some the number of syllables, some the number of words of more than one syllable, and some the words of three or more syllables. In all of these cases word length is equated with difficulty. It is often true that short words are familiar and that long words are more formal or more technical but it is not always so. Here are some examples of the monosyllabic words that appear in just four recently produced text-books for junior and lower secondary classes:

adze, carse, gneiss, haugh, hoys, knorr, motte, rere, scutch, seine, schists, stele, straths, thegns.

It seems unlikely that these words would be read with ease and under-standing by pupils in the 8-14 age group.

(b) *Familiar versus unfamiliar words*

The second method of assessing word difficulty is to use a word list which contains those words that occur very frequently in writing. (The revised Spache (1974) list has just over 1000 words, while the Dale-Chall (1948) formula lists 3000.) It is assumed that a word that appears on the list will be relatively easy for children to read, and that a word which does not will be unfamiliar, and, therefore, harder to read. In many ways this is very sensible; it certainly allows for the fact that a long familiar word like *television* will be easier for a child to read than a short, unfamiliar one like *gneiss.* Klare (1974, p. 97) comments that using a list of familiar words gives a slightly better prediction of read-ability than using a measure of word length. However, in practice, considerable difficulties arise.

First, there is the question of the validity of the word list. Vocabulary use changes with time and a list such as the Dale-Chall which was produced in 1948 is likely to be considerably out-of-date. Also, the word lists used in Britain are based on frequency counts done in the USA, where patterns of use are different. A comparison of the revised Spache (1974) list – which is American – with the frequency count of children's written vocabulary carried out in Britain by Edwards and Gibbon (1964, 1973) reveals many discrepancies. For example, the following words, which do not feature in Spache's list of 1041 items, are among the 250 words most frequently used by 7-year-old English children:

> bonfire, cowboy, doll, fairy, football, mummy, rocket, set, tea,
> television, tonight, yesterday.

More seriously, over 50 words appear on the Spache list which do not occur at all in Edwards and Gibbons's list of the 1347 words used by 7-year-olds. Examples are:

> cabin, candy, cent, dollar, gift, nibble, neighbourhood, ocean,
> parade, peek, raccoon, wagon.

If words on a 'familiar word list' are not really familiar, there is no guarantee that their presence in a text will contribute to reading ease.

Second, there is the problem that a word which is familiar to a reader with one meaning or in one grammatical context may be used with a different, less common meaning or function. If it is on the formula's word list it still has to be counted as an 'easy' word (the lists do not differentiate between homonyms or between different parts of speech), even though there is evidence that a word may be readable in one context and unreadable in another. Reid (1958, p. 297) showed that although children could read 'deep' as an adjective in (a) they could not read it as a noun in (b):

(a) We went back to the *deep* mud.
(b) Darkness was upon the face of the *deep*.

Similarly, Goodman (1967) described a child who was able to read 'toy' as a noun but not as an adjective.

The following examples illustrate the literary use of some short words which occur frequently in speech, but with a different grammatical function or a different meaning:

1 These are *but* a few examples of the ... advantages to be gained from man's achievements in space.
2 A seventy hectare farm in Kyle might have *some* fifty cows.
3 Honey was *much* used.
4 ... the long white gown which was worn by penitents *or* people who were sorry for doing wrong.

The last example is particularly difficult because, in speech, 'or' normally contrasts different things (e.g. tea *or* coffee) and it would be easy for the young reader to think that 'penitents' are being contrasted with 'people who were sorry for doing wrong' and not to realize that the two expressions are being equated.

In the next set of examples, the italicized words have their usual grammatical function but an unusual meaning that could well lead to misinterpretation:

5 Bankside was famous for its slums and *low* taverns.
6 Drake entered the Pacific and *fell upon* the unwary Spaniards.
7 Stirling *commands* access to the Highlands.

A similar problem occurs when an apparently familiar word is used with a technical meaning, e.g.

8 Products from the *cracker* go to nearby chemical works.
9 Valley *benches* are used for summer grazing.
10 It was also a bishop who was responsible for the university, obtaining a *Bull* from Pope Nicholas V.

These examples show that the presence of a word on a 'familiar word list' will not necessarily mean that it is easy to read with comprehension.

The assessment of sentence difficulty

In all the widely used formulae, average sentence length serves as a measure of sentence difficulty. It is very often the case that a long sentence is hard to read, particularly if there are several subordinate clauses with complex relationships between them. However, it does not follow that difficult sentences will always be identifiable by their length; short sentences may be harder than long ones. If length was a true measure of complexity, then all sentences of the same length would be equally difficult. Kaiser *et al.* (1975) selected from elementary reading books twelve passages that had the same average sentence length and analysed them using the Syntactic Complexity Formula (Botel *et al.*, 1973). The average complexity scores for the passages ranged from 0.32 to 2.30. The authors concluded, 'When sentence length is held constant there is still a great deal of variability between passages in terms of syntactic complexity' (p. 265). Wang (1970) found that comprehension was actually facilitated by long sentences when they contained co-ordinate clauses (i.e. clauses joined by 'and' or 'but'). She acknowledged that some of the structures that cause reading difficulty, such as multiple subordinate clauses, also tend to increase sentence length but she stressed, 'it is not sentence length *per se* which makes a sentence difficult to comprehend' (p. 403).

In order to illustrate some sentence patterns that can cause reading difficulty which is not revealed by a measure of sentence length, I shall give examples, first, of sentences of the same length but different difficulty and, second, of paired constructions where the longer version is easier than the shorter one.

(a) *Sentences of the same length and different difficulty*

If two sentences have the same vocabulary and are of the same length, the only difference there can be between them is the order in which the words appear. Readability formulae do not take word order into account; theoretically, all the words within each of the sentences could be listed in a random order and the measured reading level of the passage would still be the same. In practice, of course, children would never have to read such a text. But there are alterations of word order that give acceptable sentences which are nevertheless probably difficult for inexperienced readers to understand. This is because some unusual sequences are characteristic of formal written language and rarely occur in speech. There is ample evidence (e.g. Peltz, 1974; Ruddell, 1965; Tatham, 1970) that children read more easily those sentence structures that they would themselves say or write than sentence patterns which occur predominantly in literary writing.

One stylistic device is to put the adverbial at the beginning of the sentence and then to reverse the normal order of the subject and verb, e.g.

11   Above the noise   rose   the shouts of the drivers.
     Adverbial   *Verb*   *Subject*

12   In the middle of this bright green cave   rose   a small mound.
                    Adverbial   *Verb*   *Subject*

13   Down the centre of the lane   rumbled   heavy wagons.
               Adverbial   *Verb*   *Subject*

In all of these examples, the more usual colloquial order would be Subject–Verb–Adverbial.

Sometimes writers put the object of the sentence at the beginning for emphasis e.g.

14   Any craft you undertake to learn   you   will learn
                Object   *Subject*   *Verb*

15   The thread and screwdriver   we   hid
                Object   *Subject* *Verb*

16   The truth of this guess   he   did not learn
              Object   *Subject*   *Verb*
     until years later.

Here the more frequent order would be Subject–Verb–Object.

Another kind of stylistic variation occurs when the verb phrase consists of part of the verb TO BE as an auxiliary, followed by a past participle. In this case, the participle may be put at the beginning of the sentence and the normal order of subject and auxiliary reversed, e.g.

17   Very much feared   in those days by kings, lords
        Participle
     and citizens   was   the London mob.
                             Auxiliary   *Subject*

18 Associated   with large populations and the longer
    Participle
    sunshine of the east coast   is   market gardening.
                                    Auxiliary   *Subject*

19 Moored   against the banks on either side   were
    Participle   *Auxiliary*
    ships from all Europe.
        Subject

The more usual sequence for these sentences would be Subject–Auxiliary–Past Participle.

If teachers are sensitive to literary sentence patterns such as these,
then they will be able to recognize potential sources of reading difficulty
that are not tapped by readability formulae at all.

(b) *Long sentences that are easier than shorter ones*

Sometimes long sentences are easier for children to read than shorter
versions of the same information. This is because increased length often
means greater redundancy, with more clues to the meaning of the sentence and to the relationships between the parts. Van der Will (1976)
conducted experiments to assess the effect of sentence length on children's understanding of oral instructions. Subjects received either the
longer version of the instruction:

(a) Pick up your blue pen. First draw a big blue circle and then
     draw a little blue circle next to it.

or the shorter version:

(b) In blue, first draw a big circle, then a little one by it (p. 195).

(The second sentence of (a) has 16 words whereas (b) has only 13.)
It was noticeable that only the shorter sentence prompted children to
ask for the instruction to be repeated. Subjects who received the longer
version were significantly faster in carrying out the instruction than the
other children.

This advantage of length was also revealed in a study of reading
comprehension by Reid (1972). She selected nineteen sentences which
she thought might cause reading difficulty and matched each one with
a syntactically simpler sentence conveying the same information.
Subjects were given binary choice comprehension questions on either

the original (A) sentence or on the rewritten (B) version. The results were strongly in favour of the rewritten sentences; on eleven test items, the comprehension scores were between 10 and 47 per cent better for the (B) than the (A) versions. Of those eleven items, only two had easy versions which were shorter than their difficult counterparts; eight of the easy revised sentences were longer than the originals. In the following two pairs of examples from the study, the (B) sentences are three words longer than the (A) sentences; in both cases, subjects scored over 43 per cent more on the (B) than the (A) version of the item.

Item (1) A   The girl standing beside the lady had a blue dress.
          B   The girl had a blue dress and she was standing beside the lady.

Item (18) A   Mary's dress was neither new nor pretty.
          B   Mary's dress was not new and it was not pretty (pp. 398-9).

Reid followed her intuition in rewriting the difficult sentences; they are a random collection from the linguistic point of view, with no regular relationship between the longer and shorter versions. By contrast, there is a systematic connection between pairs of sentences when ellipsis occurs. In this case, a word (or words) has to be mentally supplied by the reader in the 'gap' left by the writer. Usually the missing word is present in the preceding context; occasionally the reader has to read ahead before he can supply it. A short test passage from a study by Bormuth *et al*. (1970) gives an example of ellipsis:

There are ripe and green apples. *The green* are mine (p. 354).

The second sentence here has a rule-governed relationship with its longer counterpart, without ellipsis:

The green apples are mine.

Bormuth *et al*. found that nearly one-quarter of the nine-year-old children they tested failed a multiple choice comprehension question where there was ellipsis of this sort. The difficulty that ellipsis can cause young readers has also been shown in studies by Fagan (1971), Malicky (1976) and Theberge and Braun (1977). If a passage has a great deal of ellipsis, it may well receive a score on a readability measure that suggests it has a low level of difficulty; however, it is unlikely to prove easy for children to read. There is obviously a danger here for writers engaged in text-simplification. An easy way to lower the measured reading-age level of a passage is to shorten the sentences. If this is done simply by ellipsis, rather than by recasting the sentences completely, the difficulty of the text may be increased rather than lessened. There follow some examples of the kinds of ellipsis that occur commonly in writing. In each case, the words that the reader has to supply mentally are enclosed in square brackets.

Ellipsis can occur in the second of two co-ordinated clauses where they share common elements, e.g.

20 One kind of solitary bee lives in holes in mud and another [kind of solitary bee lives] in holes in walls.
21 Bradford is the chief town for the marketing of the cloth and Leeds [is the chief town] for the manufacture of ready-made clothing.

There is often ellipsis in an introductory adverbial clause, e.g.

22 When [it is] disturbed it does give out two blobs of a nasty smelling liquid at the tail end.
23 When [they are] thawed out for cooking, the fish are quite fresh.

In this case the reader has to read *ahead* in order to be able to supply the missing elements.

Another kind of ellipsis occurs in the noun phrase. Very often, the missing words have to be supplied not from the same sentence but from an earlier sentence in the text (this obviously increases the burden on the reader's memory), e.g.

24 Some [metal lids] will be made from steel and some from aluminium alloy.
25 Some spiders have six [spinnerets] as shown in the picture.
26 Most [wall plants] grow in cracks where a little soil has collected.

An awareness of ellipsis, and of the difficulties it can cause, will prevent a teacher thinking that a short sentence will necessarily be easier for children to read than a longer one.

Conclusion

Readability formulae are useful for research projects, where a numerical score is needed for purposes of comparison and statistical analysis, and where so many samples are analysed that most inaccuracies will be submerged in the averaged results. They can also be valuable for the classroom teacher who wants to rank in a rough order of difficulty several books in the same series or on the same subject. Here, the similarities of style and vocabulary are likely to mean that the comparisons between the books will be valid. If a teacher has to choose one book, from a range available, in order to buy a class set, it is worth using an appropriate readability formula to filter out those books that would clearly be too difficult so that fewer books have to be considered in detail. Similarly, teachers who want to sort the books in a class library into broad categories of difficulty can use a formula to make the first classification and can then refine this grouping later in the light of various factors, including a more thorough examination of vocabulary and sentence structure. So objective and subjective assessments can be used side by side. For teachers who wish to be able to pinpoint the source of reading difficulty and to follow linguistic principles in rewriting material that has proved to be too difficult, there are considerable advantages in working to become sensitive to those aspects of linguistic difficulty that are not revealed by measures of word or sentence length.

Note

This article was first published in *Educational Review*, vol. 32, no. 2, 1980 and is reproduced by kind permission of the editors of *Educational Review*.

Acknowledgments and sources of numbered examples

These are made to the following for permission to quote extracts from their publications: 3, 5, 6, 17, Unstead, R.J. (1974), *Looking at History, 3. Tudors and Stuarts* (A. & C. Black); 2, 7, 8, 9, 10, 18, Reid, R.W.K. (1974), *Scotland* (Ginn); 12, 15, O'Brien, Robert C. (1971), *Mrs Frisby and the Rats of NIMH* (Gollancz); 4, Lewis, B. (1971), *People in Living History* (Holmes McDougall); 11, 13, 19, Welch, R. (1971) *The Galleon* (Oxford University Press); 14, 16, Le Guin, U. (1968) *A Wizard of Earthsea* (Parnassus Press); 20, 22, 24, 25, 26, James, A. (1978), *Active Science Four* (Schofield & Sims); 1, 21, 23, Evans, H. (1974), *The Young Geographer* (Wheaton).

8

The language demands of school learning

Katherine Perera

Introduction

The learning of academic subjects often poses problems for children because the language through which subjects are mediated can be very different from the everyday language encountered outside school. This article explicitly analyses such language problems in terms of vocabulary and syntax, in particular, and offers teachers tools for assessing for themselves the linguistic difficulties involved and for avoiding similar problems when writing their own work-cards or notes for children to work from. The article provides a useful complement to the previous paper by Katherine Perera. She demonstrates the usefulness of as explicit an analysis as possible but makes her approach accessible to teachers prepared to observe language in a principled and systematic manner.

When children first go to school, the majority of them have already acquired a great deal of language. They can talk happily, and often at great length, about things that are happening or that have happened. However, this predominantly narrative and descriptive type of language, important though it is, is not the only kind of language that they will meet or need in school. The world of the school is generally more formal than the world of the home, and the learning of academic subjects requires rather different kinds of language from the everyday language we find in conversation or in children's news stories. I think there are three areas in which this more formal, more academic language can cause difficulties: the first is that the child might have difficulty in understanding what the teacher says; the second is that he might have difficulty in understanding text books and work-cards in subjects such as maths, social studies and science; and the third is that he might have difficulty in writing appropriately about academic topics.

Understanding the teacher's spoken language

Unfamiliar vocabulary

There are plenty of examples, from all age groups, of pupils not under-standing what the teacher has said. One of my favourites comes from a student of education who wrote in a final exam paper about the child development theories of P.R.J. But I think that misunderstanding of oral language is more widespread at primary level. We can identify three different sources of this misunderstanding. The first is where the teacher uses unfamiliar vocabulary. This may be a word which has two meanings, one concrete and one abstract. The teacher may intend the abstract meaning but the young child is much more likely to assign the concrete interpretation to the word. There is an example of this in Laurie Lee's autobiography, *Cider with Rosie*. Discussing the first day at school, he remembers that the teacher told him to 'Wait there for the present' – and he went home at the end of the day bitterly disillusioned because he wasn't given one. On the other hand, the unfamiliar vocabu-lary may be archaic or unusual words that the child has not met at all before. Here there is a tendency for him to associate them with words he already knows. There are lots of examples to be found in children's misinterpretations of the language of school assemblies, as in 'Our Father, which art in heaven, Harold be thy name.'

Ambiguous reference

The second type of oral misunderstanding is where the adult gives a verbal explanation accompanied by a pointing gesture and the child misunderstands the reference of the verbal explanation. A friend of mine, when she was a young child, was in a car with her parents and, as they drove past an airfield, she pointed at something and asked, 'What's that, Mummy?' Her mother replied, 'It's a hangar.' 'What's it for?' 'It's where they keep the aeroplanes at night.' The point is that my friend was actually pointing to a wind-sock, not to a hangar at all. The name 'hangar' seemed perfectly appropriate for what she was looking at – it was, indeed, hanging – and when she heard the improbable explanation that it housed aeroplanes at night, she decided sagely that it was another example of the adult whimsy that she kept meeting in story-books. It was several years before she associated the definition with the appropriate object.

Unfamiliar use of sentence patterns

The third type of oral misunderstanding is where the teacher uses a grammatical construction that the child does not interpret correctly. This is particularly common with commands and rebukes. To very young children adults tend to use direct commands such as 'Don't do that' or 'Put your toys away now'. On the whole, adults do not use this kind of language to one another. We soften our commands in various ways. When the child first goes to school, he starts meeting adult-type commands and rebukes and does not necessarily recognize them for what they are. Joan Tough (1973) has a recording of an infant class-room where the teacher says things such as 'Jimmy, would you like to put your toys away' and 'I wonder who hasn't put his toys away yet' and it is very clear to the observer that Jimmy simply does not understand that this means 'Put your toys away.' He is not being perverse or disobedient; he just does not recognize these adult forms yet.

Implications for the classroom

I am not suggesting that teachers should not use such forms – if they did not, children might not learn them – but I think it is important for them to be alert for the children for whom they are totally unfamiliar. This is harder than it sounds, because children are very good at following what others are doing, at picking up cues from their environment, so they often behave appropriately without necessarily understanding the language at all. It is possible, by using a blend of structures, to lead the child gradually from the direct to the polite form of a command, e.g.

Put your toys away, would you, Jimmy, please.
Would you put your toys away please, Jimmy.
Would you like to put your toys away, Jimmy.

Understanding the language of text books

The difficulties that pupils can meet in trying to understand the language of textbooks and work-cards are most prevalent and more serious than any problems that the teacher's spoken language may cause. This is because written language is generally more formal than oral language;

it is not accompanied by gestures and facial expressions; and it cannot, of course, respond to any obvious misunderstanding on the part of the child in the way that the teacher can. In addition, reading is essentially a private activity, whereas listening is a public one, so the child who is reading is not able to take a lead from the behaviour of other children in the class. But modern teaching styles put a great deal of weight on books and work-cards: mixed-ability and mixed-age teaching mean that class lessons are difficult and group work preferable. The report on primary education in England (DES, 1978) shows that 61 per cent of 7-year-olds and 49 per cent of 9-year-olds are taught in mixed-age classes. Presumably, this means that a great deal of their work is done on an individual or group basis, rather than as a class. But, of course, group work requires the pupils to work from books and work-cards because the teacher cannot be with all the groups at once. Lest we should think that this problem can be overcome by the good and energetic teacher who makes her own work-cards, tailor-made for the needs of each group, it is worth noticing how very difficult this task is. Writing clear, simple, explanatory prose is not easy. Indeed, when the Effective Use of Reading Project team in Nottingham assessed the level of difficulty of teacher-produced work-sheets, they found, for example, that one set produced for a first-year, mixed-ability secondary group was comparable in difficulty with the standard 'O' level textbook in the same subject.

Sources of difficulty in reading can be pin-pointed at the level of the word, the sentence and the discourse. In order to illustrate different types of reading difficulty, I have chosen examples from text books in use in English schools. I have selected some books that are in use in primary schools and others that are in use in secondary schools. All the secondary books are said to be suitable for the first two years of secondary education. The books have all been published for the first time during the past fifteen years. Apart from these restrictions, the selection of the books was a random one. There is no intention here to criticize these books in particular or text books in general. The linguistic features of a book constitute only one of the aspects by which it may be judged; subject-matter presentation, interest level and so on are also very important. Neither do I intend to suggest that all text books for children should be written in the simplest possible language; if they were, pupils would lose one very valuable means of extending their reading and language abilities. Rather, I believe it may be helpful to draw attention in as precise a way as possible to areas of difficulty so that teachers are able to offer precise help and guidance to their pupils as they tackle the demanding kind of formal language that is found in subject text books. It is perhaps worth commenting that individual examples may not seem particularly difficult; indeed, they may seem no harder than the language found in children's fiction. However, a characteristic feature of academic writing is that difficult constructions tend to occur frequently, sometimes with several in one sentence, and this concentration of difficulty can be a stumbling block for the struggling reader.

Each of the examples from a text book is identified by a letter; the key to these letters is given on page 135.

Reading difficulties at word level

Familiar words with special meanings

There are two main sources of difficulty at word level; the first is when words which are familiar to the children are used in unfamiliar ways. For example,

> The camel *caravans* trudged the old silk *roads* between the ancient cities of Constantinople and Peking. (B)

> Priests generally *arose* at a later period in time when there were special holy buildings called temples. (J)

Children will understand the words 'caravan', 'road' and 'arose' but it is likely that the meanings they assign to them will not enable them to interpret these particular passages appropriately. The first extract may suggest a holiday highway rather than a rough track; the second example may give rise to the belief that priests got up late. In a sense, the very familiarity of these words is a disadvantage because the child thinks he understands them when really he does not. An additional problem with such familiar words is that the writer may take them for granted and not explain or highlight them in the text. In *The Developing World: Geography Two* (G), the following seemingly familiar words occur in one nine-page unit of work:

> estate, roots, grub, nap, battery, stock, cake, mean, litter, relief.

It seems likely that a 12-year-old pupil will be able to assign a meaning to each of these words but it may not be the technical sense that the writer intends. For, although these words are not capitalized in the text (unlike the obviously specialist vocabulary), they all have technical rather than everyday meanings, i.e.

estate:	farmland
roots:	root-crops (e.g. potatoes)
grub:	to uproot a hedge
nap:	pile on cloth
battery:	shed for hens
stock:	cattle
cake:	cattle-food
mean:	average
litter:	bedding for hens
relief:	height of land

It is worth noting here that some writers are particularly sensitive to the problems of the multiple meaning of some familiar words, e.g.

The scientist is a curious person – not of course soft in the head – but curious about things, wanting to know why they do this or that. (I)

Another fact we often want to know about a body (this is what a scientist calls a 'thing' – a book, a pencil . . . a coin – all these are 'bodies') is the space it takes up. (I)

Technical vocabulary
The second source of difficulty at word level is technical vocabulary. This is something that teachers and writers are very aware of; technical words are often capitalized, italicized or underlined in the text; they are often explained or illustrated and there may be a glossary. Additionally, they may be the focus of comprehension questions. However, there is no doubt that too great a concentration of technical vocabulary can make reading very daunting for all but the best reader. These are some examples of the more unusual vocabulary young readers meet:

muezzin, pommel, mantlets, trebuchet, effigy, Doge, Bezant. (A)

After *retting*, the fibres are removed at the mill by *scutching*. This . . . is followed by *hackling* . . . (B)

garrison, motte, bailey, culverin, saker, minion, machicolations, impressment, martello, garderobe, trebuchet, mangonel. (C)

stratum, scarp, humus, isolines, isohyets, tsunamis, caldera, sawah, carboniferous, levees. (G)

I think that technical vocabulary can be fairly roughly divided into two types. The first consists of words that are necessary and helpful. Such vocabulary encapsulates some of the key concepts of a subject discipline. Its use is essential because non-technical words will be either too imprecise or too circuitous to do the job efficiently. The second type is jargon, that is vocabulary which is not essential to clear or concise thinking in the subject but which simply replaces one word with another, usually longer and harder, one. I believe that it is important for teachers to consider carefully how much of their 'subject vocabulary' is essential and how much unnecessary. To illustrate this from the technical vocabulary of linguistics, I think that the word 'phoneme' belongs to the first type; it is essential for clear and accurate thinking in the subject and cannot be validly replaced by the more general term 'speech-sound'. On the other hand, the terms 'exophasia' and 'endophasia' to label audible speech and sub-vocal speech seem to me to be examples of the second type, jargon; they have no advantages over the simpler everyday terms.

Several studies have shown that technical vocabulary may cause comprehension difficulties. Otterburn and Nicholson (1976) tested 300 secondary children's understanding of thirty-six common terms used in mathematics at CSE level. Only fourteen of these words were understood by more than half the subjects. These are some of the words that were not understood:

factor, gradient, intersection, multiple, parallelogram, product, ratio, symmetry.

Between 1975 and 1977 Johnstone (1978) conducted an experiment with over 6,000 English and Scottish children who were about to sit for 'O' level. The subjects were given chemistry examination questions in either their original form or in a simplified form; even where only one word in the question was altered, scores for the simplified questions were considerably higher. For example, 80 per cent of the subjects got the following question right:

Which one of the following is *not* a pungent gas?
A Sulphur dioxide
B Hydrogen chloride
C Chlorine
D Oxygen

The percentage of correct responses rose to 95 when the word 'pungent' was replaced by 'choking'. Johnstone comments, 'It was clear that if pupils failed to answer a question correctly we could not assume that only their chemistry was faulty.'

Whatever the specialist area, technical vocabulary can cause problems. It probably has to be learnt slowly, with plenty of opportunity to try it out in 'safe' situations until it becomes familiar. Prestt (1976), writing of science by work-cards, points out that it is not possible for a child to enter into a dialogue with a work-card, so he does not have any way of making new terms and concepts his own; there is always a danger that technical terms remain merely a set of impressive verbal labels.

Reading difficulties at sentence level

At sentence level there are several grammatical constructions that can cause difficulty for the weak reader. There are three different underlying reasons that such constructions can present problems. One reason is that some sentence patterns occur infrequently in speech and so the struggling reader is not able to predict what might come next, as the language structure is not part of his oral linguistic repertoire. The second reason is that it can be difficult to identify quickly the grammatical constituents of a sentence when the cues to structure which are provided in speech by intonation contours are not present. The third reason is that some constructions, which are relatively easy for the listener or the normally skilful reader to interpret, are difficult for the slow reader because his slowness prevents him perceiving the whole grammatical constituent as one unit.

Sentence patterns less frequent in speech than writing

Several studies (e.g. Pearson, 1976; Ruddell, 1965; Tatham, 1970) have shown that young children read more easily and more accurately when the text consists of sentence patterns that occur in their speech than when it contains constructions more frequent in written than oral language. Other studies (e.g. Clay, 1969; Goodman, 1967; Weber, 1970) have examined children's oral reading errors and found that children tend to say what they *expect* the text to say; if the text does not match their expectation then they make an error. Clearly, a young reader's grammatical expectations will derive chiefly from his own oral language. This strongly suggests that some of the more literary sentence constructions will be a source of difficulty for the inexperienced or struggling reader. Some sentence patterns that are rarely found in children's speech are subject nominal clauses, concealed negatives, some types of ellipsis, word order altered for stylistic purposes, and various kinds of co-ordination and subordination.

Subject nominal clauses   Young children use nominal clauses as object of a sentence, e.g.

John thought *that he would win*

but rarely as subject. Examples of nominal clauses functioning as subject of the sentence are:

That the level of the sea rises and falls twice in every 24 hours is obvious to anyone at the seaside. (F)

Whether the difference is great or small and whether True North lies east or west of Magnetic North depends on the position of the observer on the earth's surface. (F)

Sometimes subject nominal clauses are introduced by a question word. This can lead the inexperienced reader, who is not skilful enough to check ahead for the presence of a question-mark, to expect a question rather than a statement, e.g.

Why this was so is very puzzling. (B)

What proved to be of particular interest were the isobars. (F)

Concealed negatives   Some sentences have a negative meaning without an obvious negative marker such as 'not', 'no', or 'never', e.g.

We *rarely* have a completely cloudless sky in Britain. (B)

Most people stayed in their home region and *hardly* went further than the nearest town or city. (J)

Reid (1972) has shown that young readers tend to interpret such sentences with positive meanings, e.g.

We have a completely cloudless sky in Britain.

Clearly, if this interpretation conflicts with other evidence in the text, or with the reader's knowledge of the world, it is likely to cause confusion.

Ellipsis   Because conciseness is favoured in writing, authors may omit words which are unlikely to be omitted in speech. For example, subordinate adverbial clauses may occur without subject and lexical or auxiliary verb, e.g.

When in battle, the knights wore red tunics over the armour. **(A)**

The holy man learnt certain actions which he hoped, *when performed,* would result in winning the favour of the gods. **(J)**

Ellipsis commonly occurs in relative (or adjectival) clauses. In their oral language acquisition, children first learn to use full relative clauses, e.g.

John saw the man *who was wanted by the police*

and only later acquire the more literary version,

John saw the man *wanted by the police.*

Relative clauses with ellipsis can cause problems for the reader, e.g.

Enzymes *present in the cells of the body* begin the breakdown of glucose. **(I)**

Here, since the child expects the subject 'Enzymes' to be followed by a verb, he may read 'present' as a verb (pre'sent); so, ignoring 'in', he begins the sentence:

Enzymes present the cells of the body . . .

He expects this to be followed by 'with' and is confused when he meets the verb 'begin'. It is generally felt that shorter sentences are easier for young readers than long ones. This is very often the case but where there is a choice between a short unfamiliar construction and a longer familiar one it is likely that the longer one will cause fewer difficulties, e.g.

Enzymes *which are present in the cells of the body* begin the breakdown of glucose.

Altered word order Writers depart from normal order for various reasons. They may wish to link a sentence smoothly with the preceding discourse, e.g.

They wanted to keep their gods happy. *This* they did by offering them gifts. **(H)**

An author may use a cleft construction to emphasize an ·important word or phrase, e.g.

It was the priest who decided whether or not a person's sacrifice was acceptable. **(J)**

Some writers are clearly not happy to use the type of prepositional construction that occurs in speech, preferring a more formal word order:

> And climate, as shown in the Introduction, to a great extent
> controls the activities *in which* it is possible for us to engage. (F)

And word order may be altered simply for variety, e.g.

> Above the mountain passes and caravan routes, along military
> and pilgrim roads, towered these castles. (A)

Whenever the word order does not match the order that the reader would use in speech, he is slowed down in his reading (until he becomes familiar with these literary patterns) because the text does not match his linguistic expectations.

Some types of co-ordination and subordination Generally young children are able to join phrases or clauses using the co-ordinating conjunctions 'and', 'but' and 'or'. It is noticeable, however, that authors of textbooks often use 'or' in a way that is very rare in speech, e.g.

> It revolved *or* moved round in a circle. (D)

> And so the electric current, *or* the rate at which the electrons are
> flowing, must be the same all round the circuit. (I)

In these sentences, instead of contrasting two *different* things (e.g. hot or cold; black or white), the authors are using 'or' to link two phrases which refer to the *same* thing; the second phrase is a gloss on the first and 'or' could be replaced by 'that is'. But in the same books 'or' is also used with its more common contrastive meaning, e.g.

> He could play the viol *or* flute. (D)

It is obviously difficult for the reader to work out which meaning of 'or' he is faced with unless he knows the meanings of the two phrases that have been joined. And of course he only needs the second, explanatory phrase if he does *not* know the meaning of the first one.

Sometimes complex conjunctions, such as 'either ... or, 'not only ... but also', can cause reading difficulties. Reid (1972) suggests that 'not only' is often interpreted with a negative meaning, so children may misunderstand sentences such as this:

> The earth *not only* travels on its orbit round the sun, it *also* rotates
> on its axis, taking 24 hours to make one complete revolution. (F)

Then there are subordinating conjunctions which may be used

differently in writing from in speech. To young children, 'once' is probably most familiar as an adverb, meaning 'at one time', e.g.

Once he had a lot of money.

In the following example, however, 'once' is used as a subordinating conjunction, meaning 'as soon as':

Once the Holy Men organised themselves properly they soon realised that they possessed power over life and death. (J)

'If' can also be used in a rather unusual way, e.g.

If there was not much daylight, neither were there many ways of providing artificial light. (C)

Normally we expect a condition to be followed by the consequence of that condition, e.g.

If there was not much daylight, people went to bed early.

But here, one condition is followed by another. The sentence could be paraphrased:

If it is true that there was not much daylight (and it is true) then it is also true that there were not many ways of providing artificial light.

Problems caused by the absence of intonation cues

The second major source of grammatical difficulty at sentence level is the absence of intonation cues to constituent structure. In speech, one of the very important roles of intonation is the division of utterances into grammatically relevant word groups. In writing, of course, this source of information is lost; and punctuation serves to demarcate only some of the larger grammatical units. This means that the reader may be confronted with a string of words without necessarily being aware of the grammatical relationships between them. Such a difficulty arises in object nominal clauses and in relative clauses if the writer does not include a clause-marker to draw attention to the structure of the sentence.

An object nominal clause can occur with or without the clause-marker 'that', e.g.

John believed *(that) the story was true.*

Hakes (1972) has shown that such sentences are easier to interpret when the clause-marker is present. When the clause-marker is not included, it is easy for the reader to 'chunk' the sentence inappropriately, treating 'the story' as the object of the verb 'believe', e.g.

John believed the story.

This tendency is increased if the remainder of the sentence comes at the start of the next line. When 'that' is included in the sentence, the structure is as clear to the eye of the reader as it is to the ear of the listener.

A relative clause may be introduced by a relative pronoun. The pronoun has to be present if it functions as the subject of the relative clause, e.g.

I met the man *who won the prize.*

But the relative pronoun can be omitted if it is the object of the relative clause, e.g.

I met the man *(whom) your friends admire.*

Fodor and Garrett (1967) have shown that such sentences are understood more readily when a relative pronoun is included. If there is no relative pronoun, two noun phrases occur together and it can be difficult to sort out the grammatical constituents, e.g.

A Professor James knows breeds dogs.

Here it looks at first as if 'Professor James' is the subject of the sentence and 'knows' the verb. If 'that' or 'whom' were included, it would be clear that 'Professor' is part of one constituent and 'James' part of another, e.g.

A Professor *that James knows* breeds dogs.

Examples from school textbooks of these two constructions are:

Object nominal clause without clause-marker
He feared *the Saracens might conquer his country too.* (A)

The weak reader may think the sentence reads:

He feared the Saracens

and then be confused by 'might conquer'.

Relative clause without relative pronoun
Prince Alexius offered to give the Crusaders the money *they needed.*
(A)

In this sentence also it is easy for the reader to stop too soon, thinking that the sentence ends at 'money'. Particularly if the line division is unhelpful or if the reader is not sensitive to the function of full-stops and capital letters, he may think that 'they needed' is the beginning of a new sentence. These are further examples where longer sentences are easier to read than their shortened versions.

Problems caused by inadequate reading speed
Inadequate reading speed causes problems when the text contains long grammatical constituents or when one grammatical constituent is interrupted by another. In order for sentence meanings to be interpreted, the reader has to hold in Short Term Memory all the words that form a grammatical constituent. Only when the grammatical subject, for example, is present as a complete unit in Short Term Memory can it be processed and then left safely on one side to await the rest of the sentence. If any grammatical constituent exceeds the capacity of the reader's Short Term Memory, therefore, he will not be able to process all the words in the constituent together and will have difficulty in perceiving the grammatical relationships within the sentence and, hence, in arriving at its meaning.

It is difficult to find precise measurements of the capacity of Short Term Memory. However, there is wide agreement that its capacity is strictly limited both in terms of the number of items it can store and in terms of the length of time it can hold them. It seems to be able to hold five to nine items at a time (Miller, 1956) for a period of a few seconds, perhaps three or four. ('Items' are not precisely defined; they may be words or phrases, so the storage capacity is for more than nine words so long as they are grammatically related.) Exactly how long these items can be retained depends partly on how much attention is being paid to the task and also on how much effort is needed to process the information that is being received. Once a meaning has been synthesized from the items in Short Term Memory, the processed 'chunk' can be shunted into a less vulnerable memory store. This store, where material can be held for several minutes, is sometimes called Long Term Memory (e.g. Hellige, 1975) but this is rather a confusing designation as the label is more often applied to the permanent memory or knowledge that a person has; Gough (1972) has coined a more explicit, if cumbersome, name: the Place Where Sentences Go When They Are Understood (PWSGWTAU).

Using figures from the eye-movement studies of Taylor *et al.* (quoted in Massaro, 1975, p. 294), we can suggest an approximate average reading speed for 6-year-olds of 80 words per minute, for 9-year-olds of 160 w.p.m. and for 12-year-olds of 200 w.p.m. From this, allowing a Short Term Memory of 3.5 seconds' duration, we can very roughly assess that, at these reading speeds, (a) 6-year-old readers will be able to hold four to five words in Short Term Memory (i.e. 80 w.p.m. $\div$ 60 = 1.3 words read per second, $\times$ 3.5 = 4.6 words held in STM); (b) 9-year-olds will be able to retain eight to ten words (i.e. 160 w.p.m. $\div$ 60 = 2.6 words read per second, $\times$ 3.5 = 9.3 words held in STM); (c) 12-year-olds will manage ten to thirteen words (i.e. 200 w.p.m. $\div$ 60 = 3.3 words read per second, $\times$ 3.5 = 11.6 words held in STM).

Of course, if the reader is reading at a slower speed than the average for his age, either because he is a weak reader, or because difficult vocabulary and unfamiliar concepts are slowing him down, then he will be able to store proportionately fewer words. All this means that, if a grammatical constituent is longer than the reader's Short Term Memory capacity, or if it is interrupted by another construction that exhausts the storage space in Short Term Memory, the reader will have to struggle to make sense of the passage. Reid (1972) shows that, given a sentence like this:

The girl standing beside the lady had a blue dress

many 7-year-old children think that 'the lady' was wearing a blue dress. Obviously, the six-word constituent 'the girl standing beside the lady' has overloaded their Short Term Memory and so 'the girl' has been lost.

Long grammatical subjects are a particularly severe source of reading difficulty because they may leave the reader in doubt about the word that actually 'does the action' of the verb. The following are some examples from textbooks of sentences with long grammatical subjects. I have used capital letters for the 'head' word of the subject and for the verb to draw attention to the distance between these two vital parts of the sentence.

A LINE of these charging knights with lowered lances WAS a frightening sight to the enemy. (A)

A SYSTEM in which nobles are given estates of land in exchange for the use of their soldiers IS CALLED feudal rule. (H)

The only WAY to rid themselves of this feeling of guilt or to avoid any likely punishment by the gods WAS to offer them gifts. (J)

These subject phrases range from nine to twenty words, requiring reading speeds of approximately 150–350 words per minute. In each case the 'head' word is singular and is followed by a singular verb, but several other nouns in each subject phrase, including the one immediately preceding the verb, are plural. (An examination of about 17,000 noun phrases (Quirk *et al.*, 1972) showed that not only are complex noun phrases more common in serious and scientific writing than they are in fiction and informal speech, but also that a higher proportion of these complex constructions occur as subjects of clauses in the academic modes than in the more informal types of language.)

Like long grammatical subjects, interrupted constructions also place a heavy burden on the reader's memory, e.g.

> They in turn were followed *after over a century of domination by lesser states* by the Persians. (H)

> The most common type *(there is probably one of this kind hanging on the wall of your classroom)* consists of a small glass tube filled with mercury. (F)

Concentration of difficulty

All these examples of sources of reading difficulty at sentence level can be found in most kinds of written language. The special difficulty of academic, or text book, written language is that it frequently contains a higher concentration of difficult features than fiction does. It is particularly common for text books to contain sentences that consist of several clauses, e.g.

> They heavily outnumbered the invaders, yet in the end the Spaniards won because they were brave, because they had better weapons, because many Indians took their side and because many Aztecs suffered from a terrible disease called smallpox which came from Europe with the Spaniards. (E)

There are seven clauses in this sentence, which is conceptually as well as linguistically difficult. The reader needs to sort out that 'they' were the Aztecs and 'the invaders' were the Spaniards; that there were more Aztecs so you would expect them to win (this expectation is implied but not stated) but they did not, for a variety of reasons. The reasons are particularly difficult because the first three are strengths of the Spaniards but the fourth is a weakness of the Aztecs.

The following sentence has only three clauses but, nevertheless, it contains many difficult features:

> The use of machinery on this scale and the fact that until recently the Prairie farmer concentrated on the growth of only one kind of

crop enables him to run his farm with far fewer labourers than the English farmer whose activities include the cultivation of a variety of crops and the keeping of animals. (F)

Here, the subject of the main verb 'enables' is the co-ordinated pair 'the use ... and the fact ...'; the complete subject phrase is twenty-six words long. The clause 'that the Prairie farmers concentrated ...' is interrupted by the phrase 'until recently'. After a comparative construction, the sentence concludes with a relative clause which has an object that is twelve words long.

The first of the two examples I have given here is a sentence that is forty-five words long; the second example contains fifty-five words. An American computer analysis (Kucera and Francis, 1967, p. 376) has shown that the average sentence length for 'general fiction' is fourteen words and for 'learned and scientific writings', twenty-four words. So, on average, sentences in textbooks can be expected to be roughly twice as long as sentences in fiction. And these particular examples are three and four times as long as the average sentence in fiction. Long sentences such as these with complex internal relationships place greater burdens on the reader's Short Term Memory and on his syntactic abilities.

Reading difficulties at discourse level

Even if the reader can understand all the technical vocabulary of the passage and has no difficulty at sentence level he may still not be able to make sense of the text as a whole. There are frequent instances of pupils understanding all the constituent sentences of a passage and yet not understanding the relationship between them, i.e. not understanding the point that is being made. Pupils will frequently remember a dramatic or vivid example without having any idea of the generalization it was intended to exemplify.

The structure of factual prose

The movement and structure of factual prose are very different from the chronological narrative of fiction. A paragraph may consist of a generalized statement, followed by detailed examples given as evidence of the truth of the first statement; or there may be several apparently disparate examples strung together to be followed by a concluding statement which draws out the similarity between each of the earlier cases; the writer may put forward one point of view and then turn round and put the opposite point of view; or he may give a series of facts, following each with his own opinion or interpretation; and so on. Unless pupils are able to recognize which type of paragraph construction they are reading and to understand the structure of the author's argument, they are unlikely to understand each sentence properly – it will remain an isolated unit, unrelated to the whole.

Writers usually signal the relationships between the ideas and signpost their readers through the text by means of conjunctions and sentence adverbs. There are the additive words which show that the writer is bringing extra evidence to prove his point, e.g. 'furthermore', 'in addition', 'similarly', 'moreover'; there are the contrastive words which show that the author is changing direction, e.g. 'on the contrary', 'conversely', 'however', 'notwithstanding'; there are the concluding words that show he is making a point, e.g. 'therefore', 'consequently', 'accordingly', 'hence'. It is all too easy for children to slip over these words completely when they read; even if they do read them, it is very likely that they will not interpret correctly the relationship that is being signalled. A project at Monash University in Australia (Gardner, 1977) tested secondary pupils' understanding of about 200 of the connective words that are used in scientific writing and found that eleven of them were understood by only 50 per cent of 15-year-olds. (Examples are 'similarly' and 'that is'.) Three words, including 'moreover', were only understood by up to 30 per cent of this age group. This suggests that a passage which a writer has constructed with care becomes, to the unskilled reader, just a collection of more or less random sentences. These connective words occur widely in all types of academic writing, not just in scientific texts as is sometimes suggested, e.g.

> *Similarly*, the Iroquoian Indians thought that the Master of life sent nothing but 'good' things to the earth. (J)

> They had, *moreover*, to make all their own houses. (F)

Sometimes the connective words connect with an idea so far away in the text that the reader has to hold a great deal in his head if he is to understand the link that is being made, e.g.

> It was food, however, which was the key to any siege. If the garrison did not bother to lay in stocks of every item they could not hope to withstand an attack for very long. Here is Salisbury castle collecting stores together in 1173. [12-line list of stores] The handmills were kept for grinding up the corn to make flour and the malt was used for brewing beer. I like the idea of keeping a spare chain for the

drawbridge and a spare rope for the well. *Equally* if they began their siege at the wrong time of year when perhaps there were no crops growing, the attackers could find themselves in difficulty. (C)

The first sentence is a general statement which is followed by two statements of detail: 'If the garrison did not bother to lay in stocks . . .' and 'Equally if they began their siege at the wrong time of year . . .' The link between the two is marked by the connector 'equally' but the two sentences are so far apart that it takes a skilled reader to make the connection.

Another general problem of the organization of this kind of written material is that an understanding of the text often depends on a simultaneous interpretation of a graph or map or diagram, which may even be on another page. It is very difficult for an unskilled reader to move from his point in the text to a chart and back again and, perhaps, to continue doing this for a whole paragraph. Whalley and Fleming (1975) showed that students spent 20 per cent more time studying diagrams when they were printed immediately next to the appropriate part of the text than when they were separated from it. Diagrams on a different page from the related written material were not looked at at all.

Studies of textbook difficulty

Considering all the difficulties of vocabulary, grammar and discourse structure that academic writing presents, it is not surprising that there are numerous studies suggesting that the textbooks used in schools are often too difficult for the pupils they are intended for. For example, Gould (1977) has shown that CSE biology texts are more suitable for 'A' level students. In an American study, Galloway (1973) looked at books of nine different types, ranging from *Macbeth* to maths, and tested 16-year-old students' understanding of them. She found that all the books were too difficult for the students to read independently, except the advanced geography text, which was markedly easier than the general geography book. Not surprisingly, the hardest of all was the poetry book – but at least teachers feel it is a legitimate, indeed fundamental, teaching activity to help pupils prise out the meaning of a poem, whereas problems of language comprehension are seen as peripheral to the 'main' business of teaching maths or science.

Implications for the classroom

Apart from a careful selection of text books in the first place, I believe that there are at least two ways in which teachers can help children to overcome difficulties they meet in reading text books and work-cards. First, an examination of several books makes it clear that a few types of difficulty tend to recur in any one text; one author may frequently use unusual patterns of word order; another may often use interrupted constructions, and so on. If teachers are aware of a structure which may cause difficulty and which is likely to be recurrent, then they can draw their pupils' attention to it, explaining that it is a feature of that writer's style. Second, I think that it can be worthwhile for teachers occasionally to read good non-fiction aloud to the class. After all, infant teachers read stories daily to their pupils and so children become familiar with the typical language of stories, such as 'Once upon a time' and 'happily ever after' and so on, and with the organization and development of a narrative. By the time children start to read subject text books, they are probably half-way through the junior school. It is unusual for them to hear this kind of language read aloud, and they may no longer have systematic timetabled help with reading by this stage. So, generally, children are expected to 'pick up' the formal language of academic subjects with rather little explicit help. But if they hear this kind of language well read, they will learn some of its characteristic vocabulary, sentence patterns and types of discourse organization in a pleasant and natural way.

Writing about school subjects

Children in primary schools do lots of writing of stories, news and so on. Anything with a strong chronological sequence, be it an imagined story or an account of the growth of some mustard and cress, is relatively easy to write about because the order of events in time imposes an order on the narrative. Similarly, anything that is written as a personal account is generally easier than something that is distanced, impersonal and formal. At some stage, most children will need to write impersonally, and also to write descriptive, explanatory and argumentative pieces which do not have their own intrinsic ordering. Teachers need to decide when children should make the move from personal, informal writing to a more scholarly presentation and how they should be helped to make it. There are distressing accounts of children's writing being sharply criticized because, although they have clearly understood the subject-matter, the academic conventions have not been respected. For example, a college student wrote (Martin *et al.*, 1976, p. 16):

> My first notion of the change in emphasis between junior and grammar school came when I had to write an essay on Neolithic man for my first piece of history homework. I started, 'My name is Wanda and I am the son of the headman in our village'. The history master read it out to the rest of the class in a sarcastic voice – everybody laughed and I felt deeply humiliated. I got 3/20 for covering the page with writing. I hated history after that until the third year.

And then there is this example from a 14-year-old boy's geography homework (Cashdan and Grugeon, 1972, p. 119):

> 'An erratic is quite an exciting result of glaciation, as a large rock not geologically the same as its surroundings may be found perched incredibly precariously on smaller stones. This is an erratic.' The teacher has put a red ring round the word 'exciting' and written in the margin, 'No need to get excited about it'.

On the other hand, not all teachers require their pupils to write always in the academic mode of the subject. In *Understanding Children Writing* (Burgess *et al.*, 1973) there is a marvellous account of the chemical structure of polythene by a 17-year-old girl who has obviously been told to write for the layman; her piece is 'dedicated to the dedicated non-scientist' – a short extract cannot do justice to the clarity and humour of the piece (Burgess *et al.*, 1973, p. 31):

> One of the curious things about carbon atoms and about most other atoms come to that, is that they appear to behave as though they possess arms, each terminating in an eager hand, ready to grab at some stray hand belonging to another atom in order to satisfy their perpetual lust for security. Carbon is not only willing to hold hands with members of its own species, i.e. other carbon atoms, but also associate quite readily with members of different species, e.g. hydrogen atoms (which unfortunately for them have only one hand, restricting them to monogamy).

I would not want it to be thought, however, that I believe pupils should always be allowed to write informally or personally about factual, academic topics. There is currently a tendency to believe that it is good for children to write in the personal style and bad for them to have to write in impersonal language. I think that this is an unfortunate polarization. I believe that it is valuable to learn to handle more formal styles of written language. But I believe that teachers need to be aware of all the difficulties such language entails and to be prepared to share good models of academic writing with their pupils, to discuss its value with them, and then to give them explicit and precise help in mastering that most demanding form of language for themselves.

Key to textbooks used for examples

Books in use in primary schools

A Bailey, V. and Wise, E. (1969), *Focus on History: The Crusades.* London, Longman.
B Evans, H. (1973), *The Young Geographer, 3*, Exeter, Wheaton.
C Gregor, H. (1972), *History Picture Topics: Castles in Britain*, London, Macmillan Education.
D Lewis, B. (1971), *People in Living History*, Edinburgh, Holmes McDougall.
E Lincoln, J.D. (1977), *History First Series: Montezuma.* Cambridge, Cambridge University Press.

Books in use in secondary schools

F Cain, H.R. and Monkhouse, F.J. (1967), *Graded Geographies, Book 1: General Geography*, London, Longman.
G Crawford, S. (1970), *The Developing World, Geography Two, A New Man*, London, Longman.
H Ha, W.H. and Hallwood, C.L.J. (1969), *A Pictorial World History, Book 1*, London, Longman.
I Mee, A.J., Boyd, P. and Ritchie, D. (1971), *Science for the 70's, Book 1*, London, Heinemann.
J Wigley, B. and Pitcher, R. (1969), *The Developing World, Religion One, From Fear to Faith*, London, Longman.

Note

This article was first published in *Supplementary Readings to Block 6*, Open University Course PE 232, Language Development, Milton Keynes, Open University Press and is reprinted here by kind permission of The Open University.

Acknowledgments

The author would like to thank Alan Cruttenden for his helpful comments on an earlier draft of this paper.

9

What is English? – Modern English language in the curriculum

Michael Stubbs

Introduction

This article proposes a syllabus on modern English language, suitable for secondary schools, colleges and universities. The syllabus is based on a substantial body of factual knowledge, a training in critical and analytic skills, and involves pupils and students in discussing problems which are socially, politically and morally important. English language in the modern world is clearly an important topic, given its hundreds of millions of speakers, and the powerful social, political and technological factors which affect it. The number of speakers of English has increased enormously in the last 200 years, and the new pressures on English mean that traditional ways of studying English are no longer always adequate. These new pressures include: its huge number of speakers and world-wide geographical spread; mass literacy and the mass media; the use of English as an international language against a background of enormous linguistic diversity. The article provides some facts about English in the modern world, and then proposes a syllabus for studying English language in an intellectually exciting way.

The theme of the AATE Conference in Perth in 1979 was: *What is English?* Since I was invited all the way round the world to address the conference, you might reasonably feel that I should have answered this question. And I did indeed feel under a considerable obligation at least to try and answer it. To answer the question, I would, of course, have had to understand what it meant, but I have to begin by admitting that it strikes me as a rather peculiar question. It seems a peculiarly funda-mental question for an Association of Teachers of English to be posing. I wonder if other teachers' associations pose comparable questions: What *is* chemistry? Does mathematics count? Has history a future? Where is geography going?

Perhaps it is simply that all conferences of educationalists appear to end up by debating: What *is* education anyway? Or is English really so

different from other subjects on the curriculum? This has been argued:
it has often been said that English is the most fundamental subject on
the curriculum, since *all* teachers are English teachers. But then this
leads to a situation where the English teacher might teach almost
anything.

Topics for an English syllabus

Some of the reasons for the question become clear if we simply list
some of the subjects which are taught on English courses: literature,
grammar, creative writing, drama, the history of English, essay writing,
the mass media, 'communication', and so on. Clearly this is a mixed
list, and not a coherent basis for a syllabus. Sometimes the brief is
even wider than this. A recent book on English teaching (Stratta *et al.,*
1973) has the apparently formalistic title *Patterns of Language.* But the
authors claim (p. xi) that 'a growing mastery of language relates to a
deepening awareness of self, of others and of the human condition'.
This appears to make English teachers responsible not only for the linguistic development of their pupils, but also for their psychological,
moral and interpersonal development – and to expect them also to provide a world view and philosophy of life.

The English teacher, it would seem is expected to raise questions
of value and civilization, freedom and responsibility, growth and
maturity, sense and sensibility; guiding pupils towards a 'deeper intuitive sense of individual humanness', going beyond 'nihilistic postures'
which diminish and deaden, bringing elements from individual experience into a structure that represents life, in 'dimensions of love and
trust' – poignant and profound, beyond conventional modes and
forms, and as complex as life itself. (The phrases in quotes are from a
book which came to my attention because of its title, *English in Australia Now,* by David Holbrook, 1973, pp. 125, 120, 199.)

This all seems to be to be most confused. English teaching is not the
study of the human condition. It is not even to be identified with The
Humanities. English *is* very complex, but not as complex as life itself.

In this article I will propose a type of English syllabus which has
clear intellectual content, a substantial body of factual knowledge;
which involves training in critical thinking and analytical skills; and
which involves discussion of problems which are socially and morally
important. The syllabus will be based on a study of the contemporary
English language.

Definitions

Let me start with a few comments about what can and cannot be achieved by definitions. Then I will discuss the type of knowledge on which such a syllabus could be based.

Definitions only matter when there is some confusion. And confusion only matters when the subject is an important one.

English language is clearly an important topic. First, English is an international language. It is important as an auxiliary language in many parts of the world, and millions of pounds are involved in teaching English as a foreign language. There was an article in the *Times Higher Educational Supplement* (26 May 1972) about private enterprise in Poland, with the headline: 'English teaching the most lucrative enterprise after growing tomatoes.' We are dealing therefore with a practical, economic and political issue. Second, English is important to speakers: witness the current debate over Black English in the USA, British West Indians' identification with varieties of Caribbean creoles, or the violence in Wales over the relation of English and Welsh. People's attitudes are the most important factor in the end, and a major aim of language teachers must be to change people's attitudes, to increase their understanding and tolerance of linguistic diversity. George Bernard Shaw's comment is still true: 'It is impossible for an Englishman to open his mouth, without making some other Englishman despise him.' We are dealing therefore with important social issues.

People have always and everywhere been very sensitive to linguistic differences and have used them as markers of social group membership. One of the earliest cases on record is reported in the book of Judges (12 : 5-6) in the Old Testament. The Ephraimites are fleeing from the Gileadites, and trying to get away across the River Jordan:

> When any Ephraimite who had escaped begged leave to cross, the men of Gilead asked him, 'Are you an Ephraimite?' and if he said, 'No', they would retort, 'Say Shibboleth.' He would say 'Sibboleth', and because he could not pronounce the word properly, they seized him and killed him.

Third, English provides interesting problems for linguists. With the increasing complexity of English, various questions arise. What do we mean by *the English language*? Or by dialects of English? Or by English-based pidgins and creoles? How do languages diversify and change? How much diversification can there be before we can no longer talk of the same language?

So, I see no point in definition for its own sake. Dr Johnson once said: 'Sometimes things may be made darker by definition. I see a cow . . . I define . . . Animal quadrupes ruminans cornutum. But a goat ruminates, and a cow may have no horns. "Cow" is plainer.' But the attempt at definition would be valuable if we discover interesting things along the way, and increase our understanding of the linguistic diversity which a label like *English* represents. And I am going to suggest that if we do this, we can in fact provide the basis for a syllabus for teaching English in schools and universities: that contemporary English language is a varied and interesting topic for school children, university students, educationalists and linguists.

English in the modern world

Let me now start to discuss the position of English in the modern world, some of the things that have to be taken into account in studying it, the functions it serves in different countries, and its relation to other languages.

In studying contemporary English language, we have to consider a large number of factors which were simply not considered by traditional language historians, because many of the pressures on English have grown up largely in the last hundred years. These pressures include: an unprecedented number of speakers; its use as an international language with a very large number of speakers of English as a foreign language; mass literacy and the associated massive printing and publishing technology; the mass media; the proliferation of institutionalized varieties of English; the use of English against a background of enormous linguistic diversity; and social developments, including urbanization, social class stratification and geographical and social mobility. Let me take these in more detail.

It is usual to distinguish three categories of English in use. First, English as a *native language*. Up to 400 million speakers have English as their native language in Britain, the USA, Australia and elsewhere. Second, there are millions more who use English for everyday purposes as a *second language* in areas such as India and West Africa. Third, there are still more millions who have learnt English as a *foreign language* for some purpose.

One estimate (Potter, 1974) is that one person in seven in the world uses English for one of these purposes. No other language has both so many speakers *and* such a wide geographical spread. (Chinese has many more speakers, although the situation is complicated by the number of mutually incomprehensible dialects.) English has twenty times more native speakers than it had 200 years ago (Strang, 1970, pp. 17, 177), with principal communities in the USA (*c.* 211 million), Britain (56m), Canada (22m), Australia (14m), New Zealand (3m), Caribbean (3m) and South Africa (1.3m). (South Africa has in addition 1.8m Afrikaans speakers, out of a total population of 24m (Valkhoff, 1971.)) South America is the only continent without a large English speaking community.

One surprising fact about English is that the national standard languages are very uniform. There are noticeable differences between various national standards: English, Scottish, Irish, American, Canadian, Australian, New Zealand, South African and Jamaican. But despite these differences and considering the geographical spread, the diversity of international written English is very small indeed. A major reason for regarding all the many varieties of English as *English*, is that they share this single superposed variety, the international written standard, which has been codified by centuries of dictionary-makers, grammar-book writers, printers and publishers, and education systems. The result of this codification is what we mean by a standard language.

When we consider English as a second language, there is a danger of prematurely christening new Englishes, but there are developing standards in areas where English is used as an auxiliary language or link language of wider communication. It is now meaningful to talk of South Asian (or Indian), West African, Malaysian and Filipino English. These varieties have developed primarily since the Second World War, due to governments' retaining English after independence as a language of world communication. (See Kachru, 1969; Platt, 1975; Spencer, 1971.) The functions of international English add more startling statistics: it has been estimated that 75 per cent of the world's mail, 60 per cent of the world's radio broadcasts and 50 per cent of the world's scientific literature are in English (Strang, 1970, p. 73; Quirk *et al.*, 1972, p. 4). Varieties such as West African or Indian English may be fairly well standardized, but the competence of individual speakers clearly differs greatly. We have to distinguish between the variety and individuals' knowledge of it. Also, English may be used by a very small percentage of the population. In India, for example, English has important functions in education and publishing, but is used mainly by educationalists and civil servants, and spoken by less than 2 per cent of the population (Das Gupta, 1969, p. 583).

Another set of factors, which are beyond the scope of traditional methods of language study, is the massive urbanization and associated complex social class stratification of modern technological societies. Big cities are simply not speech communities in the classic sense, and the resulting urban dialects and social class dialects cannot be captured by the methods of the traditional dialectologists, such as Harold Orton. The traditional types of dialect atlas, for all their pioneering value, cannot record the linguistic diversity of big urban conurbations. Inevitably they are primarily records of the dialect of elderly, rural men who have not travelled widely: agricultural workers 'with good mouths, teeth and hearing' as the *Linguistic Atlas of England* puts it (Orton *et al.*, 1977).

Another relatively recent pressure on English is mass literacy. In Britain, it was the Education Acts of 1870 and 1872 which made it a requirement for the first time that all children should learn to read and write. A stable tradition of standardized literary language goes back much further than this, of course. In the eighteenth century, the big dictionaries such as Samuel Johnson's were published, and they were recording what was already established practice amongst printers. The long tradition of literacy means, amongst other things, that English has a very large vocabulary. Unabbreviated general dictionaries contain 500,000 entries, although no individual speaker knows anything like that number of words. However, with massive printing technology, and associated systems of libraries, education and mass literacy, the relationship between spoken and written English has changed. There is now, for example, an enormous inertia against any kind of major spelling reform in English, and any reform is impossible for practical reasons for the foreseeable future.

Or consider a very recent pressure on English which has had a small but significant effect just in the past five years or so: the feminist movement. Certainly this has had an effect on address terms on letters, such that *Ms* is now as common as any alternative, at least in the academic community in Britain and the USA. But the real effect will come via the publishers, and several non-sexist codes of practice for book publishing are now in use. The best known code of practice is probably the 'Guidelines for the Equal Treatment of the Sexes in McGraw-Hill Book Company Publications'. Other sets of guidelines are in use by publishers such as Ginn & Co.; Holt, Rinehart & Winston; Macmillan; Random House; Scott, Foresman & Co.; and others (Miller and Swift, 1976).

The important point here is that it is the big publishing houses who standardize and codify our language. The first big dictionaries of

English, produced in the eighteenth century, took as their model what was accepted publishing practice of the time. Authors and editors now consult dictionaries, and continue the circle. Once this circle is set up, and is further supported by the education system, it is very powerful.

Problems with a historical view of English

A traditional way of regarding English has always been to regard it historically, to see modern English as derived from Old English, which in turn split off from other Germanic languages and so on. Part of this approach involves looking at the origins of words: etymologies.

There are various difficulties in the concept of etymology, however. In the first place, speakers do not, by and large, know the etymologies of words. Etymologies belong to the history of a language, and people do not know the history of their language, and therefore etymologies have no direct effect on speakers. Take the stereotypical word in Australian English, *dinkum* in the sense of 'true' or 'authentic'. It seems that the word is traceable to an English dialect phrase from Lincolnshire (where *fair dinkum* means 'fair deal'). Or take the ultimate etymological confusion in the word *kangaroo*. Its etymology is uncertain, but it probably passed from an Aboriginal language (where it did not mean 'kangaroo' anyway) into English, and then spread from English into other Aboriginal languages. Aborigines thought they were using a European word, and vice-versa (Turner, 1966, pp. 27, 199).

Or take the example of a suffix which is now fairly productive in English: *-nik* as in *beatnik*. The origin of the suffix is the Slav languages, as in Russian *sputnik*. But as a productive suffix the source is mainly Yiddish-influenced American English, from where we have forms such as *kibbutznik, no-goodnik* and *alrightnik* (in the sense of *nouveau riche*, if I may offer a French translation). We now have a term used by homosexuals for heterosexuals: *straightnik* (Rosten, 1968).

I am also keeping my eye on words ending in *-gate*, as this suffix travels around the world. On an analogy with *Watergate*, the term *Muldergate* caught on very fast. There is now a book entitled *Oilgate*, about the breaking of oil sanctions on Rhodesia (Bailey, 1979). And on the day of the AATE conference, someone brought to my attention a headline in the *Weekend Australian* (1–2 September 1979, p. 8): 'The Prawngate scandal down on the farms.' The word *Watergate* was originally unanalysable, but *-gate* now seems to have been detached and turned into a suffix meaning 'scandal' or 'political scandal'.

So the concept of etymology is becoming increasingly complex and sometimes meaningless due to the increasing variety of English and the increasing contact with other languages. There is internal borrowing, from American to British English, although many Americanisms are not recognized as such in Britain. In addition, an international vocabulary is developing, such that words do not really belong to any single language, and it is rather meaningless to say what their source is. Many words in areas such as science and technology, politics and sport are recognizable in a large number of languages, including English. In other words, the increasing complexity of sociolinguistic relations between languages has changed the concept of etymology. Languages have always used each other as reservoirs of vocabulary, but this common reservoir is growing. And the distinction between English and non-English is not as clear-cut as people might think.

The boundaries of English

Now, I am arguing that the distinction between English and other languages is more fuzzy than some people think. But I do not wish to argue that logically black-is-white (Flew, 1975, p. 104). There may be complex differences of degree, with no clear boundaries, but that does not mean that there is no difference at all. Many a mickle may mak' a muckle. As Edmund Burke observed: 'Though no man can draw a stroke between the confines of day and night, still light and darkness are on the whole tolerably distinct.' In other words, don't get carried away by talk of fuzzy boundaries, gradient phenomena, continua, clines, inherent variability. In describing English we require both the concept of clear-cut categories and also the concept of gradience.

Neither do I wish to argue, however, that the truth is always in the middle. I do not think that moderation should be carried to extremes. Some phenomena in English are truly gradient, but others are categorial. For example, it is an interesting sociolinguistic fact that some varieties of English are very uniform whilst others are not. International written English is remarkably uniform; and so is Australian English (compared to British English) although it is spoken throughout three million square miles.

Consider another aspect of the boundaries of English: the question of which words are 'in' English, from the everyday point of view of which words get recorded in dictionaries. First, there is the problem of obscene words: should they be included or not? When new dictionaries are published, reviewers always seem to start by looking to see which obscene words are included (Leach, 1972). The problem involved is not just one of propriety – but a full-blown logical paradox. Dictionaries are regarded as one of our most respectable institutions. Obscene words are not respectable: that is part of their meaning. But if they are in the dictionary, they must be respectable. In other words, if taboo words are recorded in dictionaries, the very act of recording them will change their meaning. We are dealing with a version of the observer's paradox (Labov, 1972b) which affects many aspects of language study. We would like ideally to observe how language is used, when no one is observing it.

Many Australian Aboriginal languages have very complex systems of linguistic taboos, observed in talking in the presence of taboo relatives: so-called 'mother-in-law' language; or used for ritual purposes, at initiation ceremonies and so on (Dixon, 1971; Hale, 1971); and which provide very valuable semantic data for linguists.

Or there is the problem of obsolescent words. For example, English has a large number of collective nouns. Some of these are still quite current: a *school* of fish, a *pride* of lions, a *swarm* of bees, a *flock* of sheep, a *litter* of puppies. But others have little existence nowadays outside school text-books in English: a *gang* of elks, a *wedge* of swans, a *drift* of hogs, a *knot* of toads. These are all genuine examples (recorded by Lipton, 1977), but known only to a very small number of speakers. Should dictionaries be storehouses of old words? How long should words be recorded? It is difficult to say, since no one has ever seen a word die. Such examples open the way to a nice game, incidentally. I propose as new collective terms: an *anthology* of English teachers, a *conjugation* of Latin teachers, a *nucleus* of chemistry teachers, a *proper subset* of logicians, a *systems network* of Hallidayan linguists, a *drone* of lecturers.

English and linguistic diversity

Contemporary English is therefore subject to many sources of diversity: not only traditionally recognized regional and social variation, but relatively new kinds of variation due to its increasing contact with other languages.

It is a basic principle that the amount of linguistic diversity in a community will regularly be underestimated. The reasons are very simple. Everyone's speech varies according to the formality or casualness of the social situation. But we see only our own close family and friends in a wide range of social settings. We tend to see people from other social groups in relatively formal settings. For example, teachers often only see pupils in the classroom, and it is difficult or impossible to observe them outside school: the observer's paradox again. Teachers may therefore get only a restricted view of the range of language which pupils use. Another reason why language variation gets systematically underestimated is that there is more variation in the spoken than in the written language. And it is, simply, easier to observe written language. It follows that dictionaries will under-record the extent to which English is changing since they will record only well-established trends and are based predominantly on written language.

Since diversity is regularly underestimated, one thing we have to be careful about is that politically and socially dominant cultures in some countries attempt to project the view that these countries are monolingual and monocultural, where this is a grossly oversimplified view or just out of date. Britain, for example, does superficially appear to be a monolingual country. Almost everybody speaks English, and there is no need to speak any other language in order to live there. But this view ignores both the indigenous Celtic languages (Welsh, Irish and Scottish Gaelic) and also the enormous linguistic diversity due to recent immigration, especially since the 1950s.

Scottish Gaelic, for example, has always been ignored, to all intents and purposes, by politicians. It has around 80,000 speakers, all bilingual with English, mainly in north-west Scotland, but it has no official status in Scotland. Even the Scottish National Party only formulated a policy on Gaelic in 1974. And given the failure to bring about Scottish devolution in 1979, and the reduction of SNP numbers in parliament at Westminster in the 1979 election, there is little hope of future official support for Gaelic.

However, the main source of linguistic diversity in Britain is the immigration into London and the big urban conurbations in the Midlands, such as Birmingham, Nottingham and Leicester. It is not very surprising that the politicians have not yet caught up with this diversity, since the whole linguistic configuration of many areas of Britain has changed drastically in just twenty years. We do not even have statistics on the languages spoken by immigrants, since census figures refer only to country of origin: and this can give only a very rough indication of language for someone coming from multi-lingual countries such as India or West Africa. The first major report on the teaching of English in England was the Newbolt Report published in 1921 (HMSO, 1921): it just makes no reference to any language other than English. The most recent is the Bullock Report (DES, 1975): it does discuss the problem, although it refers rather coyly to 'children of families of overseas origin' and is very sparse on statistics.

An estimate (Campbell-Platt, 1976) of the most widely spoken immigrant languages in Britain, in descending order is: Punjabi, Bengali, Gujerati (northern Indian languages), German, Polish, Italian, Greek, Spanish, Cantonese, Hakka. Many other languages could be added. It is common now for teachers in some English cities to have classes where native English-speaking children are in the minority.

A large number of children in Britain's ethnic minorities in fact attend evening or weekend classes in their mother tongue outside the normal school system, although little is known about the extent of such provision (Khan, 1976). There are many motivations for such classes: parents who are not fluent in English, although their children are; parental pride in the mother tongue; a hope that the children will return home to marry; a fear of compulsory repatriation at some time; or religious reasons. One estimate for Australia (Grassby, 1977) is that 100,000 children attend such ethnic schools in twenty-five languages.

The mixture of languages in British cities is leading to the creation of new varieties. For example, recognizably London varieties of English creoles from the Caribbean have developed. London Black English might be learnt by black teenagers who were born in Britain, and who choose to learn the variety in their teens as an act of ethnic identity, or by black Africans. We now even have the phenomenon of white youths learning to 'talk black'.

In Australia, the dominant cultural view is again of a monolingual country. This view crops up in unexpected places. For example, the *Encyclopedia Britannica* article (Potter, 1974) on English language claims that 'Australia has no European language other than English within its borders'. This is quite simply false. Admittedly Australia has a very homogeneous population due to immigration controls. But altogether migrants have come from about sixty countries: 45 per cent from Britain, 40 per cent from Europe, and 15 per cent from other countries (Jones, 1974, p. 31). Figures on school children whose native language is not English appear to differ. The Australian Department of Education (1977, p. 18) figures based on the 1971 Census is 300,000 children (11 per cent) in Australian schools 'with at least one parent whose native language is not English'. But Grassby (1977, p. 4) cites a figure well over twice as high.

Summary and some implications

Let me now try to sum up some of the things that I have been saying, before I go on to make some proposals for a syllabus which studies contemporary English language. I have suggested that English has to be defined according to its use in the world. In international terms, English is extremely important. This is a truism: but even a truism may be true. English now has an unprecedented number of speakers, and is in contact with an unprecedented number of other languages. There are new pressures on English, which mean changes in the relation between English and other languages, changes in what we mean by literacy in English, and changes in the methods that have to be used to study English. A traditional historical view is inadequate on its own; so also is an approach which sees English primarily as a vehicle for imaginative literature; and so also is a narrowly linguistic view. All such views, on their own, will simply miss major facts about the uses of contemporary English.

The importance of English is due, of course, to social and historical accidents. It is not due to any linguistic superiority: that concept makes no sense. But in discussing the place of English in the world we are dealing with powerful political, social, attitudinal and technological pressures. The study of contemporary English therefore rests on a substantial body of knowledge, is socially important, relates to the everyday experience of pupils, and involves interesting intellectual and conceptual problems.

The teaching of language is a social and political act. This can and should be explicit, and such discussion can form part of the content of a syllabus. We are talking, for example, about the historical and social forces on world languages and minority languages, the relationship between languages and cultural groups, the dissipation of migrant and Aboriginal languages, and the tolerance of linguistic diversity. Given the decline of foreign language teaching in Australia, English teachers have all the more responsibility to promote understanding of such issues. We are not just talking of yet another content area which English teachers might cover, but of changing students' attitudes. If we *understand* the extraordinary complexity of anyone's use of language it becomes impossible to be intolerant of language diversity.

The teaching of contemporary English language

Finally, then, I want to propose one type of syllabus for the study of modern English language, which can be based on the view of English

I have discussed. The whole article so far has, of course, been concerned with the kinds of things teachers ought to know about English, and which are often rather different from the traditional, historical, literary or narrowly linguistic approach to English. In the next section I will put forward a few suggestions at the level of lesson plans, and in the Appendix I will set out an outline syllabus more systematically.

One comment first about the academic level for which such a syllabus might be appropriate. I have in mind mainly secondary school pupils. A discussion of contemporary English requires an understanding, for example, of the enormous geographical and social spread of English, and young children just do not have this grasp of geographical and social space. And there is no problem in extending the syllabus upwards into college and university education to make a conceptually exciting course for students. It may therefore be felt, however, that the syllabus is too abstract and academic for all but the most academic and highly motivated school pupils.

I would answer this objection as follows. First, many of the things I have discussed have had to do with the real everyday experience of language diversity and language contact in contemporary societies: this is not abstract, but real and socially important. Second, I think children are often more sophisticated about such language diversity than their teachers give them credit for: teachers regularly underestimate the range of pupils' language abilities. Third, I am not proposing that all I have said should be taught to pupils in the form I have presented it here. In this article, I am discussing primarily the powerful ideas about English which should inform the teacher's approach: things teachers ought to know. Sometimes, it may be appropriate to teach such ideas abstractly and explicitly. Sometimes they may provide a framework for practical activities: a principled base for the teacher to refer to. A real objection to such a syllabus is that it requires a great deal of time and commitment from teachers to learn about new ways of analysing variation in English.

Some practical suggestions

The syllabus could cover content areas such as the following: written versus spoken language; literary versus non-literary language; standard versus non-standard language; child versus adult language (i.e. native language acquisition); English as a native versus a foreign language; regional accents and dialects; pidgins and creoles; dictionary-making;

attitudes to language; ways in which English is currently changing. Each topic could then be treated in three ways: through the study and comparison of real texts, and the development of analytic skills for describing language in use; through factual work on types of variation which languages display, and the concepts necessary to describe this; through studies of policy-making and the kinds of practical social decisions that such linguistic diversity requires.

Consider as one example the topic of the differences between spoken and written language (cf. Stubbs, 1980, for much more detailed discussion of this topic). The textual study could involve the comparison of samples of language: formally printed, literary, non-literary, informally written, audio-recorded and transcribed. It could involve also samples of pupils' own creative writing, discussed and analysed. The study of language variation could involve a study of different kinds of writing system, and what it means to be able to read and write. The study of policy-making could look at the problems of the acquisition of literacy in particular countries or world-wide. All I can now do in the space available is mention a few topics which might figure on such a syllabus: just a list of practical suggestions, at the level of lesson plans, within the topic of the relation of spoken to written language.

One interesting way of investigating what English *is*, is to study marginal varieties or limiting cases of English. Some restricted varieties of English are only possible in written form: the language of technical manuals (e.g. car repair); computer languages; crossword clues; newspaper headlines; telegrams; recipes; knitting patterns; forms and questionnaires; legal language (e.g. guarantees). Others are essentially spoken: baby talk; the language of air traffic controllers; shipping forecasts on radio; glossolalia – pseudo-language used by Pentecostalists; and some varieties of English mixed almost inextricably with other languages, such as Yinglish, Yiddish-influenced English. There are many sources of such limiting cases of English in literature of all kinds from Lewis Carroll to Goon Show scripts to Tom Stoppard's plays.

Such samples raise very difficult problems, such as: how far can English be distorted and still remain intelligible? Very important work on this topic has been done by Professor Stanley Unwin (Unwin and Dewar, 1961). He has studied Angloid in detail right down to the smallest, however transmitted: written down by the scribbly scribe, and, of course, viva voce, when air is expelled from the mouse. The most importaload and fundermold principle to come out of Professor Unwin's work, is that all languishing have a very high redundaload faction, so that even though the world of mouth is twisty and false, with many a slip twixt club and limp, neverthelesson is that this does needly preventilate us from grasping at a crow and following hard on the wheels of what someone is trying to .... Rightly is Professor Unwin's work fully fame the worm over, and read with leisure by people in their manifolds, from Great Brixton to the antipoles.

Another possibility is to use literary sources to study representations of dialects, or accounts of language teaching or language snobbery. Famous examples include Mrs Malaprop, Dickens's character Sam Weller, or *Pygmalion.* (Quirk, 1974, gives a large number of observations of Dickens along these lines.) More recent examples include humorous books by Leo Rosten about the character Hyman Kaplan, or by George Mikes, or serious literature by authors such as Richard Wright. All such writing can lead into a discussion of people's attitudes to language variation.

Another example: it might be thought that spoken language is relatively simple compared with written language. One way to question this is to point out the complexity of the grammatical competence often involved in understanding jokes, spoken or written. Consider a superficially simple example. A lodger is complaining to his landlord:

Lodger: And another thing – I don't like all these mice in my room.
Landlord: Well, pick out the ones you like and throw the rest out.

Now this joke can be understood instantly by any native speaker of English. But it hinges on the ambiguity of the scope of the quantifier *all*, which can only be fully explained to predicate logic. We might propose as paraphrases, that the lodger intended to say: 'For all x, if x is a mouse in my room, then I don't like it.' Whereas the landlord interpreted his utterance as: 'There is an x, such that x is a mouse in your room, and you don't like it.' Jokes can provide a neat way of demonstrating the impressive complexity of grammatical knowledge.

One could go on listing such ideas ad infinitum. Students could: make language maps, showing the distribution of different writing systems in the world; collect samples of spoken and written English from all over the world; find new words, used in print or speech, but not yet recorded in dictionaries; study types of concrete poetry which exploit characteristics of written language; make translations between varieties of English which are conventionally only written or spoken.

Many of these ideas doubtless correspond to activities which readers are already using in classrooms. And many other ideas have doubtless also occurred to readers. As often happens, the careful study of language in use provides a large number of ideas for use in the classroom. And, just as important, it provides a principled basis for such work, by providing a way of relating such activities to a coherent overall framework for describing language. This is what should be meant by 'applied linguistics': theory which suggests and illuminates interesting practice.

I think the kind of English syllabus I have proposed has considerable attractions. First, it can be based on samples of real language in use in the world. Second, it is therefore 'relevant': English language in the world is important. Third, it emphasizes throughout the diversity of English in use. On the one hand, this should extend students' own stylistic competence. But it should also increase their understanding of diversity, and therefore their tolerance of diversity. Fourth, since it is based throughout on comparing and contrasting varieties of English, it provides a meaningful way of teaching grammar: analytic methods are introduced because they are needed to solve problems, not for their own sake. Fifth, all the things I have suggested can be taught at widely different degrees of sophistication. Sixth, a lot of the work can be fun: 'serious but not solemn' (Halliday, 1974). Seventh, the syllabus has a coherent theoretical basis in current linguistic work in language variation.

What is English?

Well, this article is already long enough, and I suppose some of you may have noticed that I haven't yet said what English *is*.

There is the story of an eminent scholar of English who devoted his life to trying to define the essence of English. He wrote many books, trying always to pare away the inessential and the peripheral, and get down to the essential core. English was clearly not homogeneous: but not entirely heterogeneous – structured heterogeneity. It was sometimes categorial: but also gradient. A relatively stable core: but with indeterminate boundaries. How to define fuzziness with precision? His writings became shorter and shorter, and clearer and clearer. He began by writing long text books, but soon was writing brief prolegomena, succinct articles, gradually discarding the inessentials. At his death he was known to be working on his ultimate project. He was trying to distil the essence of English into a single word. When he died his disciples were going through his academic papers, sorting out a lifetime's notes. Eventually they came upon the piece of paper with the *word* on it! The culmination of a lifetime's study.

Unfortunately, no one could read his writing.

Appendix A Sample outline syllabus

I suggest below the broad outlines of a course on modern English language. Most of the topics could be taught at widely different levels of sophistication, between secondary school and university.

Course objectives

(a) Given any text, students ought to be able to comment systematically on its interesting features.

Text means any piece of spoken discourse or written text which has actually occurred in a real social situation. Texts could therefore include: children's speech; samples of regional and social dialects; literary texts; casual conversation between adults; samples of pidgins, creoles and code switching; etc. This implies *contrastive stylistic analysis of real language*, and not the development of some descriptive linguistic framework for its own sake. (See also Appendix B.)

(b) Students ought to be aware of the types of language variation which occur in society, and of concepts required to describe such variation.

Types of variation include: societal multilingualism of different kinds; dialectal variation, regional and social; and stylistic variation.

Given (a), students ought to be able to comment precisely on the relevant linguistic characteristics of the variation.

(c) Students ought to be aware of work on practical language planning, i.e. policy-making.

This involves work at all institutional levels from national governments down to institutions such as publishing houses and schools. Such linguistic policy-making includes choosing and modernizing national languages, literacy programmes, language teaching policies at national and school level. 'Language across the curriculum', etc.

Sample content areas could be divided into blocks, each treated from these three points of view as follows.

Course outline

TX   Textual analysis.
LV   Language variation.
LP   Language planning.

Block 1   Styles of language
TX   Samples of different styles, registers, functional varieties, for contrastive analysis.
LV   Grammatical versus communicative and stylistic competence. Concept that language is not correct in any absolute way, but is appropriate or inappropriate to different purposes.

LP   Attitudes to language. Institutionalized styles of language, e.g. legal.

Block 2   *Native language learning*
TX   Samples of children's vs adults' language.
LV   How children acquire language. Language and cognitive development, language and intelligence.
LP   Teaching the native language in schools. Language policies in schools.

Block 3   *Dialects and codes*
TX   Samples of regional and social dialects and accents. Most extreme dialect variation in creoles.
LV   Language and social class.
LP   Attitudes to accents and dialects.

Block 4   *Multilingualism*
TX   Samples of code switching: stylistic, bilingual, bidialectal.
LV   Language and ethnic groups. Societal multilingualism: case studies of different countries. Relations between English and other languages. Individual bilingualism.
LP   Foreign language teaching in schools; English as a second language and as a foreign language. Roles of English as an international language.

Block 5   *Written language and literacy*
TX   Samples of written vs spoken language.
LV   Nature of written language and writing systems. Literacy in different countries, world literacy rates.
LP   What it means to be able to read and write. Teaching literacy. The standardization of English by dictionary-makers, printers and publishers.

Block 6   *Literary language*
TX   Samples of literary vs non-literary language.
LV   Literary and linguistic stylistics. Nature of literary criticism.
LP   Teaching literature in schools, aims and objectives.

Appendix B Description of contemporary English

I have discussed in the body of this paper the possibility of describing samples of real language in use and of contrastive text analysis. This clearly needs some framework for describing texts, but I have not discussed this at all. This is partly because it does not really matter which framework is used, as long as it obeys various criteria. It must be non-prescriptive and fairly comprehensive: able to describe what actually occurs. If teachers are familiar with, for example, tagmemic grammar, systemic grammar or various other descriptive frameworks, then these could serve.

If I had to recommend one particular framework, however, I would recommend *A Grammar of Contemporary English* by Randolph Quirk and his colleagues. I would recommend this for various reasons.

1 It is fairly traditional in many ways. It is based on some of the best of contemporary descriptive linguistics, but many of the concepts are compatible with more traditional notions of English grammar, and will therefore be accessible to many teachers.

2 It is based on a survey of contemporary English usage, spoken and written.

3 It is published in various forms: a substantial, basic reference volume (Quirk *et al.*, 1972), and also two more condensed versions by Leech and Svartvik (1975) and by Quirk and Greenbaum (1973). The second of these also has an associated workbook.

Acknowledgments

I am grateful to Margaret Berry, Oscar Collinge, and Anne Gunter for providing data and ideas for this article; and to the audience at my address in Perth for formulating over fifty questions on the address and giving me the opportunity to try and respond to some of them.

This article was originally prepared as the Keynote Address given to the Australian Association for the Teaching of English at their national conference in Perth, Western Australia, in September 1979, and published in *English in Australia*, 51, March 1980. Some remarks in the article were designed for its original Australian presentation, but since they are relevant to the theme of the article, which is English language in the modern world, they have been left unaltered here.

10

Sociolinguistics and the integrated English lesson

Ronald Carter

Introduction

This article discusses some ways in which a principled account of the organization of vocabulary can assist in the development of language use and in an appreciation (which is not wholly impressionistic and inexplicit) of how lexis can work in literary texts. Attitudes to words both within and outside a literary context are explored as part of a sociolinguistic framework for analysing literary and non-literary language. Teaching suggestions for integrating language and literature work are made together with a proposal for a joint language and literature syllabus for upper-school students of English.

This article is about the relation between 'literary' and ordinary, every-day language. It is designed to be of particular interest to English teachers of pupils 14+ but I hope the points raised will be relevant to a principled teaching of vocabulary at all levels and in many different contexts. In the first part of this article I should like to discuss the following points and questions:

(i) to point out that lexis is a level of language which can be studied in a clear, systematic and accessible way;

(ii) to argue that a principled study of the organization and structure of vocabulary can be of real value both in extending awareness of language as language and for assisting in developing pupils' and students' performance in language use. In particular, I hope to show that this linguistic level, as would be the case with other levels, is best studied in terms of the human communicative ends it serves;

(iii) to show that work on lexis can be undertaken in language *and* literature classes. I hope to show that, as far as language study in secondary education is concerned, literary language is a particularly fertile ground. Such work might thus allow some mutually support-ive integration of areas which are often kept distinct in the English classroom.

In the second part of the article, I shall suggest some ways in which lexis can be studied with reference to a basic sociolinguistic account of *attitudes* to language and explore how this framework can be used to raise questions about different attitudes to literary language. Finally, having established a theoretical perspective and some basic terminology, there is a section more explicitly devoted to classroom and teaching applications generally.

1 Analysing lexis in poetry

Much of the following discussion is of lexical choices in a poem. The discussion will focus on the literary meanings produced by the lexical choices but will also introduce the following terms used in the linguistic study of lexis: collocation; lexical item; association; cluster; paradigmatic and syntagmatic; linguistic level; context of use. The poem – 'Janet Waking' by John Crowe Ransom – is one quite widely anthologized in school and college course books. Here is the text:

> Beautifully Janet slept
> Till it was deeply morning. She woke then
> And thought about her dainty-feathered hen,
> To see how it had kept.
>
> One kiss she gave her mother,
> Only a small one gave she to her daddy
> Who would have kissed each curl of his shining baby;
> No kiss at all for her brother.
>
> 'Old Chucky, old Chucky!' she cried,
> Running across the world upon grass
> To Chucky's house, and listening. But alas,
> Her Chucky had died.
>
> It was a transmogrifying bee
> Came droning down on Chucky's old bald head
> And sat and put the poison. It scarcely bled,
> But how exceedingly
>
> And purply did the knot
> Swell with the venom and communicate

Its rigor! Now the poor comb stood up straight
But Chucky did not.

So there was Janet
Kneeling on the wet grass, crying her brown hen
(Translated far beyond the daughters of men)
To rise and walk upon it.

And weeping fast as she had breath
Janet implored us, 'Wake her from her sleep!'
And would not be instructed in how deep
Was the forgetful kingdom of death.

I want to begin by examining the poet's choice of words in the first
stanza. Students often remark that they are unusual or do not sound
right, but do not regularly go beyond such impressions. The 'unusual'
words seem agreed to be:

'Beautifully'   'deeply'   'kept'   *'dainty* - feathered'

Extracting the words from their context in the poem and jumbling
them up with other words from the stanza leads to a recognition that
some words sit alongside each other more comfortably than others.
There is, in fact, a kind of magnetic field at work which forcefully
draws some of the words together. For example:

beautiful and morning
deeply and sleep

seem to attract each other more closely than is the case in this text
where *beautifully* is closer to *sleep* and *deeply* closer to *morning.* Most
native speakers would tend to agree on the usualness of:

I slept *deeply* (rather than beautifully) or
I had a nice deep sleep.

or

It was a beautiful morning (rather than 'a deep morning')

although, if we convert morning into *mourning* then it attracts the
word *deep* much more strongly, e.g.

They were in deep mourning.
His death was deeply mourned.

But the two other words most often singled out, 'dainty' and 'kept',
do not seem to have any ready-made partners internal to this stanza.

Regrettably, there is space only to deal with one of them. In such cases jumbling up and rearranging does not lead to anything. Instead, a procedure of substitution needs to be adopted. That is, we do not readily find 'kept' fits 'hen' so we try to substitute 'hen' with other words:

*The hen kept
*The house kept

The man kept $\begin{cases} \text{the key} \\ \text{hens} \end{cases}$ (kept here would be a transitive verb)

The milk kept
The meat kept
The cheese kept
*The car kept

'Kept', then, when used in this way (i.e. intransitively) seems only to go with what can be loosely called perishable items (things, that is, which, to put it colloquially, 'go off').

Having reached this stage, a class can be invited to discern links between perishable, deeply mourning (and, if necessary, 'sleep', 'waking') and conclude a common association with death. The death of the hen is thus, in part, subtly foretold in the first stanza of the poem. There may even be from one viewpoint a rather cruel 'overtone' in the word 'kept' in that the hen is already putrefying as Janet runs across her world to see it. The way the words in the first sentence change their natural places seems on one level to parallel the way in which the world of Janet is turned inside out, reversed and otherwise dislocated from normal expectations. We can thus make a direct equation between language observation and literary meaning.

We have at this stage introduced, largely by indirect means, what in contemporary linguistic terms is the notion of *lexical items*[1] and their *collocates*. By *collocation* we may therefore understand the company habitually kept by a word. For example, 'busy', 'buzz' have a high probability of co-occurrence with 'bee'; bee in turn regularly co-occurs with words such as 'hive' or 'honey' and less regularly with items such as 'intrepid' or 'transmogrifying'. Some members of the *cluster* of words which collocate with 'bee' will be more central or stronger than others. Where item and collocation do not make a conventional fit (e.g. 'the seductive cottage') then the user must be aware of the stylistic effects he produces. Literary usages tend to comprise many unexpected collocations.[2] Collocability works sequentially on a horizontal axis; its relations are what linguists term *syntagmatic*. The actual items chosen at any number of points in a text come from a vertical or paradigmatic axis and are thus synonymous or at least generally relevant to the meaning. Thus I might describe

	zealous	
	industrious	
a(n)	busy	bee
	hard-working	

and select from a number of words the one most appropriate to the context I was using it in. Mention of *contexts of use* raises now the issue of the *associations* carried by lexical items.

In stanza two of 'Janet Waking' there is a contrast – reinforced by line-final position – between

1	2
mother	mummy
father	daddy

There are different associations between 1 and 2 which have to do with interpersonal use. The former tends to be more formal and less intimate, while the second column often reflects the age of the user. It is certainly unusual that Janet should be seen to differentiate in this way. Similarly the word 'alas' carries associations. It conveys a sense of slightly melodramatic exclamation and can thus always have ironic overtones when used to frame events. Apart from having virtually disappeared from current usage (how recently have a class heard this word?), it is in this sense both incongruous and inappropriate to the immediate situation of Janet's discovery. In the case of such *associations* the meaning of the words is determined as much by the context in which they are used as by their referents. 'Chucky' (like 'doggy' or 'kitty') works in the same way. There can be associations which reflect degrees of formality (malefactor, crook, criminal), which reflect specialized domains (wings, footlights, curtain, backdrop), interpersonal and social use (see above), a historical dimension ('wireless' – radio; 'gramophone' – record player (stereo)) or even a recognizable acceptability for literary use[3] ('twain', ofttimes', 'whither', 'verdant', 'main', etc.). Associations of words can be objectively measured using a basic linguistic research procedure of informant tests (see part 3). Once the principles are understood and a limited defining meta-language mastered, there is no reason why a class should not investigate such properties for themselves and thus really explore their own verbal impressions and intuitions.

A theory of lexical collocation and association helps to explain the incongruity which occurs in the third stanza with the introduction of the word 'transmogrifying'. If a blank were left adjacent to the word bee, it is unlikely that this collocate would ever be predicted. It is a word which carries associations of a scientifically verifiable or special-ized process (a dictionary will confirm its domain to be biological science). It is incongruous because its five syllables are in almost comic disproportion to the noun it modifies and because it contrasts with the markedly 'simple' language in the preceding stanza. Primarily though it does not seem to fit in the context. But it might be seen to parallel the way in which Janet's experience of Chucky's death is incongruous and does not fit in any way with her expectations. On another level, it seems simultaneously to inflate and deflate the subject and process it depicts and thus comes close to a mock-heroic tone. By the third stanza the reader has been deliberately subjected to so many unexpected shifts in tone that he or she does not know which way to take things, particularly the relationship between Janet and her parents.

The difficulty in precisely specifying this relationship is augmented by paradigmatic exploration of some lexical choices in the concluding stanzas. For example:

weep   implore   instruct

are all verbs employed by Ransom. What effects are produced if 'cry', 'ask' and 'teach' are all substituted at relevant points in the text? This kind of procedure is one regularly followed by English teachers so I shall dwell on just 'instruct' – which, if we examine its usage, tends to occur in contexts involving mechanical processes or a particularly authority-bound set of relationships. For example, machines have instructions; we are given instructions in how to behave; we are taught to drive by a driving *instructor.* By contrast, teaching is viewed as a somewhat more 'humane' channel. The use of 'instruct' in the final stanza here may reveal something of the underlying relationship between Janet and her parents – something concealed by the reference to her as a *'shining* baby' – or of the relationship into which events may have forced them to 'wake'.

There are, of course, many more aspects of this poem's lexis and its literary effects which could be discussed. To cite just a few examples; the ambiguities present in Janet *Waking*; the use of the word 'rigor' to suggest 'rigor mortis' (which ironically cannot be 'communicated'); the allusiveness present in 'daughters of men' and 'rise and walk upon it' which confer distinct Biblical overtones; the collocational partners of 'shining' and 'baby'; the story book structures of 'So there was Janet. . .'. From a more distinctly formalistic viewpoint there is (allowing for American phonology) the effect of 'daddy' and 'baby' being the only non-rhyming pairs across the poem; the way 'sleep' and 'deep' rhyme and thus 'come together' in an association with 'death' in the final stanza which in turn recalls the comparative lack of fit in the opening stanzas. All these elements can be built into an increasingly fuller interpretation of the text. It is a 'difficult' poem – particularly in ascertaining the attitude of the poem's speaker – and in evaluating properly the effects of switches in tone. But it is a text which can be approached in stages which allow an integrated linguistic-literary approach with each stage sufficiently thought-provoking and instructive in terms of language usage and discussion of literary meaning. Pupils often ignore this basic convention in interpreting literary texts: that what words do in contracting patterns with one another is often intended to reflect or underline the meanings made by the text. It is one of several 'logopoeic' modern poems which can be explored in similar ways to this.[4]

I have tried to show through the discussion in this section that lexis is a starting point for studying the nature of language.[5] By working within and extending these categories we can demonstrate the degrees to which language is patterned. Like all levels of language there are in lexis intersecting axes of chain and choice. There are constraints on the probable chain of lexical items just as there are on the syntactical ordering of items (though collocational patterns cannot be specified in finite terms); in the area of paradigmatic lexical choice we are more than dependents of a language system but must be aware of the strength of conventions of use. Studying literary texst as language use illustrates the extent to which creative language must define itself in relation to the system before exploiting its patterns for unique and individual effects. It can also help to define literary effects in a more precise manner.

2 Attitudes to language use

In this section I hope to illustrate briefly how a systematic study of lexis and word organization can lead to a consideration of different *attitudes* to language and how this can be of value to pupils studying English language *and* literature. For example, one of the most striking features of the lexis in 'Janet Waking' is its *variability*. It constantly switches in tone, in expected association and in contextual appropriacy. This clearly reveals an *attitude* to language in poetry on the part of John Crowe Ransom. People's attitudes to language, in both literary and non-literary contexts, can be systematically investigated and much can be revealed of the specifically *social* meanings words can convey. But my main purpose here is to show that literary study should not be insulated from the kinds of questions raised about language use in the language lesson and that, conversely, much benefit can be derived in language lessons from productive interplay with the language of literary texts. Once again, because studying anything in a principled way requires appropriately defined labelling and definition, linguistic terms and meta-language will be introduced. Whether teachers teach the meta-language to pupils is their decision but a framework appropriate to both theoretical concepts and particular functions is needed. Among the main terms to be introduced in this section are: *formality; dialect; specialized domain* or *register; diction; synchronic* v. *diachronic; descriptive/prescriptive* approaches to language.

The social functions of language

I shall begin with a quotation from Dr Johnson and ask you to discern what kind of attitude he displays towards language, especially the spoken language.

> When I took the first survey of my undertaking, I found our speech copious without order, and energetic without rules: wherever I turned my view, there was perplexity to be disentangled and confusion to be regulated; choice was to be made out of boundless variety, without any established principle of selection; adulterations were to be detected without a settled test of purity; and modes of expression to be rejected or received without the suffrages of any writers of classical reputation or acknowledged authority. . . .
>
> As language was at its beginning merely oral, all words of necessary or common use were spoken before they were written; and while they were unfixed by any visible signs must have been spoken with great diversity, as we now observe those who cannot read catch sounds imperfectly and utter them negligently. When this wild and barbarous jargon was first reduced to an alphabet, every penman endeavored to express, as he could, the sounds which he was accustomed to pronounce or to receive, and vitiated in writing such words as were already vitiated in speech. The powers of the letters, when

they were applied to a new language, must have been vague and
unsettled, and therefore different hands would exhibit the same
sound by different combinations. (Samuel Johnson, Preface to
A Dictionary of the English Language (1755))

Johnson clearly distrusts some features of language, especially those
'infected' by common or 'popular' usage. In compiling his famous
dictionary, from the preface to which this extract is taken, Johnson
includes only words which can be located in written sources. The most
'barbarous' words are often those which survive in the spoken language
only. However, evidence points to the fact that all language changes
diachronically (i.e. over periods of time) and that changes are frequently
lead by what becomes common currency in the spoken word. For
example, Dr Johnson may have tried to codify the language in his
dictionary (in a certain respect he sought to purify it, too) but such
an enterprise can be shown to be ultimately futile. The fact that today
we have words such as:

coax, flimsy, bamboozle, fun, sham, snob, budge, clever

which were frowned upon as vulgarisms in the eighteenth century
illustrates that a dictionary cannot really preserve the language (although
some, like the *OED*, are constructed on historical principles and give
etymological information) but simply record it *synchronically* (i.e. at
a particular moment in time). Also, the fact that Johnson either could
find no reliable record of any of the above words (presumably because
he used only written sources) or because he thought they would disappear anyway indicates a predominantly *prescriptive* rather than
descriptive account of the language. A prescriptive view is one which
says what the language ought to be; a descriptive view describes what it
finds without judgment.[6] Of course, prescriptive views need not only
be applied to the written or more *formal* operations of language.
Writers, for example, can prescribe that only the spoken language
should be at the root of poetic vocabulary. But Johnson's attitudes
are fairly typically prescriptive. In section 3 of this article I suggest
some ways in which prescriptivism in attitudes to spoken and written
language can be investigated.[7]

Attitudes to language and poetic diction

In this section I explore the extent to which the language used in
poetry might be affected by a writer's own attitude to language.

Here is an extract from a poem entitled 'Oxford' written by Lionel Johnson and first published in 1891. It describes the speaker's farewell to his years spent as an undergraduate:

> And there, O memory more sweet than all!
> Lived he, whose eyes keep yet our passing light:
> Whose crystal lips Athenian speech recall;
> Who wears Rome's purple with least pride, most right.
>
> That is the Oxford strong to charm us yet:
> Eternal in her beauty and her past
> What though her soul be vex'd? She can forget
> Cares of an hour: only the great things last
>
> Only the gracious air, only the charm,
> And ancient might of true humanities,
> These nor assault of man, nor time can harm:
> Not these, nor Oxford with her memories.
>
> Together have we walk'd with willing feet
> Gardens of plenteous trees, bowering soft lawn;
> Hills whither Armold wanders; and all sweet
> June meadows, from the troubling world withdrawn;
>
> Chapels of cedarn fragrance, and rich gloom
> Pour'd from empurpled panes on either hand:
> Cool pavements, carved with legends of the tomb;
> Grave haunts, where we might dream, and understand
>
> Over the four long years! And unknown powers
> Call to us, going forth upon our way:
> *Ah*! Turn we, and look back upon the towers
> That rose above our lives, and cheer'd the day
>
> Proud and serene, against the sky they gleam:
> Proud and secure, upon the earth they stand
> Our city hath the air of a pure dream
> And hers indeed is a Hesperian land
>
> Think of her so! The wonderful, the fair,
> The immemorial, and the ever young:
> The city sweet with our forefathers' care:
> The city where the Muses all have sung.

Discussion of the poem can take many forms of which language is only one but the language used here by Johnson is characterized by a number of striking features:

(i)	inversion (usually of subject and verb)	— 'Ah, turn we. . .'; 'Lived he. . .'; 'Together have we walked'
(ii)	exclamation	— 'Ah! . . .'; Think of her so!' 'Over the four long years!'
(iii)	repetition	— '. . .The wonderful, the fair, the immemorial, and the ever young:'
(iv)	an archaic or 'poetical' vocabulary	— 'whither'; 'going forth'; '*bowering* soft lawn'; 'empurpled', 'hath'.

The focus here is necessarily on (iv); in fact, some attention has been drawn to this feature previously (see part 1, p. 160). It is an example of the kind of specialized poetic diction of which Dr Johnson might approve. It certainly allows poetry to be marked as poetry and not confused with anything else. And such a language has a relative permanence and 'purity' about it.[8] This can be demonstrated by looking at examples of eighteenth-century poetry from the time of Dr Johnson and noting the relative lack of variation in diction. (A good example is Thomas Gray's 'Ode on a Distant Prospect of Eton College'.)[9] It can also be demonstrated by the simple test of trying out such words in everyday use. Informants will report such words as belonging to what linguists might refer to as a specialized domain or register of poetry; or, if they do have a function in contemporary discourse, it is frequently comic or ironic, as in the example of 'alas' in 'Janet Waking'.[10] Such vocabulary has been preserved but it is a long way from common spoken discourse (and would certainly have been so in Lionel Johnson's day).

Yet not all poets adhere to such lexical 'norms'. In fact, investigation of the attitudes to language shown by a poet or writer can reveal something of his or her characteristic attitudes (perhaps even social attitudes) or those of the group to which he or she belongs. Or it might help define some of the characteristics of the period(s) in which he writes.[11] Donne and Wordsworth are two good sources for further examination.[12] Many twentieth-century poets make particular use of vocabulary which is not restricted or homogeneous in the manner of Lionel Johnson. Some mix their styles in a similar way to John Crowe Ransom (above)[13] or they move perceptibly in the direction of the spoken language as in these lines from 'Mr Bleaney' by Philip Larkin:

> 'Behind the door, no room for books or bags –
> "I'll take it". So it happens that I lie
> Where Mr. Bleaney lay, and stub my fags
> On the same saucer-souvenir, and try
>
> Stuffing my ears with cotton wool, to drown
> The jabbering set he egged her on to buy.

As T.S. Eliot has aptly and relevantly remarked: 'Every revolution in poetry is apt to be . . . a return to common speech' ('The Music of Poetry' from *Selected Essays*). Indeed, it is interesting to compare another statement of Dr Johnson from *Lives of the Poets* with another representative view of language and style from this century:

> Every language of a learned nation necessarily divides itself into diction scholastick and popular, grave and familiar, elegant and gross; and from a nice distinction of these different parts, arises a great part of the beauty of style. . . .
>
> There was . . . before the time of Dryden no poetical diction: no system of words at once refined from the grossness of domestick use and free from the harshness of terms appropriated to particular arts. Words too familiar or too remote defeat the purpose of a poet. From those sounds which we hear on small or on coarse occasions, we do not easily receive strong impressions or delightful images; and words to which we are nearly strangers, whenever they occur, draw that attention on themselves which they should transmit to things. (Samuel Johnson, *Lives of the Poets*, i, pp. 420f)

Finite and quite rigid, words are not, in any sense that holds good of bricks. They move and change, they wax and wane, they wither and burgeon; from age to age, from place to place, from mouth to mouth, they are never at a stay. They take on colour, intensity and vivacity from the infection of neighbourhood; the same word is of several shapes and diverse imports in one and the same sentence. They depend on the building they compose for the very chemistry of the stuff that composes them. The same epithet is used in the phrases 'a fine day' and 'fine irony', in 'fair trade' and 'a fair goddess'. Were different symbols to be invented for these sundry meanings the art of literature would perish. For words carry with them all the meanings they have worn, and the writer shall be judged by those that he selects for prominence in the train of his thought. A slight technical implication, a faint tinge of archaism, in the common turn of speech that you employ, and in a moment you have shaken off the mob that scours the rutted highway, and are addressing a select audience of ticket-holders within closed doors. A single natural phrase of peasant speech, a direct physical sense to a word that genteel parlance authorises readily enough in its metaphorical sense, and at a touch you have blown the roof off the drawing room of the villa, and have set its obscure inhabitants wriggling in the unaccustomed sun. In choosing a sense for your words you choose also an audience for them. (Sir Walter Raleigh, *Style* (London, 1918 edn), pp. 25–7)

In terms of poetry it is perhaps a case of the principal differences between poetic diction and poetic language. Or a prescriptive view on one hand and a descriptive view on the other? It may not be stretching things too far to examine the equations (if any) between a writer's attitude to language and his social or political views? How far is prescriptivism in language an essentially conservative stance? Can it be linked with a desire to preserve things the way they are? How far is this traceable in subject-matter and/or in a writer's statements on other subjects than language? (For a lucid treatment of this and related language matters such as archaism, dialect words, etc., with particular reference to Hopkins's poetry, see Milroy (1977), especially ch. I; Trudgill (1975) and Hughes and Trudgill (1979) are very useful on 'correctness' and the sociolinguistics of dialect study.)

3 Suggestions for classroom activities

This section is divided into three parts. Each section involves a little more advanced work and contains proposals for increasingly detailed and longer-term exercises. Frequent reference is made here to the need for discussion of particular issues. Anyone who thinks such discussion an arid and unfocussed activity should consult the transcript printed in Thornton (1980) which records group discussions of pupils in inner-London comprehensive schools examining with real insight and enthusiasm their attitudes to their own local dialects, accents and languages.[14]

What words do

One considerable advantage of the study of lexis is that it can be practically and empirically investigated. As we have seen, the categories and meta-language it generates are relatively limited and therefore some of its main organizing principles can be relatively easily unravelled. The value of its study is enhanced when studied systematically, since in exploring how it works, playing with its patterns, exploiting its potentialities can lead to freedom from the kind of inhibitions which face anyone who confronts the undifferentiated mass of vocabulary in a language. No one has yet demonstrated that conscious awareness of language structure improves pupils' own writing, but that is not to say no such links exist or cannot be made to exist. (In fact, it may be dangerous to develop performance skills in any area of human activity without some theoretical grasp, however basic.) For example, the following exercise is one of many in which discussion of *collocability, syntagmatic* and *paradigmatic* relations and lexical *associations* can take place alongside practice in performing a range of language effects:

When I	*consider*	the	*conduct*	of pop-idols,
	think about		*demeanour*	
	ponder		*ways*	
	reflect upon		*behaviour*	
	get to thinking		*goings-on*	
	about			

football stars and	*the like*	*I must confess to being*
	such people	*I am frankly*
	persons of	*honestly obliges me to*
	that description	*declare myself*

piqued	by their success and the	*wealth*	they have.
exasperated		*money*	
disconcerted		*affluence*	
narked		*opulence*	
		bread	

Of course,	they	*work*	very *hard*	; but so
All right		*labour*	*diligently*	
Granted,		*graft*		
Admittedly,		*apply themselves*		
		slog		
		toil		

do other	*people*
	folk
	blokes
	individuals.

Pupils can also test the associations or levels of formality in such items by asking informants to rate them along scales:

A 10 9 8   7   6 5 4 3 2   1
       formal   *quite formal*   *informal* *slang*

    reflect upon (?) think about (?) get to thinking about (?)

    10   9   8   7   6   5   4   3   2   1
B *formal*   *informal* *slang*

    blokes (?) folks (?) people (?)   individuals (?)

They can quickly learn from such tests (especially one that includes scales as here) that formality is not a fixed category and that much depends on the sociolinguistic function the word or lexemes have. As far as the associations of words are concerned, they might be asked what information is missing from the following definitions:

       mate = friend
        fag = cigarette
    jalopy = car
       guy = man
     boss = master or manager
bow-wow = dog

or to write an explanation of the word for reference in a dictionary for foreign learners of English.

Other ideas might include discussion of how we recognize words and their meanings. This is often usefully illustrated by means of nonsense words. For example:

A 'I found this *nibbet* of yours when I took your coat to be *slinned*. I hope they get all the marks and stains out.'
   'Yes, I put it in my pocket in case I got hungry at school.'
   'Oh, I prefer the ones with chocolate on myself.'

Or we can discuss which words might form a collocational cluster with the following:

B bidaily, cardback, excessage, disrecommend, punkly. (Examples from Bolitho and Tomlinson, 1981)

This latter activity also provides opportunities for exploring the morphological structure of words and for examining the semantic function of different prefixes, suffixes, etc.

Informant tests

Informants are simply native speakers of English who are asked to draw on an operational knowledge of their own language to assist with tests designed to establish certain descriptive facts about that language. They can be pupils from a single class or from different classes and ages across a school, teachers, parents, younger or older brothers and sisters or members of the wider community. Much depends on the nature of what needs to be tested and whether such factors as age, region, dialect, etc., are relevant but for most tests at least twenty informants would be needed to produce reliable results. Just from the material examined in this article, informants could be used to test whether certain words are felt to be primarily spoken or written, what degree of formality attaches to them (and whether this changes in different contexts), whether examples of poetic diction can be recognized, what are the most common collocational partners of certain words, etc. With regard to collocability tests, a basic technique of gap-filling is productive. For example, informants might be asked to fill in gaps like the following:[15]

a. ———— materials
b. ———— bee
c. sleeping ————

Such exploration can lead to definition of clichés and linguistic stereo-types, to a fuller account of what is involved in calling vocabulary simple or complex (see also Brazil (1969) and note 5) and a recognition of how and why some words keep many different kinds of company. Interesting results can be obtained if the same kind of tests are applied to literary texts. (For a fuller account see Carter, 1982). Examining the functions of vocabulary in the creation of literary meaning often enables us to see human language working at full stretch and for communicative ends in which we can imaginatively participate and re-participate. Too often, literary language is explored and evaluated in highly impressionistic terms and in ignorance of the structures of the language. 'Tone' - which is a crucial aspect of the effects produced by a poem like 'Janet Waking' - is just one overworked literary critical term that is only rarely specified with any real attentiveness to linguistic form and function. An approach to a literary text through a structured examination of its lexical constituents is *one* way of achieving this. Informant tests make a useful starting point and serve to remove unnecessary distinctions between 'literary' and 'non-literary' language by treating all language within the same framework. In summary, the framework is one which allows corroboration to be found for intuitions and hypotheses concerning words and the work they do.

Projects

One useful project which can be undertaken by a class is an examination of attitudes to language in the community beyond the school. The questionnaires used in a long-term linguistic survey[16] can serve as a basis or can be appropriately adapted by the teacher, to include a more exclusive focus on lexical items *per se*. Figure 10.1 shows a sample.

	Informal		Formal	
	Speech	Writing	Speech	Writing
One rarely likes to do as *he* is told.				
Roller-skating is very different *to* ice-skating.				
These sort of plays need first-class acting.				
You will learn that *at university*.				
Pulling the trigger, the gun went off unexpectedly.				
He could write *as well or better than* most people.				
She told Charles and *I* the whole story.				
It was *us* who had been singing.				
Nowadays Sunday is not observed *like* it used to be.				
He told me the story and I *implied* a great deal from it.				
They bought some tomatoes *off* a barrow-boy.				
It looked *like* it would rain.				
I *will* be twenty-one tomorrow.				
Everyone has *their* off-days.				
They will *loan* you the glasses.				

Figure 10.1

Attitudes to dialect usages can be investigated along similar lines, although a 'matched-guise' technique has a lot to recommend it for an examination of attitudes to different accents. This can take the form of playing to informants two short tape-recordings of a talk (say, on capital punishment) given either by the same speaker using standard English and a local accent or by different speakers using the same script but with different accents. Questions can be posed concerning the convincingness, intelligence, sincerity, etc., of the speakers and very interesting results obtained. (For further reading see Giles and Powesland, 1975.) *Language in Use* (Doughty, Pearce and Thornton, 1971) contains many related ideas for language projects which allow intriguing facts about prescriptive and descriptive views of language to emerge. In such activities pupils and students also learn to advance and test hypotheses, evaluate real language, examine counter-examples, marshal evidence and present verifiable conclusions.

Another valuable project is to work as a class to produce a basic or special-purpose dictionary. This can take several different forms. One useful one is a School Subject Dictionary. This involves examining the specialized domains or registers of different school subjects (e.g. physics, biology, chemistry, history, English, etc.). How far do such subjects have special vocabularies? Do different words have different collocational partners in different subjects? Are such patterns only found in text books or are they used in spoken discourse in class? What are the attitudes to such registers of (a) teachers, (b) pupils, (c) parents, (d) non-specialists with no interest in the subject? Another dictionary project for older pupils might be a Children's Dictionary. This would involve careful study of books for children in a defined age-range. It can lead to very productive examination of what should be included and excluded from such a dictionary. For example, what about the words in children's playground games and songs? What about the language of comics? (An interesting source for further activities is Chapman, Twite and Swann (1979), especially pp. 64-84.)

Finally, for combined language and literature lessons there are numerous possibilities, although space permits mention of only a few.[17]

First, as suggested in section 2, literary language and attitudes to literary language can be investigated diachronically, that is from two different points in time. This can involve comparison of statements revealing attitudes to language. Wordsworth's 'Preface to Lyrical Ballads' (1802) always makes a fascinating point of comparison. Other useful loci are W.H. Auden's 'Reading and Writing' (Auden, *The Dyer's*

Hand, Faber & Faber 1956); Swift's 'A Proposal for Correcting, Improving and Ascertaining the English Tongue' (1711–12); Pope's 'Essay on Criticism' (1711); George Orwell's 'Politics and the English Language' (in *Collected Letters, Journalism and Essays*, vol. IV, Penguin, 1968); T.S. Eliot, 'The Music of Poetry' (1942) (in *Selected Essays*, Faber & Faber); G.M. Hopkins, *Letters* (e.g. letter to Robert Bridges, 14 August 1879), in H. House and G. Storey (eds), *The Journals and Papers of Gerard Manley Hopkins* (Oxford University Press, 1959) or especially 'Poetic Diction', pp. 84–6). Or it can involve diachronic comparison of particular texts. Here eighteenth-century poems make a most useful starting point. Late Victorian poets who regularly adhere to a 'standard' poetic diction include Swinburne, D.G. and Christina Rossetti, Lionel Johnson, and W.E. Henley. The most salient examples of register-switching in the lexis of twentieth-century poets are to be found in the work of Ezra Pound, T.S. Eliot, W.H. Auden, Keith Douglas, Philip Larkin and Geoffrey Hill, or in particular texts such as Ted Hughes's *Crow* or Henry Reed's 'The Naming of Parts'. Here one crucial question to ask is what kind of relationship exists between subject-matter or theme and different kinds of poetic/stylistic representation. Another is to ask what different uses of language assume about the audience for the poem and the effects it might produce on them.

Whether some basic groundwork in language study is established first or whether the basic linguistic points can be derived from first-hand acquaintance with the literary texts will depend on the experience of a particular group and will be a matter of judgment for individual teachers. As with the related projects above, data is scrutinized in a disciplined manner and evidence presented according to well defined criteria and a framework which can be both replicable and verifiable. Only rarely are such standards met within the literary criticism to which students might be exposed.

Second, and at a rather more advanced level, projects can be set up to explore similarities and differences between literary language and the language used in other social contexts and for other sociolinguistic purposes. One useful comparative study is that of literary and advertising language (for which examples are always readily to hand). Here are some lines from recent colour supplement advertisements:

1 Drinka pinta milka day
2 Be One-Up on a Two-Car family. Drive Three (A hatchback car)
3 You can't see through a Guinness
4 Nips in and out like Ronald Biggs (BL Mini)

If literary language can be said to be characterized by such features as striking phonoaesthetic effects, by semantic ambiguities, allusiveness or lexical contrasts and patterning, then why do we not regard the above examples as literary? This and related projects do much to induce thought about the literariness of literature; pupils and students are forced to re-examine basic assumptions about language and literature; they might come to talk about literary languages rather than literary language as such and might be encouraged to explore these languages in their own writing. As Sinclair (1971) has so convincingly demonstrated, creative writing is a discipline and not at all a matter of rampant free expression. The more detailed the awareness of pupils of the norms and rules and structural properties of language the more refined their appreciation of literature and the more developed their own creative writing. As an example, here is a representative poem from a class of fifth-form comprehensive pupils I have recently worked with:

> **School : Skule**
> Why
> should we let school
> dampen
> our lives
> why let teachers rule
> our lives
> with their books to tool
> our lives for their
> way of things?
> You can
> stick it. Our
> lives are ours. Only fools
> and jerks end up in schools.
>
> 'Because school is
> an instrument of
> educational advancement and
> enriches
> our lives
> with unheard of opportunities
> like. . .'
>
> I only wish I were able to extri-
> cate
> myself from school and shout

> I hate the whole soddin' place
> Teachers, go rot
> in ditches – 'But school
> might be the pool of
> investment for future generations. I doubt
> you'll ever regret your days at school.'
>
> Sandra, aged 15

The example here has no special claims to originality but it is linguistically interesting. The class had discussed two poems by Philip Larkin, 'Toads' and 'Poetry of Departure' and the poems clearly serve as a model, in both subject-matter and style, for Sandra's expression of contradictory feelings. This is the second of a number of drafts of the poem and even at this stage shows the kind of awareness of different levels of formality, lexical associations, common partners of words, etc. that should please both literature and language teachers. As can be seen, opportunities for further work on style, rhythm, metaphor or semantic structure or for straight language essay work are by no means excluded. Even more fertile ground seems laid for a fusion of linguistic and literary interests.

Objections

Objections can and will be raised to proposals outlined here. Integrated work is always accused of dilution. Some linguists will object that this kind of application results in undue attention to language use with a corresponding absence of detail in the description of language. Literature specialists may object to the introduction of 'jargon', the classification of effects in terms of mechanical categories instead of felt responses, the subjection of creativity to rules and the reduction of literature to language at the expense of a wider context of history, study of author and periods, influences, artistic development, etc. While I would agree with Sinclair (see this volume, chapter 2) that a more rigorous core linguistics is a necessary element in the education of all teachers and especially English teachers, materials and aims have to be carefully defined when teaching language in schools. Some compromises are unavoidable; but gains are also made. The main advantages of these proposals and the kind of work based on them are that discipline is introduced into English studies; real analysis can be undertaken and pupils' awareness of and skill with language can be systematically encouraged. Literature may be produced in history but its medium was and is language and language should be foremost in the study of literature. The terminology introduced is no more opaque than terms such as 'alliteration', 'terza rima', 'iambic' or 'sestet' and traditional meta-language need not be excluded anyway. The 'jargon' is only a shorthand however; the important thing is for the concepts to be understood and the analytical categories mastered. Because students are operating with their own native language, intuitions and sensitivity will be at the centre of all analysis. All that is denied is impressionism and vagueness and the kind of creativity which can only be praised because anything goes. Integration of this kind is open to several directions of influence and can be allied with 'pure' literature and language study according to a teacher's assessment of pupils' needs or the exigencies of particular examination requirements (see next section and syllabus).

Conclusion

Conclusions are usually retrospective. In proposing a syllabus for integrated language and literary study I hope to be prospective. The aims for such a syllabus outlined here can, however, serve as a conclusion to the article. The syllabus is a tentative proposal in that it would be naïve not to recognize the obstacles that exist against integrated work. The divisions between English language and English literature are fairly deeply ingrained and are in several respects historically determined. But I hope I have shown that an integrated approach to lexis and lexis in literature is viable. This can be a basis and model for further development with reference to other levels of language organization. Such a syllabus can be easily modified to take account of different learning needs but, in general, it might serve as an outline for work in English from fourth-year secondary to first-year university level. Recommendations for examination/assessment or its status in terms of 'O' or 'A' level curriculum English are not considered at this stage but to allow further discussion and both practical and theoretical examination key texts for background reading are recommended. Finally, such a syllabus is not a prescriptive model. Not all linguistic levels need be studied and there is considerable scope for selecting different topics and texts. But it is designed to provoke debate and thus further clarify some rather fuzzy areas of English teaching.

Syllabus for integrated language and literature study

Aims

1 To develop pupils' awareness of and attitudes towards the structural and functional properties of language at different linguistic levels. To introduce some basic linguistic concepts and terminology so that pupils will have access to real analytical categories.
2 To stimulate understanding of the processes of sociolinguistic communication and to give practice to pupils in achieving defined communicative ends in writing and in speech.
3 To enable pupils to work creatively with the rules and norms of language organization.
4 To increase sensitivity of response to the way language works in literature and to raise questions about the nature of the literary artifact.

Fourth-year secondary to first-year university 14–18 age group (approx.)

I *Lexis*		Attitudes to language. Descriptive v. prescriptive approaches. Lexis and social context: associations, formality, dialect and accent. Connotation and denotation. Collocations, lexical cluster and span. Lexical domains. Register. Etymology and words. Synchronic and diachronic description. Poetic diction and poetic language. Semantic ambiguity in literature. Structural semantics: synonymy, antonymy and hyponymy (see note 5 below). Structure in literary text.
Key text(s)		D. Crystal and D. Davy, *Investigating English Style* (Longman, 1969) plus e.g. J. Hayward (ed.), *Penguin Book of English Prose: Essays by English Authors* (Penguin, 1967).
II *Discourse*		Pronouns and the social functions of language; tense as modality; address forms; shared knowledge and membershipping; turn taking; speech acts – overlap of grammatical mood and discourse function. Paralinguistic communication. Kinesics. Hesitation phenomena and pauses in conversation. Monologues and dialogues.
Key text(s)		R.M. Coulthard, *Introduction to Discourse Analysis* (Longman, 1977) plus e.g.
	Shakespeare	*Soliloquies*
	Browning	*Dramatic Monologues*

	D.H. Lawrence	*Sons and Lovers* (dialogue)
	Shaw	*Pygmalion* (also useful for I)
	Pinter	*Request Stop; Last to Go*
	Beckett	*Happy Days*

III *Syntax*   Groundwork in methods, using the most accessible units of English syntax – the lowest and highest units.

Morphology: Innovation
Texts e.g. Thomas   *Under Milk Wood*
　　　　　 Burgess   *A Clockwork Orange*

Morphology: Repetition
Texts e.g. Lawrence *The Rainbow*

Sentence types: Variation
　　　　　 Donne   *Sermons*
　　　　　　　　　　 'The Sun Rising'
　　　　　 Auden   'Stop All the Clocks'

Sentence types: Repetition
　　　　　 Auden   'Oh What is That Sound?'
　　　　　　　　　　 'From Reader to Rider'
　　　　　 Owen   'Futility'

Application to nominal structures.

Nominal groups: Repetition
Texts e.g. Morgan   'Off Course'
　　　　　　 Selection of imagist and concrete poetry.

Nominal groups: Development
Texts e.g. Roethke   'Child on Top of a Green-house'
　　　　　 Wordsworth   'Tintern Abbey'

Pronouns
Texts e.g. Graves   'The Legs'
　　　　　 Auden   'Stop All the Clocks'
　　　　　 Lawrence *Studies in Classic American Literature*

Nominal groups: Complex
Texts e.g. MacNeice 'Morning Song'

Nominal groups: Advanced
Texts e.g. Thomas   *Under Milk Wood*
　　　　　 Beckett   'Ping'

Application to verb and clause structures.

Personification
Texts e.g. Plath   *The Bell Jar*

Transitivity
Texts e.g. Golding   *The Inheritors*
　　　　　　　　　　 Pincher Martin

Verb tense in narrative
Texts e.g. Hughes   'Hawk-Roosting'
　　　　　 Joyce   *A Portrait of the Artist*
　　　　　 Frayn   *A Very Private Life*

Runyon   *Runyon on Broadway*
Clause structures: Theme
Texts e.g. Tolkien   *Lord of the Rings*
Clause structures: Complex
Texts e.g. James   *The Ambassadors*

N.B. Many of the texts suggested are the subject of published papers
in stylistics, listed in the Bibliography.

In the case of long texts, clearly only short extracts need be
used in class.

Key text	R. Quirk and S. Greenbaum, *A University Grammar of English* (London, 1973) (relevant sections)
IV *Phonology*	The organization of sounds in English. Introduction to broad transcription. 'Hard' and 'soft' sounds; 'open' and 'closed' vowels; sonority; voicing. Analysing phonetic patterns in poetry. Phonemes and allophones. Rhythm and metrics. Intonation and spoken dialogue in novels and plays. Intonation and discourse.
Key text	E. Traugott and M.L. Pratt (1980) ch. 2 (see below) plus selected poems, e.g. Tennyson 'In Memoriam'; Hopkins 'The Windhover', 'Inversnaid', 'Pied Beauty', 'No Worst, there is None'; Keats 'Ode to Autumn'; Auden 'The Wanderer'.

Background Reading

Bolinger, D., *Language, the Loaded Weapon* (London,
Longman, 1980).

Carter, R.A. (ed.), *Language and Literature: A Reader in
Stylistics* (London, Allen and Unwin, 1982).

Cluysenaar, A., *Introduction to Literary Stylistics* (London,
Batsford, 1976).

Fowler, R., *Linguistics and the Novel* (London, Methuen,
1977).

O'Donnell, W. and Todd, L., *Variety in Contemporary English*
(London, Allen & Unwin, 1980).

Traugott, E. and Pratt, M.L., *Linguistics for Students of
Literature* (London/New York, Harcourt Brace Jovanovich, 1980).

Notes

1 *Lexical items* or lexemes is a more appropriate bit of metalanguage
than vocabulary. For example in the following sentences lexical
items are underlined to show the difficulties in seeing vocabulary
or collocates only in terms of single words:

(a) He's *a dark horse*, Mr. Jones.

(b) I've got *pins and needles* in my leg.

(c) It's raining *cats and dogs*.

In (b) *pins* and *needles* separately would have different collocational ranges. For further reading in the analysis of lexis see Halliday (1966), Sinclair (1966b).

2 Though not exclusively so. Unusual or deviant language is not an automatic mark of literariness, despite the familiar reference to e.e. cummings and Dylan Thomas whenever literary language is mentioned. For a discussion of this question and of lexis generally see an article by C.J.E. Ball, 'Lexis: The Vocabulary of English' (Ball, 1975).

3 For an interesting discussion of this see Leech (1969).

4 'Logopoeia' is a term used by Ezra Pound to describe poetry involving clashes of different linguistic tones and registers. See Pound (1927). For further suggestions see my article 'Register, Styles and Teaching Some Aspects of the Language of Literature' (Carter, 1978).

5 Useful extensions to the ideas outlined here can be found in Keen (1978), especially ch. 4 and, with particular reference to lexis in literary texts, in Widdowson (1975), pp. 104–8 and 116–24, where the analysis is of two poems by Robert Frost. Another important area of vocabulary which is generally termed 'structural semantics' is extensively covered in Lyons (1977), chs 8 and 9. Its relevance to the analysis of a literary text (the opening to Iris Murdoch's *The Sandcastle*) is explored in Brazil (1969). 'Componential analysis' of lexis is discussed in the paper by Mike Riddle in this volume (chapter 3).

6 See W.H. Mittins (1969).

7 It is interesting to note at this juncture that words do also disappear from spoken currency. For example, 'weary', 'betrothal', 'martial', subjectively at least, seem to be hardly used in the spoken language. There are many others. The account of differences between spoken and written language needs amplifying. For a clear and comprehensive account see Stubbs (1980).

8 A useful introductory book in this area (though it is a little sketchy in discussion of language) is called, appropriately, *Purity of Diction in English Verse* (Davie, 1952). A more linguistic account is Milroy (1977).

9 See Leech (1969), p. 16.

10 A good test of this is to substitute a 'poetic' word for the 'non-poetic' word. For example, I like the look of your steed (horse); My husband collects the finny tribe (fish); I'm going out to mow the verdure (grass).

11 An excellent study of modern poetry as social discourse is Raban (1971). Crucially, too, he has much of considerable value to say about the relationship between style and meaning.

12 Both in their own way attempt to break with the conventionalities of the existing poetic decorum.

13 For further discussion and suggested approaches to teaching such poetry see Carter (1981). The main text discussed is a poem by W.H. Auden.
14 See particularly Thornton (1980, pp. 56–62). But also Richmond (1979) and, from a more theoretical perspective, Wight (1971).
15 For a truly systematic test both collocates would need to be blocked out and offered to measurably equal numbers of informants. Tests for informants' attitudes to 'literary' and 'non-literary' language can be made by blanking out collocates in a poem and in de-contextualized prose versions of the same text (see Carter, 1982).
16 W.H. Mittins, M. Salu, M. Edminson, S. Clyne. *Attitudes to English Usage* (Oxford University Press, London, 1970).
17 For a connected argument see Burke and Brumfit (1974).

Glossary

Generally speaking, writers for this book have attempted to gloss definitions in the course of their articles.

The following is a list of definitions of terms which have not been otherwise contextualized in the particular articles. It is by no means a complete glossary of terms currently in use in educational linguistics. Neither are descriptions of this kind wholly adequate except as working definitions. Wherever possible use should be made of relevant items in the bibliography for fuller explanation. Readers are also directed to the following sources which also contain useful definitions of linguistic terms (1) D. Crystal, *A First Dictionary of Linguistics and Phonetics,* London, Deutsch, 1980; (2) Glossary and Index to Open University Course PE 232 Language Development (Open University Press, 1979); (3) Glossary to A. Cruttenden, *Language in Infancy and Childhood,* Manchester University Press, 1979; (4) Glossary to P. Gannon and P. Czerniewska. *Using Linguistics: An Educational Focus,* London, Arnold, 1980.

ACCENT Those features of an individual's pronunciation which signal where he is from, regionally or socially.

    The term is also used synonymously with *stress* to indicate the marking of a certain syllable(s) in a word or utterance.

ALLOPHONE Allophones are variants of phonemes which occur in particular phonetic environments. For example, the *p* in *ship* and *pin* is articulated plosively only in the case of 'pin' where it occurs initially. Each phoneme can have in principle different allophonic variations according to such factors as the pronunciations of different individuals in different speech communities.

ANTONYM A gradable opposite in meaning to a word or phrase. See SYNONYM.

ASSIMILATION The process whereby one sound changes to another as a result of the influence of an adjacent sound. For example, 'ten balls' in normal colloquial speech would see *n* assimilated to *m*, the *n* having acquired a bilabial shape from the neighbouring *b*.

COHESION An umbrella term for the ways in which different meaning relations in a text are combined intersententially. The most comprehensive introduction to cohesion is Halliday and Hasan (1976).

CONNOTATION This is contrasted with DENOTATION and refers to the emotional, attitudinal or communal associations of a lexical item. Such associations are to a considerable extent part of the meaning of that lexical item.

DENOTATION is generally equivalent to the referential meaning of a lexical item. For example, 'bitch' is a 'female canine quadruped' but the connotative meaning of the word can carry very different associations. See CONNOTATION.

DIALECT Those features of language which vary in grammar and vocabulary and which can be associated with a particular social group or geographical region.

DISCOURSE This is an umbrella term covering related aspects of language organization. It is used (a) to refer to the organization of connected text beyond the level of the sentence (b) the linguistic examination of conversational interaction (see Sinclair and Coulthard, 1975), (c) the contextual functions of different grammatical forms and the rules pertaining to particular interactive features of human interchange. This is also known as speech act theory.

HYPONYM One of a set of lexical items in a relationship with a more embracing or superordinate word. For example, 'rose' and 'geranium' are hyponyms of *flower*.

KINESICS See PARALINGUISTIC.

META-LANGUAGE A higher-level language used for describing the object of study. In linguistics, the language used to describe language is typified by the terms entered in this glossary and others.

MOOD This is a general term used to refer to different sentence types. The main moods in English are *imperative* (stop!), *interrogative* (would you like to go to bed?), and *declarative* (it's time to stop now).

But there is no direct equation between grammatical mood forms and semantic or DISCOURSE function since both the latter examples can in certain contexts (an adult to a young child) operate as imperatives.

MORPHOLOGY This is a branch of grammar within which word structure and word forms are studied.

A MORPHEME is the smallest meaningful unit of language for grammatical analysis. *House, cat* and *dog* are *free* morphemes i.e. they can stand as words in their own right. *Bound* morphemes cannot occur as separate words. *Unselfish*, for example, consists of three morphemes: *self* is a free morpheme; *un* and *ish* are bound forms. In cats and dog*s* the *s* is a bound morpheme.

PARALINGUISTIC Non-verbal aspects of communication which may include facial expression and gesture (also referred to as KINESICS) or relative position to one's interlocutor(s) also referred to as PROXEMICS). For some linguists paralanguage can also include non-verbal aspects of sound such as voice quality and pitch, hesitation noises, etc., etc.

PHONEME Sounds which can transmit the difference between possible pairs of lexical items. For example, the phonemes /p/ and /b/ in *pin* and *bin*. Phonemes may also have different ALLOPHONES:

for example, in English /l/ is pronounced 'clear' before a vowel (*l*eaf) but 'dark' elsewhere (kee*l*). But allophonic differences do not signal a difference in lexical item.

PROXEMICS See PARALINGUISTIC.

REFERENCE A type of COHESION in English which depends for its interpretation on the presence of other items in the text.

REGISTER A rather imprecise term which describes the kind of language used appropriate to a particular function in a situational context. Features of language are selected with reference to content, purpose, the relation of the language user to an audience. For example, there are registers of legal English, advertising English, etc., etc.

SONORITY A term used in phonetics to identify the loudness of a sound relative to other sounds with the same pitch, stress and duration. It is, however, difficult to account for sonority objectively.

SPEECH-ACT THEORY See DISCOURSE

SYNONYM A word or phrase similar in meaning to another word or phrase. See ANTONYM.

TENSE (a) A feature of the description of verbs which refers principally to the way grammar marks the duration of an action or the time at which the action denoted by the verb took place.
(b) Tense *as modality* accounts for the semantic function of tense. For example, 'I *wondered* if I could speak with you' uses tense not to mark pastness but rather a certain deferentiality on the part of the speaker. Other functions accrue to what are conventionally present and future tenses.

TRANSITIVITY A transitive verb is one which has a grammatical object affected by the 'action' of the verb. For example,

The man *hit* the ball

'hit' here is a transitive verb. In the sentence:

An hour *elapsed*

'elapsed' is intransitive, i.e. it can never take an object.

VOICING Sounds produced by the vibration of the vocal cords to set the air stream in motion.
For example, in the phrase 'cat*s* and dog*s*, the 's' in the first word is unvoiced, the 's' in the second word voiced.

Bibliography

References

The following items are the entries for references and sources cited in individual articles in this volume.

Anglin, T. (1971), *The Growth of Word Meaning*, Cambridge (Mass.), MIT Press.

Australian Department of Education (1977), *Education in Australia*, Canberra, Australian Government Publishing Service.

Bailey, M. (1979), *Oilgate*, London, Hodder & Stoughton.

Ball, C.J.E. (1975), 'Lexis: the vocabulary of English', in W.F. Bolton (ed.), *The English Language*, London, Sphere Books.

Bates, E. and Benigni, L. (1975), 'Rules of address in Italy: a sociological survey', *Language in Society*, vol. 4, no. 3, pp. 271-88.

Bernstein, B. (1959), 'A public language: some sociological implications of a linguistic form', *British Journal of Sociology*, vol. 10, pp. 311-26.

Blom, J. and Gumperz, J. (1972), 'Social meaning in linguistic structures: code-switching in Norway', in J. Gumperz and D. Hymes (eds), *Directions in Sociolinguistics*, New York, Holt, Rinehart & Winston.

Bogatyrev, P. (1972), *The Functions of Folk Costume in Moravian Slovakia* (English translation, 1971), The Hague, Mouton.

Bolitho, R. and Tomlinson, B. (1981), *Discovers English*, London, Allen & Unwin.

Bormuth, J.R. (1966), 'Readability: a new approach', *Reading Research Quarterly*, vol. 1, pp. 79-132.

Bormuth, J.R., Manning, J., Carr, J. and Pearson, D. (1970), 'Children's comprehension of between-and-within-sentence syntactic structures', *Journal of Educational Psychology*, vol. 61, pp. 349-57.

Botel, M., Dawkins, J. and Granowsky, A. (1973), 'A syntactic complexity formula', in W.H. Macgintie (ed.), *Assessment Problems in Reading*, Newark (Delaware), International Reading Association.

Brazil, D. (1969), 'Kinds of English – spoken, written, literary', *Educational Review*, vol. 22, no. 1, pp. 78–92.

Brown, G. (1977), *Listening to Spoken English*, London, Longman.

Brown, G. (1978), 'Understanding spoken language', *TESOL Quarterly*, vol. 12, no. 3, pp. 271–83.

Brown, R. and Ford, M. (1961), 'Address in American English', *Journal of Abnormal and Social Psychology*, vol. 62, pp. 375–85.

Brown, R. and Gilman, A. (1960), 'The pronouns of power and solidarity', in T. Sebeok (ed.), *Style in Language*, Cambridge (Mass.), MIT Press.

Brumby, E. and Vaszolyi, E. (eds) (1977), *Language Problems of Aboriginal Education*, Western Australia, Mount Lawley College.

Burgess, C. *et al.* (1973), *Understanding Children Writing*, Harmondsworth, Penguin.

Burke, S.J. and Brumfit, C.J. (1974), 'Is literature language? *or* is language literature?', *English in Education*, vol. 8, no. 2, pp. 33–43.

Campbell-Platt, K. (1976), 'Distribution of linguistic minorities in Britain', in CILT (1976), pp. 15–30.

Carter, R.A. (1978), 'Register, styles and teaching some aspects of the language of literature', *Educational Review*, vol. 30, no. 3, pp. 227–36.

Carter, R.A. (1980), 'Linguistics, the teacher and language development,' *Educational Review*, vol. 32, no. 2, pp. 223–8.

Carter, R.A. (1982), 'Responses to language in literature', in R.A. Carter and D. Burton (eds), *Literary Text and Language Study*, London, Arnold.

Cashdan, A. and Grugeon, E. (eds) (1972), *Language in Education*, London, Routledge & Kegan Paul.

Chapman, J., Twite, S. and Swann, J. (1979), *Words and their Meanings*, Block 3, PE 232, Open University Language Development Course, Milton Keynes, Open University Press.

Chomsky, N. (1972), 'Language and Mind', in A. Cashdan and E. Grudgeon (eds) (1972).

Chomsky, N. (1979), *Language and Responsibility*, Brighton, Harvester Press.

CILT (1976), *Bilingualism and British Education: The Dimensions of Diversity*, London, Centre for Information on Language Teaching and Research.

Clay, M.M. (1969), 'Reading errors and self-correction behaviour', *British Journal of Educational Psychology*, vol. 39, pp. 47–56.

Crystal, D. (1976), *Child Language, Learning and Linguistics*, London, Edward Arnold.

Crystal, D. and Davy, D. (1969), *Investigating English Style*, London, Longman.

Culler, J. (1973), 'The linguistic basis of structuralism', in D. Robey (ed.), *Structuralism: An Introduction*, Oxford, Clarendon Press.

Culler, J. (1975), *Structuralist Poetics*, London, Routledge & Kegan Paul.

Czerniewska, P. (1981), 'The teacher, language development and linguistics: a response to Ronald Carter's review of Open University Course PE 232, "Language Development"', *Educational Review*, vol.

3, no. 1, pp. 37–41.

Czerniewska, P. and Twite, S. (1979), *Patterns of Language*, Block II, OU Language Development Course PE 232, Milton Keynes, Open University Press.

Dale, E. and Chall, J.S. (1948), 'A formula for predicting readability', *Educational Research Bulletin*, vol. 27, pp. 11–20, 37–54.

Das Gupta, J. (1969), 'Official language problems and politics in South Asia', in T.A. Sebeok (ed.) (1963–76).

Davie, D. (1952), *The Purity of Diction in English Verse*, London, Chatto & Windus.

DES (1975), *A Language for Life*, The Bullock Report, London, HMSO.

DES (1978), *Primary Education in England*, London, HMSO.

DES (1979), *Aspects of Secondary Education in England*, London, HMSO.

Dixon, R.M.W. (1971), 'A method of semantic description', in D.D. Steinberg and L.A. Jakobovits (eds) (1971), pp. 436–71.

Doughty, P., Pearce, J. and Thornton G. (1971), *Language in Use*, London, Arnold.

Edwards, R.P.A. and Gibbon, V. (1964, 1973 2nd rev. edn), *Words Your Children Use*, London, Burke Books.

Ervin-Tripp, S. (1976), 'Is Sybil there? – The structure of some American English directives', *Language in Society*, vol. 5, pp. 25–66.

Fagan, W.T. (1971), 'Transformations and comprehension', *Reading Teacher*, vol. 25, pp. 169–72.

Ferguson, C. (1959), 'Diglossia', *Word*, vol. 15, pp. 325–40.

Fishman, J. (1972), 'Domains and the relationship between micro-sociolinguistics and macro-sociolinguistics', in J. Gumperz and D. Hymes (eds) (1972).

Flesch, R.F. (1948), 'A new readability yardstick', *Journal of Applied Psychology*, vol. 32, pp. 221–33.

Fletcher, P. and Garman, M. (eds) (1979), *Language Acquisition*, London, Cambridge University Press.

Flew, A. (1975), *Thinking about Thinking*, London, Fontana.

Fodor, J. and Garrett, M. (1967), 'Some syntactic determinants of sentential complexity', *Perception and Psychophysics*, vol. 2, no. 7, pp. 289–96.

Fries, C.C. (1962), *Linguistics and Reading*, New York, Holt, Rinehart & Winston.

Fry, E.B. (1968), 'A readability formula that saves time', *Journal of Reading*, vol. 11, pp. 513–16, 575–8.

Galloway, P. (1973), 'How secondary students and teachers read textbooks', *Journal of Reading*, vol. 17, no. 3, pp. 216–19.

Gannon, P. and Czerniewska, P. (1980), *Using Linguistics: an Educational Focus*, London, Arnold.

Gardner, P.L. (1977), *Logical Connectives in Science*, mimeographed report to the Australian Education Research and Development Committee.

Giles, H. and Powesland, P.F. (1975), *Speech Style and Social Evalua-*

tion, London, Academic Press.

Givon, T. (1979), 'From discourse to syntax: grammar as a processing strategy', in T. Givon (ed.), *Syntax and Semantics 12: Discourse and Syntax*, London, Academic Press.

Goodman, K.S. (1967), 'Reading: a psycholinguistic guessing game', repr. in H. Singer and R.B. Ruddell (eds), *Theoretical Models and Processes of Reading*, Newark (Delaware), International Reading Association, pp. 497–508.

Goody, J. (1977), *The Domestication of the Savage Mind*, London, Cambridge University Press.

Gough, P.B. (1972), 'One second of reading', in J.F. Kavanagh and I. Mattingly (eds) (1972), *Language by Ear and by Eye*, Cambridge, (Mass.), MIT Press, pp. 331–58.

Gould, C. (1977), 'The readability of school biology textbooks', *Journal of Biological Education*, vol. 11, pp. 248–52.

Grassby, A.J. (1977), 'Linguistic genocide', in E. Brumby and E. Vaszolyi (eds) (1977), pp. 1–4.

Gumperz, J. and Hymes, D. (eds) (1972), *Directions in Sociolinguistics*, New York, Holt, Rinehart & Winston.

Hakes, D.T. (1972), 'Effects of reducing complement constructions on sentence comprehension', *Journal of Verbal Learning and Verbal Behaviour*, vol. 11, pp. 278–86.

Hale, K. (1971), 'A note on a Walbiri tradition of antonymy', in D.D. Steinberg and L.A. Jakobovits (eds) *Semantics*, Cambridge University Press.

Halliday, M.A.K. (1966), 'Lexis as a linguistic level', in C.E. Bazell *et al.* (eds), *In Memory of J.R. Firth*, London, Longman.

Halliday, M.A.K. (1971), 'Linguistic function and literary style', in S. Chatman (ed.), *Literary Style: A Symposium*, London, Oxford University Press.

Halliday, M.A.K. (1974), Review of R. Shuy (ed.) *Sociolinguistics*, *Language in Society*, vol. 3, pp. 94–103.

Halliday, M.A.K. and Hasan, R. (1976), *Cohesion in English*, London, Longman.

Harrison, C. (1979), 'Assessing the readability of school texts', in E. Lunzer and K. Gardner (eds), *The Effective Use of Reading*, London, Heinemann.

Hawkins, E.W. (1979), 'Language as a curriculum study', in *The Mother Tongue and Other Languages in Education*, NCLE, Papers and Reports 2. London, Centre for Information on Language Teaching and Research, pp. 61–70.

Hellige, J.B. (1975), 'An analysis of some psychological studies of grammar: the role of generated abstract memory', in D.W. Massaro (ed.) (1975).

HMSO (1921), *The Teaching of English in England*, The Newbolt Report, London.

Holbrook, D. (1973), *English in Australia Now*, London, Cambridge University Press.

Hughes, A. and Trudgill, P. (1979), *English Accents and Dialects*, London, Arnold.

Jacobson, M.D. (1965), 'Reading difficulty of physics and chemistry textbooks', *Educational and Psychological Measurement*, vol. 25, pp. 449–57.

Jakobson, R. (1960), 'Closing statement: linguistics and poetics', in T.A. Sebeok (ed.), *Style in Language*, Cambridge (Mass.), MIT Press.

Johnstone, A. (1978), 'What's in a word?', *New Scientist*, 18 May.

Jones, P.E. (1974), *Education in Australia*, Newton Abbot, David & Charles.

Kachru, B.B. (1969), 'English in South Asia', in T.A. Sebeok (1963–76).

Kaiser, R.A., Neils, C.F., and Floriani, B.P. (1975), 'Syntactic complexity of primary grade reading materials: a preliminary look', *Reading Teacher*, vol. 29, pp. 262–6.

Keen, J. (1978), *Teaching English: A Linguistic Approach*, London, Methuen.

Khan, V. (1976), 'Provision by minorities for language maintenance', in CILT (1976), pp. 31–47.

Klare, G.R. (1974), 'Assessing readability', *Reading Research Quarterly*, vol. 10, pp. 62–102.

Kucera, H. and Francis, W. (1967), *Computational Analysis of Present-Day American English*, Providence (Rhode Island), Brown University Press.

Labov, W. (1972a), *Sociolinguistic Patterns*, Philadelphia, University of Pennsylvania Press.

Labov, W. (1972b), 'Some principles of linguistic methodology', *Language in Society*, vol. 1, no. 1, pp. 97–120.

Lakoff, R. (1972), 'Language in context', *Language*, vol. 48, no. 4, pp. 907–26.

Leach, E. (1972), 'Our words', *New Society*, 19 October.

Leech, G. (1969), *A Linguistic Guide to English Poetry*, London, Longman.

Leech, G. (1974), *Semantics*, Harmondsworth, Penguin.

Leech, G. and Svartvik, J. (1975), *A Communicative Grammar of English*, London, Longman.

Levin, S. (1962), *Linguistic Structures in Poetry*, The Hague, Mouton.

Levin, S. (1977), *The Semantics of Metaphor*, Baltimore, Johns Hopkins University Press.

Lipton, J. (1977), *An Exaltation of Larks, or the Venereal Game*, 2nd edn, Harmondsworth, Penguin.

Lyons, J. (1977), *Semantics*, vols I and II, Cambridge University Press.

McDonough, J.E. and McDonough, D.H. (1978), 'Teaching English as a foreign language and mother tongue teaching: some parallels', *Educational Review*, vol. 30, no. 3, pp. 237–46.

Mackay, D., Thomson, B. and Schaub, P. (1970), *Breakthrough to Literacy: Teachers Manual*, London, Longman.

Malicky, G.V. (1976), 'The effect of deletion produced structures on word identification and comprehension of beginning readers', *Reading Research Quarterly*, vol. 11, pp. 212-16.

Martin, N., *et al.* (1976), *Writing and Learning Across the Curriculum 11-16*, London, Ward Lock.

Massaro, D.W. (ed.) (1975), *Understanding Language*, London, Academic Press.

Miller, C. and Swift, K. (1976), *Words and Women*, Harmondsworth, Penguin, 1979.

Miller, G.A. (1956), 'The magical number seven, plus or minus two: some limits on our capacity for processing information', *Psychological Review*, vol. 63, pp. 81-97.

Milroy, J. (1977), *The Language of Gerard Manley Hopkins*, London, Deutsch.

Mittins, W.H. (1969), 'What is correctness?', *Educational Review*, vol. 22, no. 1, pp. 51-63.

Morehead, D.M. and Morehead, A.E. (eds) (1976), *Normal and Deficient Child Language*, Baltimore, University Park Press.

NCLE (National Congress on Languages in Education) (1981), *Report of Working Party C: A Comparison of the Various Methodologies and Materials involved in the Teaching of English as a Foreign Language, Modern Languages and the Mother Tongue, and an Examination of their Relevance to Each Other*, London, Centre for Information on Language Teaching and Research.

Ochs, E. (1979), 'Planned and unplanned discourse', in T. Givon (ed.) (1979).

Orton, H., Sanderson, S. and Widdowson, J. (eds) (1977), *The Linguistic Atlas of England*, London, Croom Helm.

Otterburn, M.K. and Nicholson, A.R. (1976), 'The language of CSE mathematics', *Mathematics in School*, vol. 5, no. 5, pp. 18-20.

Palmer, F. (1974), *The English Verb*, London, Longman.

Pearson, P.D. (1976), 'The effects of grammatical complexity on children's comprehension, recall and conception of certain semantic relations in H. Singer and R.B. Ruddell (eds) *Theoretical Models and Processes of Reading*, Newark, Delaware, International Reading Association, pp. 67-102.

Peltz, K.F. (1974), 'The effect upon comprehension of repatterning based on students' writing patterns', *Reading Research Quarterly*, vol. 9, pp. 603-21.

Platt, J.T. (1975), 'The Singapore English speech continuum and its basilect "singlish" as a "creoloid"', *Anthropological Linguistics*, vol. 17, no. 7, pp. 363-74.

Platt, J.T. (1977), 'A model for polyglossia and multilingualism (with special reference to Singapore and Malaysia)', *Language in Society*, vol. 6, pp. 361-78.

Potter, S. (1974), 'English Language', *Encyclopaedia Britannica Macropaedia*, vol. 6, Chicago, William Benton, pp. 874-87.

Pound, E. (1927), 'How to read', repr. in *Literary Essays*, London, Faber & Faber, 1954.

Prestt, B. (1976), 'Science education: a reappraisal', *School Science Review*, vol. 57, no. 201, pp. 628-34.

Pyrczak, F. (1976), 'Readability of "Instructions for form 1040"',

Journal of Reading, vol. 20, pp. 121-7.

Quirk, R. (1974), 'Charles Dickens, linguist', in R. Quirk, *The Linguist and the English Language*, London, Arnold.

Quirk, R., Leech, G., Greenbaum, S. and Svartvik, J. (1972), *A Gramm Grammar of Contemporary English*, London, Longman.

Quirk, R. and Greenbaum, S. (1973), *A University Grammar of English*, London, Longman.

Raban, J. (1971), *The Society of the Poem*, London, Harrap.

Reid, J.F. (1958), 'An investigation of thirteen beginners in reading', *Acta Psychologica*, vol. 15, pp. 295-313.

Reid, J.F. (1972), 'Children's comprehension of syntactic features found in some extension readers', in J.F. Reid (ed.), *Reading Problems and Practices*, London, Ward Lock, pp. 394-403.

Richmond, J. (1979), 'Jennifer and "Brixton Blues": language alive in school', in *Supplementary Readings for Block 5*, PE 232 Language Development Course, Milton Keynes, Open University Press.

Rosten, L. (1968), *The Joys of Yiddish*, Harmondsworth, Penguin, 1971.

Ruddell, R.B. (1965), 'The effect of oral and written patterns of language structure on reading comprehension', *Reading Teacher*, vol. 18, pp. 270-5.

Searle, J.R. (1976), 'A classification of illocutionary acts', *Language in Society*, vol. 5, pp. 1-23.

Sebeok, T.A. (ed.) (1963-76), *Current Trends in Linguistics*, vols. 1-14, The Hague, Mouton.

Sinclair, J.Mc.H. (1966a), 'Taking a poem to pieces', in R. Fowler (ed.), *Essays on Style and Language: Linguistic and Critical Approaches to Literary Style*, London, Routledge & Kegan Paul.

Sinclair, J.Mc.H. (1966b), 'Beginning the study of lexis', in C.E. Bazell *et al.* (eds), *In Memory of J.R. Firth*, London, Longman.

Sinclair, J.Mc.H. (1971), 'The integration of language and literature in the curriculum', *Educational Review*, vol. 23, no. 2,: rev. version in R.A. Carter and D. Burton (eds), *Literary Text and Language Study*, London, Arnold, 1982.

Spache, G.D. (1974), *Good Reading for Poor Readers*, Champaign (Illinois), Ganard.

Spencer, J. (ed.) (1971), *The English Language in West Africa*, tic essay', *Lingua*, vol. 16, pp. 57-70.

Spencer, J. (ed.), (1971), *The English Language in West Africa*, London, Longman.

Steinberg, D.D. and Jakobovits, L.A. (eds) (1971), *Semantics*, London, Cambridge University Press.

Stocker, L.P. (1971-2), 'Increasing the precision of the Dale-Chall readability formula', *Reading Improvement*, vol. 8, pp. 87-9.

Stokes, A. (1978), 'The reliability of readability formulae', *Journal of Research in Reading*, vol. 1, pp. 21-34.

Stork, C. *et al.* (1980), 'Language study in secondary education', *English in Education*, vol. 14, no. 2, pp. 23-34 and vol. 14, no. 3, pp. 18-29.

Strang, B.M.H. (1970), *A History of English*, London, Methuen.

Stratta, L., Dixon, J. and Wilkinson, A. (1973), *Patterns of Language: Explorations of the Teaching of English*, London, Heinemann.

Stubbs, M. (1980), *Language and Literacy: the Sociolinguistics of Reading and Writing*, London, Routledge & Kegan Paul.

Tatham, S.M. (1970), 'Reading comprehension of materials written with select oral language patterns: a study at grades two and four', *Reading Research Quarterly*, vol. 5, pp. 402–26.

Taylor, G. (1981), 'English mother tongue teaching' in NCLE (1981).

Theberge, V.E. and Braun, C. (1977), 'The effect of deletion-produced syntactic structures on reading comprehension', *Reading Horizons*, vol. 17, pp. 183–9.

Thornton, G. (1980), *Teaching Writing*, London, Arnold.

Tinkel, T. (1979), 'A proposal for the teaching of linguistics at the secondary school level', *MALS Journal*, no. 4, pp. 79–100.

Tough, J. (1973), *Focus on Meaning*, London, Allen & Unwin.

Tough, J. (1977), *The Development of Meaning*, London, Allen & Unwin.

Trudgill, P. (1975), *Accent Dialect and the School*, London, Arnold.

Trudgill, P. (ed.) (1978), *Sociolinguistic Patterns in British English*, London, Arnold.

Turner, G.W. (1966), *The English Language in Australia and New Zealand*, London, Longman.

Unwin, S. and Dewar, R. (1961), *The Miscillian Manuscript*, London, Cassell.

Valkhoff, M.F. (1971), 'Descriptive bibliography of the linguistics of Afrikaans', in T. Sebeok (ed.) (1963–76), vol. 7, pp. 455–500.

Wang, M.D. (1970), 'The role of syntactic complexity as a determiner of comprehensibility', *Journal of Verbal Learning and Verbal Behaviour*, vol. 9, pp. 398–404.

Weber, R.M. (1970), 'A linguistic analysis of first-grade reading errors', *Reading Research Quarterly*, vol. 5, no. 3, pp. 427–51.

Whalley, P.C. and Fleming, R.W. (1975), 'An experiment with a simple recorder of reading behaviour', *Programmed Learning and Educational Technology*, vol. 12, no. 2, pp. 120–3.

Widdowson, H.G. (1975), *Stylistics and the Teaching of Literature*, London, Longman.

Wight, J. (1971), 'Dialect in School', *Educational Review*, vol. 24, no. 1, pp. 47–58.

Wilkinson, A. *et al.* (1980), *Assessing Language Development*, London, Oxford University Press.

Will, C. van der (1976), 'The wording of spoken instructions to children and its effect on their performance of tasks', *Educational Studies*, vol. 2, pp. 193–9.

Select bibliography

An introduction to educational linguistics

The following items have been selected by the contributors to this book as the books and articles which provide the most useful introduction to language studies in education *from a specifically linguistic viewpoint*. A number of books containing relevant material have therefore been omitted either because they are not particularly introductory, or because – though dealing with language and education – are not linguistically principled in approach. A number of items here do contain references to more advanced material (as do the references to particular articles in this volume) and liberal use should be made of such bibliographies at an appropriate time. It is important that readers bear in mind the limited and introductory nature of this short bibliography and note that material generally refers to mother-tongue teaching only.

Brown, G. (1977), *Listening to Spoken English*, London, Longman.

Cazden, C., John, V. and Hymes, D. (eds) (1972), *Functions of Language in the Classroom*, Columbia (New York), Teachers College Press.

Cruttenden, A. (1979), *Language in Infancy and Childhood*, Manchester University Press.

Crystal, D. (1976), *Child Language, Learning and Linguistics*, London, Arnold.

Davies, A. (ed.) (1975), *Problems of Language and Learning*, London, Heinemann.

Davies, A. (ed.) (1977), *Language and Learning in Early Childhood*, London, Heinemann.

Doughty, P., Pearce, J. and Thornton, G. (1971), *Language in Use*, London, Arnold.

Edwards, V. (1979), *The West Indian Language Issue in British Schools*, London, Routledge & Kegan Paul.

Fraser, H. and O'Donnel, W.R. (eds) (1969), *Applied Linguistics and the Teaching of English*, London, Longman.

Gannon, P. and Czerniewska, P. (1980), *Using Linguistics: An Educational Focus*, London, Arnold.

Halliday, M.A.K. (1973), *Learning How to Mean*, London, Arnold.

Halliday, M.A.K., McIntosh, A. and Strevens, P. (1964), *The Linguistic Sciences and Language Teaching*, London, Longman.

Keen, J. (1978), *Teaching English: A Linguistic Approach*, London, Methuen.

Labov, W. (1972), *Language in the Inner City*, Oxford, Blackwell.

Macaulay, R.K.S. (1978), *Language, Social Class and Education: A Glasgow Study*, Edinburgh University Press.

Mackay, D., Thomson, B. and Schaub, P. (1970), *Breakthrough to Literacy: Teacher's Manual*, London, Longman.

Perera, K. (1979), 'Reading and Writing', in Cruttenden (1979), pp. 130–60.

Perera, K. (forthcoming 1982–3), *Analysing Classroom Language: the Structure of Writing*, London, Deutsch.

Pit Corder, S. (1973), *Applied Linguistics*, Harmondsworth, Penguin.

Reid, J.F. (ed.) (1972), *Reading Problems and Practices,* London, Ward Lock.

Rosen, H. (1980), 'Linguistic diversity in London schools', in A.K. Pugh, V.J. Lee and J. Swann (ed), *Language and Language Use,* London, Heinemann.

Sharp, D. (1973), *Language in Bilingual Communities,* London, Arnold.

Sinclair, J. McH. and Coulthard, R.M. (1975), *Towards an Analysis of Discourse: the English used by Teachers and Pupils*, London, Oxford University Press.

Spolsky, B. (1978), *Educational Linguistics*, Massachusetts, Newbury House.

Stubbs, M. (1976), *Language, Schools and Classrooms,* London, Methuen.

Stubbs, M. (1980), *Language and Literacy: the Sociolinguistics of Reading and Writing*, London, Routledge & Kegan Paul.

Trudgill, P. (1975), *Accent, Dialect and the School,* London, Arnold.

Wells, G. (1977), 'Language Use and Educational Success: a Response to Joan Tough's "The Development of Meaning"', *Nottingham Linguistic Circular*, vol. 6, no. 2, pp. 29–50.

Widdowson, H.G. (1975), *Stylistics and the Teaching of Literature*, London, Longman.

Widdowson, H.G. (1977), *Teaching Language as Communication,* Oxford University Press, London.

Wight, J. (1971), 'Dialect in School', *Educational Review*, vol. 24, no. 1.

Index